Atlantic Ocean

W9-CPF-378

G. BAHAMA

Nassau NEW PROVIDENCE
ELEUTHERA

BAHAMAS

GREAT INAGUA

WINDWARD PASSAGE
TORTUGA (LA TORTUE)

Puerto Principe

HISPANIOLA

MONA PASSAGE

PUERTO RICO
San Juan

VIRGIN IS.
SANTA CRUZ

ANGUILLA
ST. BARTHOLOMEW
ST. CHRISTOPHER

ANTIGUA

GUADELOUPE

Santiago

PETIT
GOAVE

(HAITI)
ILE AUX VACHES

Santo Domingo

NEVIS
MONSERRAT

DOMINICA

MARTINIQUE

ST. LUCIA

ST VINCENT

BARBADOS

Port Royal

JAMAICA

Caribbean Sea

GRENADA

TRINIDAD

MARGARITA

Rio de la Hacha

ARUBA

CURAÇAO

Coro de Vela

Borboruta

Bello
ombre de Dios
Panama City
Port Pheasant

Santa Marta

Cartagena de Indias

Maracaibo

LAKE MARACAIBO

VENEZUELA

ORINOCO R.

CARONI R.

San Tomás

DARIEN

DE PERLAS

NUEVA GRANADA

(C O L O M B I A)

The Age of Piracy

The Age of Piracy

By ROBERT CARSE

Illustrations by
TED TRINKAUS

Publishers • GROSSET & DUNLAP • *New York*

This book is
for
RUTH AND JAMES DUGAN

Contents

CONTENTS

A Very Ancient Profession

In a broad sense, it may be said that piracy began the day after man first learned to transport valuable goods by sea. The temptation to take another's possessions was, apparently, too great to resist. Almost from the beginning of recorded history, the two great rivers of Mesopotamia — the Tigris and the Euphrates — were infested with river pirates. Many of the mythological heroes of ancient Greece were little better than pirates. In Roman times, Julius Caesar was once captured by the "brethren" of the eastern Mediterranean, and released after paying a large ransom. He captured the pirates later, and hanged them. But that hardly deterred the practice.

Piracy was widespread in many parts of the world, yet it was in the Caribbean area that the greatest fortunes were exposed to large-scale illegal seizure. The fact that the Spanish were in control of the Caribbean and were forced to move huge amounts of their fortune across it into the Atlantic was of major interest to pirates. The slow and clumsy fleets in which the treasures of High Mexico, Central America, Peru, and the Philippines were carried offered a target too easy to miss in the confined waters around the Antillean islands. Thus it seemed to me very logical to write in detail of these buccaneers and their successors, the less capable although better-known pirates, who, from the late sixteenth century through the seventeenth and on into the eighteenth century, bedevilled the Spanish commanders, and branched out to attack any ship that seemed weaker than their own. So my title.

The record of pirate history in the Indian Ocean is treated briefly since it was my intention to concentrate on the Caribbean activities which during the "great age" were unparalleled for the amounts of loot seized, and the number of ships, villages, towns, and cities raided. Still, strangely, it was the East Indian swashbucklers who caught the popular imagination long before the rum-numb, blowhard, Captain Blackbeard Teach, gained notoriety.

Nothing has been written in this book about the Barbary pirates who for centuries, from approximately 1415 to 1830, exacted ransom from seafarers in the western Mediterranean and in the Atlantic as far North as the British Isles. The Barbary corsairs were just as ruthless as their counterparts in the Caribbean and the Indian Ocean, better organized, and much more effective at procuring ransom. They had inherited their trade from ancient times.

For centuries piracy was an established form of livelihood in Ireland, particularly among the impoverished people who were driven from their homes by English troops during the Cromwellian era. They kept a keen sea watch upon both coasts and sailed, rowed or swam out to board their prospective prizes. One of the rare acts of mercy they performed was to help the survivors of the Spanish Armada who were stranded on the Irish seacoast. But the Spaniards, weak with scurvy, hunger, and despair, were escaping from the English, and that was reason enough for the Irish to assist them.

Perhaps the oldest set of pirates in recorded history are the daring, canny men whose descendants are still occasionally active in the South China Sea. In their fast junks, they raided throughout all of the Malay archipelago attacking much larger vessels with frequent success. Early in the nineteenth century, when the Canton tea trade was being opened, American shipmasters came to know them well.

They met the pirates off Java Head, and in the Macassar Strait, and almost into the Pearl River, below Canton. Although their respect for them as fighting men was considerable, the Boston, Salem, and New York captains furiously resented the problem they presented. In addition to the danger involved, the presence of pirates made it necessary for the American ships to carry cannon, powder, and shot, whose cost reduced the profit made on the tea cargoes.

Hotel Chelsea,
New York City,
March,
1965   R.C.

The Age of Piracy

Spain Supplies the Loot

"No prey, no pay."

First article of pirate agreement to undertake a voyage

The tapestry of the record space of piracy is old, and worn.
Many of the threads that were the lives of the men who made
it are lost; others are brilliant, some parts agleam, showing in
sharp relief the great figures. Over the centuries while they
flourished and then stubbornly declined, from the great pirates
of the time of the Tudors down to the last harassed and befuddled renegade hiding in the coves of the Mosquito Coast three
hundred years later, they shared one thing in common. They
sought on the sea by force of arms to take from other men what
was legally theirs.

There has been enormous discussion as to which ones
among their number deserved the name pirate. The famous
Hawkins family of Plymouth has been accepted, rejected and,
along with it, Francis Drake of the *Golden Hind.* They alone
need to be mentioned to illustrate the difficulty of definition.
John Hawkins was, of course, given a knighthood for his part
in the Armada actions. But his cousin, Drake, waited for
anxious months before Queen Elizabeth made up her mind
to knight him when he returned from his round-the-world
voyage of plundering. Both men had sailed carrying commissions issued by the Queen, but to the Spaniards whose property they had seized they had no legality whatsoever. They
were at best Her Majesty's pirates.

The light flickers unevenly back into the centuries, dis-

15

The Age of Piracy

torts, enlarges or only vaguely reveals discoverable fact. Perhaps it is not strange that the captains of the pirate ships almost invariably paid for their ventures with their lives. Sir Henry Morgan is the major exception to those who escaped hanging or violent death. The rest were too notorious, too confident. The illusion of inviolability, the successes of the past and the dream of the next magnificent prize were always there to draw them forward from safety.

The common sailors who formed the crews often had much better luck than their commanders. In the nature of the enterprise the mortality rate was logically very high among them. It has been computed that only about one out of three ever survived his service and got home again. Still, the mortality rate was also very high among those ashore. Each man who chose the pirate way could remember the plagues, the fluxes, the fevers, the outright starvation in the city slums, the backbreaking and debilitating labor of the farms and the awful punishment for the slightest crime. But then, for a sailor, life was far worse in the King's ships.

They slept wet, hip to thigh among their watchmates on the lowest deck up against the leaky gun ports. Their clothing was never enough, and their food the rotten stuff the victualers had sold for immense profit. Once a rating, a bosun's or a carpenter's or gunner's mate, they were too valuable to be allowed ashore. They were kept virtual prisoners aboard, sometimes for years on end. The pay, when they received it, was a few shillings a month, and for any infraction of regulations there was always the crippling, terrible lash.

Life aboard the slave ships was nearly as bad, for there the space was given to the human cargo, and the crew took what it could find. In the ordinarily engaged merchant vessels, the rations were usually short, the pay small, and the lash was used at the discretion of the captain. Men waited with carefully concealed hope to join as a pirate. If fortune smiled, they would be

16

home after a few voyages with a sackful of doubloons, a pearl or so and nobody the wiser.

As a consequence of this implacable crew belief in freedom from undue penalty and wanton exercise of discipline, there was created the most peculiar form of shipboard conduct ever to exist. The men chose their captains and discharged them at will; and if really displeased with their actions, marooned them and elected another from among their number. It was primitive, nonpolitical anarchy, and it worked.

Whenever a prize was taken, the first question asked of the seized crew was whether the captain of the vessel had treated them right. If he had been brutal, his clothing was stripped, he was triced up to the main shrouds and given a tarred rope's end as a reminder of things past. So, many fervent recruits were gained and some old scores settled *in absentia*.

One of the popular misconceptions which should be finally destroyed here is that the captain of a pirate ship was anything like her sole commander. He commanded her only when a potential prize was in sight, or was being taken or lost. There were no quarters reserved aboard for his special use. He ate at the common mess with the rest of the crew. After a victory, he drew a larger portion of the shares than the other men, but that was because, probably, he was a better fighting man and sailor.

The crews were not content, though, with such safeguards against authority. They added another, and to do it they elevated the ship's quartermaster to a position quartermasters had not held before and have not since. This man, for manifest reasons, was generally a veteran sailor. He handled the helm when the ship was in action, and very likely, beyond the captain, he was the one man aboard who had knowledge of navigation.

He was used by the crews as a counterbalance to the captain. His authority was extensive. It was he who during the

Spain Supplies the Loot

17

The Age
of
Piracy

tensely nervous time of the share-out at the mainmast proclaimed the worth of the loot that had been taken. He doled it forth, man after man, and his word was trusted, accepted. When there were drunken, violent fights ashore in the various careenages and hiding places and members of the crew came to handystrokes, the quartermaster stopped the fracas. Men who persisted in finishing personal quarrels were given orders to duel with pistols, and the quartermaster measured off the twenty paces, acted as judge, offered surgical help afterwards. He was decidedly executive and was rarely disobeyed, yet there are recorded instances when he was forced to fight for private reasons. Whatever those may have been, he earned his whack of the share-out.

The anarchical theory of denial of absolute command, equity for all as far as it was in any way practical, was carried by the pirates into the articles drawn up among them. Almost entirely illiterate, essentially desperate men, divorced from a society they both hated and feared, they still insisted upon the formality of a written agreement. These articles were patterned in their expression upon the relatively legal letters of marque issued to privateers. Maybe the men hoped that, if captured, the articles would save them from the bowline knot under the chin and the last spinning swing from the yardarm. More probably, they tried to increase the always tenuous unity that kept them together as a ship's company. Anyhow, they put into the articles their quite definite ideas.

Many of these sets of articles were very much alike. One drawn up by a crew that sailed with Captain William Kidd just prior to 1700 is worthy of inspection. It has particular historical value because, although the men formed a privateer crew, the great majority of them deserted during the voyage and openly became pirates. They were not displeased with the agreement but with Kidd, and they wanted a further chance at loot. They signed fifteen articles. Here are the first four:

1) Captain Kidd and his shipe to have fourty shares and any man that would come aboard the said shipe should have shares of such treasure as should be taken.

2) If any man should Loose (sic) a Leg or Arm in ye said service, he should have sex (sic) hundred pieces of Eight, or Sex Able Slaves.

3) If any man should Loose a Joynt in ye said service, he should have a hundred pieces of 8.

4) If any man shipped himself aboard ye said shipe and should offer to go away from her, he shall suffer what punishment ye Capt. and ye Company Quartermaster shall think fitt, and shall have no share.*

Other articles of the Kidd ship treated on cowardice, mutiny, drunkenness, obedience and further details as to sharing. The pieces of eight mentioned are roughly equivalent to the present American dollar, although their buying power was much greater. "Slaves" meant the prisoners taken from a prize. They could be held for ransom or worked ashore, as their owner saw fit.

Various systems of payment and share-out were established. But they were all effective immediately after the prize ship was secured. Then the dice in the leather cup began to rattle; the rum, the wine or the beer and flip were passed. The men who had evolved their own unique pension plan had once more forgotten fear.

They, in their place in history, were also unique. A complex of forces sent them west. They came to the Caribbean basin, the great center of piracy, from most of the European countries along the Atlantic. Among the first were French Huguenots driven out by the religious wars at home. These dared the Spanish interdiction of the region as early as 1530, and the first recorded capture of a Spanish ship was made by a Dieppe man named Pierre le Grand. With a crew of twenty-eight, from a sinking boat, he took a major vessel.

* William Hallam Bonner, *Pirate Laureate*

Spain Supplies the Loot

The Age of Piracy

Word of his exploit spread. More Frenchmen followed him, and Hollanders who had served with the Sea Beggars in the battles against the Duke of Alva in the Narrow Seas. Then there were Englishmen who had been restive at home, oppressed by poverty, religious and political troubles, or indentured men who fled their often cruel masters. They sometimes joined forces, sometimes sailed separately in ships of their own nationality, but they sacked the Spanish Main in fierce assaults and took prizes from St. Augustine and the Florida capes on south to Cartagena de Indias and Puerto Bello and Panamá.

It was the beginning of the great age of piracy. Here were the islands where the ships could careen for bottom repair, gather fresh stores, refit and sail out from hidden harbors to strike again. Here was the loot that came down in fabulous quantity from High Mexico, from Perú and even across the Pacific from the Philippines. That must be taken home to Spain in the clumsy, slow *flotas,* and the courses were known.

The pirates became, in their own term, "sea-artists." There is great doubt that other groups of men excelled them as sailors. Their chosen craft were small and light, initially faster than the much bigger Spanish ships. They handled them with consummate skill and they kept them clear at all times for possible action. Once a sail was sighted, they were wholly determined in pursuit, drew off only if under tremendous odds.

They were the survivors of the survivors, tough, desperate, and in superb physical shape, and stronger than any motive of personal greed was a consuming hatred of the enemy. No mercy was to be expected if they lost; if they won, the man who led the way over the side was given extra shares.

It is difficult to compute what these men gained for their daring. The dicebox took a lot right after the share-out. The doxies of the ports the ships entered soon got the rest. Reports are given of scenes along the water front of Tortuga and Port Royal where pirates already stooping drunk stood over rum

or brandy casks they had bought and splashed the people who passed, sometimes insisted with a flourished pistol that "a sup" should be drawn.

Sadness, a sense of tragedy, were within the bravado. The fancy clothing, the fine Cordoba boots, the huge pendant gold ear-loops, even the display of weapons didn't mean much. The dream of the return home grew dimmer with each voyage. Staggering down the beach back to the ships, men heard in their heads the sound of Bow Bells that they were aware they would never really hear again; they imagined Devon meadows, a Breton orchard pink-white in the spring, or a Flemish windmill delicately traced upon the sky at dusk. More rum was the only answer.

After the sack of Panamá, one of the richest single hauls ever made, Morgan sorely cheated the crews under him. The individual share-out for a buccaneer came to about ten English pounds apiece. But there was no lack of volunteers for the next voyage.

Drunkenness was increasingly the passport home as, in the years of the eighteenth-century peace between England and France and Spain, honest governors and tighter guard-ship control reduced the pirate ventures in the Caribbean. The intelligent pirates left the area for the Indian Ocean, but their end was foreshadowed and they did not last long. The great age was over well before 1800, when, curiously, the popular writing about it began.

But with one notable exception, the men who had made it famous had never made a prisoner walk the plank. Very rarely had they flown the skull-and-bones flag, much more often the common red battle banner; and usually only in necessity had they marooned a man. Then they gave him a loaded pistol so that he could put himself out of his misery. They were amazingly humane towards the majority of their prisoners. It was profitable to be so, and they sought profit until there was none left worth the taking.

The Age of Piracy

22

23

Never A Bolder
Race of Men

"A bolder race of men, both as to personal valor and conduct, certainly never yet appeared on the liquid element or dry land."

ALEXANDRE EXQUEMELIN, in his preface to
History of the Buccaneers of America

The story of piracy, even the history of the West Indies might very well have been vastly different without the presence of the buccaneers on Tortuga. Columbus gave it the name on his first voyage. To him, as it rose humpbacked and speckled brown above the horizon glitter, it resembled a sea turtle, so La Tortuga—the Turtle.

It is a small island, some four miles wide and a bit over twenty-two long, and today, except for a few Haitian fishermen and herds of wild goats, deserted. But from early in the 1620's until late in that century, shelter was taken there by the Brethren of the Coast, the men who came to be known as buccaneers and freebooters, then pirates. Gradually, under the relentless pressures applied against them, they made it the most feared outlaw stronghold in the New World.

They had a manifest reason for their choice of the site. Tortuga lies at the head of the Windward Passage, close onto the northeast Haitian coast and only an hour's easy sail from the main island of Hispaniola. Across it, riffling the palm fronds, stirring the bamboo brakes and the wild cane and cotton and the guinea grass, the Trade Wind steadily blows. Beyond, past the confines of the passage that reaches between

Cuba and the sprawl of Hispaniola, is the Caribbean, and at the southerly end of the Windward Passage is entrance to the heart of the Spanish Main.

The original Brethren were French, of Huguenot stock. They had sailed down the Trade from Europe around 1530 and settled on St. Christopher. But they fought with the English there, and their leader, Pierre d'Esnambuc, took them along to the northward through the islands to Tortuga. There were already on that island a few Englishmen, deserters who had jumped ship and runaways from indenture. They called it Association Island and used it mainly as a hiding place. They were soon absorbed by the French.

They made their settlement under the lee, out of the wind, where there was a pretty fair anchorage. Up from the beach they built their *ajoupas,* the palm thatch huts, as they had learned from the soft-spoken, shy Arawaks. Soil was cultivated in the Indian style, a stick hardened by fire being used for both plow and hoe. The crops were maize and yams and manioc and tobacco, and the fruits of what appeared as paradise to those from the chill French land: mangos and custard apples and sapodillas and coconuts and little, very sweet oranges, lemons, bananas and figs. The sea held fish of infinite variety, from stripers and groupers to bass and tuna. There were always the great turtles, and as a delicacy in season, their eggs buried in the tidewater sand. Lobsters were to be plucked from under the rocks alongshore. Crabs, gray, white and pink, scuttered rustling, could be caught barehanded. In the woods that flanked the rocky interior were aromatic trees that offered spices, and pigeons by the thousands, and wood doves and boar, and small, furred animals that, when roasted, were delicious. A man couldn't ask for much more.

Word spread back to Europe about Tortuga. Ships touching the island on the way furtively to trade or raid on the Main brought recruits. Cavaliers who still affected shoulder-long hair, velvet doublets and a flick of lace were among them; and

Never a Bolder Race of Men

25

The Age of Piracy

red-kneed Scots in tattered kilts; further French, and Irish who had escaped the Pale or indenture, men from the Massachusetts Colony whose Puritan faith had faltered, Hollanders with memories of the Inquisition rack. Then there were those whose left cheeks, close to the nose, bore the big branded T of thief, and others who had served for years in the prison galleys, and more with backs that were grids of scars from the cat-o'-nine strokes, the keel-hauling and the rope's end of the Royal Navy punishment.

They hated the Spanish, but also all oppression. They were absolutely resolved to remain free. Deep in the psyche of each man was the insatiable desire for equity that was to persist centuries later in the articles of agreement of the pirate ships. Here, on the sea frontier of the Main, the Spaniards were to be constantly feared and watched.

A lookout was maintained on the summit of the island, vigil kept to the south and east towards Hispaniola and the territory the Spaniards occupied. Questions were put to the Arawaks who crossed from the main island in their canoes. They, too, had known Spanish cruelty, and sometimes with them they carried maimed, half-maddened Negro slaves who, one by one, had managed to break loose from the *estancias* where their mates had been buried to the necks in the ground after hours of torture and left to die.

The danger of eventual Spanish attack sobered even the very reckless who considered this a womanless Eden. Meetings were held. Formal articles were established that were to be carefully followed. Officers and a Council of Brethren were elected, and men took up one of three kinds of endeavor.

Those who wished to stay on Tortuga,—and they were about one third—became known as *habitans,* their purpose to till the soil. Another third said they would be content to serve on the sea. Most of that lot were Hollanders, and they had already built their boats of the local timber—swift, lean, lateen-rigged craft—and launched them. Their boats were called in the jumbled colloquial speech that the Brethren used *frei-bote,* *fly-bote,* or *flei-bote.* So the crews took the name of *freiboteros.* The Englishmen made it at once into freebooters.

The work given to the freebooters was to transport the third segment of the Brethren over and back from Hispaniola. The lot was subdivided. Half the number chose to hunt the wild cattle that had originally been brought out by Columbus and since roamed the western part of the island. The other half, called *chasseurs,* elected to go after the hordes of wild boar. Dutch ships putting into the roadstead off Tortuga had asked for hides as cargo, were also in need of smoked meat for homeward-bound provisions and tallow for the preservation of their hulls. The Arawaks had explained to the Brethren the Indian method of curing hides or meat on a green wooden hurdle over an open fire pit called a *boucan.* The cattle hunters took the title of *boucaniers* and in their articles agreed to stay on Hispaniola for periods of at least a year.

It was a lonesome and perilous but for them a delightful life. They were men who cherished solitude; remembrance stayed keen of the past in the stinking, chill darkness of the crowded kennels of the slums at home, prisons where body chafed sickened body, ships where there wasn't even sufficient sleeping space. Haiti, "the high country," the Arawaks had named this land, and the buccaneers came to adore the place.

They went from the shore in teams of twos, drawn together for the sake of safety. Each man was well known to his partner and they spoke of themselves as *matelots.* They wore for the most part loose cotton garments, conical leather caps with small visors, soft leather wrap-around leggings, and in clay pipes smoked the coarse Arawak shag. Moving through the green and lush beauty of the coastal plain towards the great russet ridges of the Massif du Nord beyond, they were heavily armed. They carried muskets with five-foot-long barrels expressly designed for them by an armorer named Brachie at Dieppe and another, Gelin, at Nantes. Their usual method

Never a Bolder Race of Men

27

The Age of Piracy

of fire was two or three balls at a time; the balls weighed sixteen to the pound and were contained in a pigskin haversack. At the left side of a broad leather belt each one wore a short saber, called the *manchette* and held within an alligator scabbard. At the right side of the belt was the calabash powder flask and inside it several long, very sharp Flemish knives. Over their shoulders, bandolier-style, they strapped their rolled cotton tents of extraordinarily fine quality and their pigskin sleeping bags.

Tent and sleeping bag were for protection against mosquitoes and white ants. At dusk, the hunt finished, *ajoupa* huts were built and smudge fires started, then the tents put up within the hut frameworks. Banana leaves made soft bedding under the bags, but men had been wholly devoured by the white ant swarms, so even on the hottest nights the *boucaniers* crawled into the pigskin covering.

With them as they entered the mountain country to begin the hunt were packs of twenty to twenty-five fierce and strapping mastiff dogs. The dogs had cost their masters as much as six gold *ecus* apiece, and in the packs were several famous leaders who could sniff the wind and unerringly find the cattle. Between the ravines and savannahs and winding valleys where the cattle grazed were trails made by them and here the *boucaniers,* to conserve ammunition, often took up the chase on foot, knife in hand instead of musket.

The cattle, if cornered, would fight back, piercing fatally with a blow of the long, sharp horns, but the buccaneers closed with them and bent and slashed their knife blades along the hock tendons. One of the hunters, Vincent de Rosiers, became so deft at this that his reputation was carried to France. Out of a hundred hides taken by him during a chase, only ten had bullet marks; the rest of the animals he had brought down with the knife alone.

But there were Spaniards in the mountains also, and often at dawn a pair of solitary hunters were found transfixed by bamboo lances in their sleeping bags. The buccaneers more and more took to hunting in groups of ten or twelve, changing camp sites each night, although that meant the lugging of the raw hides for miles. Each hide weighed at least a hundred pounds, and they were strong men who packed them.

They seldom if ever bathed, or cut their hair and beards. The cheap cotton clothing was smirched, then caked and stiffened by the blood of the slaughtering. Standing by the *boucan* fires while the hides were dried, they made impressive, almost fantastic figures. By the young *valets* who were sent out in the later years to serve apprenticeship under them, the veteran buccaneers were regarded with both awe and trepidation.

Such men could lift the heavy spade-stocked muskets and fire twenty shots a minute and put every shot on target, served by their *valets* who reloaded spare weapons behind them. They ran faster than the cattle they pursued, and they kept at it all day long. And often when they drank at night by the campfires, sometimes during the chase they beat the *valets* without mercy.

Yet even the *valets,* indentured for terms of three weary years, recognized that this was a life beyond parallel. They ate prodigiously, boar meat with pimiento sauce being a favorite dish, and roasted pigeon and wood dove, or wild honey taken from the hives in the logwood trees and smeared on maize johnnycake, while an entire steer was barbecued, buckets of the spice-sharp sauce poured over the carcass. Possessions were shared unquestioningly; any man's property could be taken, used by another. A hunter away from his own camp might enter the *ajoupa* of another, go away with shot, powder, a hatchet, rum, and never make mention of the fact. They were Brothers of the Coast, and they believed in and practiced complete equity.

From the quick cerise flash of dawn, though, until the more rapid descent of night they kept at the chase. Logwood, mahogany, rosewood were flung into the *boucan* pits over a dry

Never a Bolder Race of Men

29

The Age of Piracy

brush base. The flames leaped slowly and the firefly scrolls were dulled, moths as big as small birds circled the hunters' heads. Somewhere high in a ceiba tree a wood dove gave dim repeated cry to the snuffing of a mastiff who was eager for the entrails about to be ripped from within the taut hide.

The hides were dried, pegged, sorted, and the *valets* went surreptitiously to wash themselves in the waterfall beside the savannah. Then they sat with the hunters and gorged the hot meat. It was all they had. It was all they wanted. A breeze surged through the trees with a sound like music. Humming-birds twittered, although the wood dove was still, asleep.

Mosquitoes picked up their chorus. The hunters slapped patiently, smeared themselves with tallow. Rat-bats grazed down for the morsels the mastiffs left. The hunters rose stiff-legged and moved towards the vague white of the tents under the huts.

"Good night."

"Bonne nuit, mon vieux."

The sleeping bags were opened, men crawled in, shut them. The mastiffs lay by the fire, now almost out, a reddish rind in blue-purple. One of the hunters murmured, distant in sleep. His partner hardly heard him, but it was a woman's name.

Women came inevitably from Europe to Tortuga to join the buccaneers. The Brethren were prosperous, and although once, in 1638, the Spanish attacked the island, slaughtered a great number of them and drove them off, they returned. The heights above the town and the beach were fortified. A French governor was accepted on very loose terms of rule. Then a deal was made with the French West Indies Company.

A whole shipload of women was sent out with the permission of the king. Louis was convinced that they would bring increase to the buccaneers, perhaps regularize life on Tortuga; besides the shipment would rid Paris of hundreds of its prostitutes. Most of the contingent came from the Convent of the

30

The Age of Piracy

Madelonettes on the Rue des Fontaines. According to the nuns who guarded them, they were "debauched young girls who knew the truth about themselves." On their backs as proof were the marks of the hundred lashes administered publicly for their sins.

They sailed in 1669 in a high-sided French merchantman of the type known as a *flûte*. The voyage was slow and arduous. The ship was foul upon arrival at the anchorage off Tortuga. But the cargo was in fine shape.

On the beach the assembled Brethren waited. The *habitans* had built new huts in expectation of added occupancy. The *boucaniers* had come in from the fastnesses of Hispaniola to trade their bales of hides for clean clothes, kegs of rum, pipes of claret and brandy, and the *freiboteros* kept themselves in similar supply by running boats out to circle the ship before the cargo was discharged.

The delay was snapped at dusk. The women came ashore in the ship's boats, dressed in their best, eager eyes searching over the hard brown faces. But a regular and formal procedure was followed. D'Ogeron, the Governor, and an administrator of sagacity, saw to it that a betrothal contract was entered into by each couple.

Buccaneers were forced to remember their baptismal names. They gave up such as Bras-de-Fer, Chasse-Marée, Fort-en-Gueule and Brise-Galet and Vent-en-Panne. A record has been left of one man's statements to his bride. He told her:

"I take thee without knowing, or caring to know, who thou art. If anybody from whence thou comest would have had thee, thou wouldst not have come in quest of me. But no matter; I do not desire thee to give me an account of thy past conduct, because I have no right to be offended at it at the time when thou wast at liberty to behave either ill or well according to thy own pleasure, and because I shall have no reason to be ashamed of anything thou wast guilty of when thou didst not belong to me. Give me only thy word for the future; I acquit thee of the past." Then he struck his hand upon the barrel of his gun and promised further, "This will revenge me of thy breach of faith; if thou shouldst prove false, this will surely be true to my aim."

The beach was given to celebration that night. Fires soared. Buccaneers showed their brides how to barbecue meat island-style. The heads were kicked out of the claret and brandy pipes. Rum kegs were rolled down the sand. There was drumming, dancing, fiddling, then a mass expression of love.

But in the days afterwards many of the buccaneers were restive. This, they realized, could not last. Out along the jagged shore to the south were the posts the Spaniards occupied on Hispaniola. Soon again, surely, the Spaniards were going to strike.

The more adventurous married couples disregarded the danger. They went to live on Hispaniola, close across the strait, then further inland. Crops were planted. Tobacco and indigo and sugar were cultivated for export. The former rough, random way of life was almost forgotten. Children played laughing under the mango trees in the farm dooryards. Outcast buccaneer and exiled prostitute turned into earnest *bourgeoisie* proud of their families, their land.

Then from the central region of Hispaniola the Spaniards attacked the settlements in force. They were determined to crush and efface all resistance. It was a slow form of slaughter, raids by night or in the middle of the day's drowse, as heat shimmered over the tawny yellow of the cane and the darting of a butterfly in fright was the only warning a colonist got of the approach of a Spanish patrol.

French occupation of the coastal region was broken. Tortuga, strongly defended, at last accepted defeat. The commanding officer of the Spanish troops was impressed; he gave consent and the garrison marched out under its own arms, with honor. The tight-faced men, their few women and the remaining children embarked at the beach and headed towards St. Christopher.

Never a Bolder Race of Men

33

The Age of Piracy

The prize was too rich to lose, though, and a number of the Brethren who had been freebooters became open pirates. They were enlisted and the island was won back. It was not the same afterwards; with the victory came a change in the basic policy of the organization.

Pirates were welcomed, encouraged. Henry Morgan, when he prepared for his raid on Panamá, got many impatient volunteers from among the Brethren. Profit was now what counted. The fort up on the heights above the town that had been built by Le Vasseur, the first nominal governor, was converted into a huge slave-pen. Ships came in steadily with their freight from the Guinea Coast.

But as the slave trade shifted to Hispaniola, the smaller island was deserted. People shunned Tortuga. It was without life when more than a hundred years later the slaves revolted against their masters on the great plantations across the strait. An awful bloom of flame from the fired estates was sent up into the night sky. The reflection fell upon Tortuga, stark reminder of the dream the Brethren had lost.

Hate Is the Password

"Il n'est pas permis à aucune nation, sous quelque pretexte que ce puisse être, d'aller aux Indes occidentales traiter avec les Espagnols."

PÈRE LABAT *in his journal*

When the buccaneers of Tortuga decided towards the end of the seventeenth century that they should strike openly as pirates against the Spanish, they were already following a well-established tradition. Not only had William Hawkins and his cousin, Francis Drake, and other Englishmen attacked the ports on the Main. Columbus, as early as his third voyage (1498–1500), was forced to change his homeward course and deflect it to the south in the direction of Madeira in order to avoid the French "corsairs."

These were all letter-of-marque men, bearing the King's commission, and they waited for him off Cape St. Vincent. Among them were some great French sea heroes, Jean Bart and Surcouf and Duguay-Trouin. They were so successful that from the beginning of the sixteenth century the Spanish built big, fast carracks to drive them off the coast.

The first really large-scale French pirate venture was that of the Parmentier brothers who sailed on the account of Jean Ango in 1520. He was a merchant with headquarters in several French ports on the Channel, and he was possessed of great wealth, imagination and daring. He believed as did his opposite numbers, the Plymouth shipowners, that his vessels could outsail and outfight the Spaniards although the latter had

The Age
of
Piracy

added to the carracks an even faster fleet of caravels, then frigates with a huge sail spread.

His judgment was correct. The Parmentiers, running free, ranged raiding from Newfoundland to Brazil to the Antilles and home again. Jean Fleury came after them. He went in along the Mexican coast and he got his hands on an immense amount of the Montezuma treasure in 1536 and brought it safely away. But the next year in another try he was captured and given to the horrors of the *auto-da fé*. He was both a heretic and a pirate, and the quality of mercy was not strained for his kind.

It is estimated that at this time the French had forty corsair vessels active against the Spanish. Many were privately financed by François I, King of Navarre, and by Cardinal Tournon and the Duchess, Madame d'Estampes, "friend of the king." The return for their investment was a quite steady stream of gold, silver, emeralds, rubies, diamonds, pearls, and tobacco, sugar, indigo and cacao.

The Spanish put a network of spies through the French ports to stop it. They had agents all over: La Rochelle, Nantes, Croisic, Dieppe. The corsair ships were closely watched, and still they sailed.

Early in 1540, a single ship carrying twenty-four men entered Havana harbor. The city was threatened with bombardment, then taken, sacked and burned. July 24, 1543, a raid was made upon Cartagena de Indias by François Leclerc. It was the real prize, the richest port on the Main, and excellently defended. Leclerc was known as Jambe de Bois because of a wooden leg, and he also had a badly injured arm. But he seized Cartagena. Upon his return home and on the recommendation of Admiral Coligny, he was ennobled by Henry II. His luck was considerably better than that of Jean Fleury.

For years afterwards the French continued their forays against the Main. Then, because of a complexity of religious wars at home and intermittent peace with the Spanish, the

36

attacks diminished. There was, later in the seventeenth century, a recrudescence, and French pirates served with Drake when he went for the famous gold-train raid on the Isthmus of Panamá. Quite a number were with Morgan at the sack of Panamá City itself. Then others learned how to round Cape Horn and hit savagely at the exposed Spanish settlements all along the western coast of South America.

But except for L'Ollonais, Lafitte and a few other captains, the French withdrew from piracy. The ships no longer ran out of the Channel ports for the Main. It had become the turn of the buccaneers with a personal vengeance to satisfy, and of the English whose motive was, simply, loot.

Hate Is the Password

Fit For Burning

"There by the sea they encountered us threatening war."
ARCHIBALD MACLEISH, in *Conquistador*

It is very probable indeed that without the presence of the Spanish in the West Indian area and in Central and South America in the sixteenth, seventeenth and eighteenth centuries, piracy might not have existed over such a long period or with as much success. The peculiarly rigid form of Spanish colonial life and trade, the strictures of the Inquisition, the cruel mistreatment of the indigenous peoples, then the early Negro slaves, and, moreover, the possession of incredible wealth, all invited armed attack. A study of piracy must consider how the local *colonios* lived, were ruled from distant Madrid, and tried to make themselves rich. They became a common enemy for their adversaries. There were French and English and Danish and Dutch and Scottish colonies in the region also, and while some of them were raided by pirates of other nationalities, they never received the concentrated, repeated attacks suffered by the Spanish.

Religion was part of the problem. French Huguenots had a rancorous personal vengeance to pay, and Dutchmen and Englishmen, who were called "Lutheran dogs and heretics" by the Spanish, were not far behind. But more than religion the inability to trade caused deep-seated trouble. Madrid insisted that any commerce with the colonies be conducted by Spanish merchants alone, and every cargo carried in a Spanish ship. Smuggling was punished severely; a petty official in some outpost who was caught buying slaves or goods from a foreign-flag vessel was either dismissed or sent home to serve time in prison.

Spain was greedy, and intensely jealous of her possessions. There was set up at home in Seville to handle colonial traffic a cumbersome and stiff-functioning organization called *La Casa de Contratacion*. This was a combination immigration service, clearing house, mercantile tribunal and nautical college. It had been created by the King and through its complex branches held control of each phase of colonial economic life.

The three major Caribbean ports on the mainland—Cartagena de Indias, the entrepôt for the trade products of South America; and Nombre de Dios and Puerto Bello, close together in the flat, dismal Panamanian region—were visited each year, usually in the spring, by the huge fleets from Spain. Two of them sailed under heavy escort, and aboard them were the eager Spanish merchants, seeking their annual profit in the New World and the finished trade goods they would sell to the *colonios*. The fleets separated in Caribbean waters. One went to Vera Cruz for Mexican treasure and that brought by ship from the Philippines, then overland across Mexico by mule train. The other sailed first to Cartagena de Indias, where a fair was set up for buyer and seller. Then that fleet moved on to Nombre de Dios and Puerto Bello.

Puerto Bello, a small and rainy and fever-ridden village, was the site each year of another fair that began customarily in May and ran for forty days. The Spanish merchants were packed into miserable shedlike quarters ashore where they paid excruciating prices. They sold silks and laces and satins, finished goods of all sorts, and they bought gold and silver and hides that had been baled on the Río de la Plata and in Chile, llama wool and tropical dyewoods, cochineal, wax and drugs. Then the fleet left for Havana. It met there the fleet that had been in Vera Cruz and together they sailed for home.

The vast regions which supplied these fleets were under the rule of viceroys, one at Mexico City whose territory was

Fit for Burning

The Age of Piracy

New Spain (Mexico), and the other at Lima. The Viceroy of Perú ruled from Lima land that extended three thousand miles overland to Buenos Aires and thirty-five hundred miles along the coast from Panamá to Valdivia. Beneath the vice-regal structure were *audencias,* political and territorial subdivisions. *Audencias* were governed by men who often, like the Viceroys, had been appointed personally by the King. They were empowered to form supreme courts, report back for orders to the *Consejo de Indias,* a special council for colonial affairs.

Provinces before the establishment of the vice-regal system were ruled by *adelantados,* usually military officers with good connections close to the throne. Towns of size were run by *alcaldes,* men more important than the average mayor, and in their own right not to be disregarded. Then there were the hordes of minor officials, prelates and priests and magistrates and officers of the garrisons and members of the Inquisition tribunals, but principal among them the *Veedor,* the Royal Inspector, who saw that the King's taxes were paid.

The taxes were, of course, immense. They were paid for import and for export, and for the convoys that took goods out from Spain and cargoes home. A governor worthy of his appointment made sure that the prosperous came forward with their *donaticos,* king's gifts, at regular intervals. There were also levies that were less formal, and went to the Governor and the Inspector, possibly as far as the Viceroy, and the numerous religious orders were not to be forgotten.

But while colonial life had its burdens, the Spaniard who had decided to emigrate was given a great deal to enjoy. He was usually of the adventurous type, and looked upon himself as belonging to an elite class, for no Jews or Moors or New Christians (newly baptized members of those races) were allowed in the colonies. Slaves performed every sort of manual labor, and while the rapacious had to wait to make their fortunes after the huge initial successes of Cortes and Pizarro, nothing was really difficult. The daily pattern was very much

40

like that at home, except that here slaves carried you in a litter along the mountain roads. They obeyed each command or were whipped, burned or buried to the neck and left for the ants to finish. The towns, whether in the *tierra alta* of Mexico, the swamps of Panamá or the windy reaches of the Chilean and Peruvian mountains, were amazingly reminiscent of mother Spain.

There was the church that dominated the *plaza,* and the town hall and the jail and the Governor's palace, the pink and white and pale blue houses with their bulging iron grilles at the windows, the balconies and arcades and tiled floors and roofs, even many of the same flowers and trees. The town crier made his rounds, the priests had a bell in the church tower that rang with a familiar tone, and flies still crawled over the meat in the sun-splashed market; the wine was not as good, but cheaper, and from the cactus plant could be manufactured a potion that dulled homesickness, made the years of exile seem to pass quite quickly.

For those who lived within reach of the sea, pirates were a recognized, almost inevitable evil, like the fever. When a raid came, it was to be repelled fiercely, with the complete satisfaction of Spanish honor. If the pirate force proved too strong, retreat was possible into the jungle or some narrow valley that had been chosen beforehand as a point of last defense by the commander of the garrison. If the pirates were defeated, captured, they were given to the Inquisition. They were the enemies of God, unbelievers, and should be put at the stake. Each town of any size had its *quemadero,* the burning place, usually in the *plaza* where all might come and watch an execution.

Fit for Burning

41

The Spanish Main

"The *Jesus* was brought in such a case that she was not able
to bear the sea longer, for in her stern on either side of the
sternpost theplanks did open and shut with every sea. . . .
And the leaks so big as the thickness of a man's arm, the
living fish did swim upon the ballast as in the sea."

An unnamed officer of the ship Jesus of Lubeck

There was no chart yet that gave an accurate description of
the area, no beacons or aids to navigation of any sort. A man
sailed, carrying his knowledge of the Caribbean in his head.
But the buccaneers took their *frei-botes* across it unerringly, and
in later days towards the end of the seventeenth century, when
they had accepted piracy as a way of life, they entered the
Spanish ports with superb skill.

Lookouts were kept doubled aloft in the ship's roundtops.
Leadsmen were stationed in the bow chains. Approaching a
coast, if the weather permitted, the pinnace was sent off with
the bosun in command. Signals were maintained between the
boat and the ship by flag. It was the system that Columbus had
used, and it worked. The ship followed the pinnace gradually
in to the shore. If night came before the landfall was made, the
boat was brought aboard, sail was shortened and the ship
jogged on and off on short tacks until dawn.

Then with dawn, under the brassy tropic sun, the islands
showed again. Mauve and lilac and saffron cloud raised in high
buttresses above them as the heat drew the moisture from the

land. Surf that the Trade kicked shone on the beaches. The jungle was a somber blue-green.

The islands spread south in a series of tremendous arcs. From Florida on to within less than eleven degrees of the Equator, they reached in a nearly unbroken chain. Some, like the Bahamas which began at the flank of the Florida coast, were of coral, low, quite barren, and rested in shallow and dangerous shoal water. Others, like Hispaniola and Jamaica and Puerto Rico and the islands to the south of them, were extremely mountainous, or were themselves the sheer tops of mountains that rose steeply from the bright sea.

The entire area—from the northernmost of the Bahamas down to the mud-silted Orinoco mouth in South America, and from Barbados, the farthest east of the islands, to the Isthmus of Panamá and back up the Mosquito Coast, where the insects of that name swarmed, to Yucatan and Campeche and the Gulf of Mexico—was almost a hundred thousand square miles. It bore the great sweep of the Gulf Stream along towards the Atlantic, and during July, August and September, the *uracana* winds of the Arawaks.

A navigator in a pirate ship knew that the Gulf Stream currents flowed up out of the belt of warm Equatorial calms at the bulge of Brazil, took a speed that increased to more than three knots after they passed through the narrows of the Florida Strait. Word had come from the Arawaks who ventured to sea in their dish-shaped *canaos* fashioned out from charred hardwood logs. Their sails of loosely woven native cotton had not been of much help to them; they took to their paddles to make shore. That was something they could measure and against which they could contend. But when the hurricane blew they dragged their craft high and fled inland.

Spanish ships in accordance with royal orders stayed in port during the hurricane season. Pirate ships, because of the demands of their calling, were more often at sea. When pos-

The Spanish Main

The Age of Piracy

sible, a haven was sought, a cove, a river entrance or a mountainous lee. But there was always a vast tide to rip a vessel from her moorings. The island forests, torn in fury, cast trees flailing. It was better on some occasions to ride out the storm at sea.

Warning was given by the peculiar yellow skies, the piled density of alto-cumulus cloud that darkened daylight; then the rain. The rain obscured all visibility. A man who attempted to peer through it had his eyes slashed as though with steel pellets. Wind sent with it sheets of spindrift raked from the crests of the thirty- and forty-foot waves.

Forecastle, aftercastle, groaned, laboring. Planks loosened on the frames. The masts nodded, swayed and bent, and the clumsy rope cordage of the shrouds was not sufficient for the strain. A topmast went, and the spritsail yard. Down in the waist, the ship was completely awash. Sailors could not be allowed to go there to handle the gear.

The wind whooped. In huge right-to-left blows it hit the ship. Flowers from the savannahs ashore, anything light and small—birds, a lizard, leaves—came strangely along the gusts. Then the center of the storm whirled off to the north.

There was calm. Half the crew worked the pumps. The bosun led the rest to reset the shrouds. The carpenter and his mates stuffed caulking by the handfuls into the opened seams. Relief was allowed the helmsman. Officers on the poop cleared the brine from the compass binnacle and did their best to estab-

lish bearings. But the storm came back, the second half as violent as the first. Hours more of buffeting were endured before the ship was safe.

With the return of normal weather a pirate ship proceeded on her courses under the beneficent Trade. That, holding generally from the northeast, gave names to the islands. Thus the Leeward Group, Puerto Rico and her sisters to the west, and the Windward Group, those to the south, for which the French have taken the beautiful name of Les Îles Sous le Vent—the Islands under the Wind.

The Spaniards, during the more than hundred years that their power held the Caribbean solidly, had for the land from Panamá on along the curve of the South American continent to the Orinoco the title of *Terra Firma,* or the Main. But the pirates soon called the region from the Bahamas on down to South America the Main, for here no ships except those under Spanish license were supposed to navigate. A man who defied the Spaniards was a pirate; legally, he had no existence.

The Spaniards cherished the Main. They conceived of it as the miraculous source of wealth that would resuscitate their impoverished, war-crippled homeland. But they found the Bahamas of small immediate value to them, and Cuba not much different. Cuba had three low ranges of mountains, and an indented shore line with a few good harbors like Havana and Santiago. There was not much gold inland, though, and Arawak slaves driven by the lash worked the sugar cane. These were exhausted in a generation, died from hunger, disease and torture. They were replaced by the Lucayans from the Bahamas, and into the vacuum left as the Lucayans were decimated came the first Negroes from Africa.

South of Cuba, between 17° and 20° north latitude and 68° to 74° west longitude was Hispaniola. Here was an island as beautiful as any sailor was ever to see. Columbus in his euphoric nationalism had given it the title, Little Spain. It stood against the dawn and the Trade like an immense, up-tilted

*The
Spanish
Main*

The Age of Piracy

shield, each rib a mountain ridge. Cloud dragged the summits, dissipating with the sun, tattered by the wind. The contour showed sharp; many ridges bare and brown, darkly marked where electrical storms had swept fire into the forests. Below, on the slopes that dropped like green waterfalls to the sea, was the virgin timber.

The men sent from a ship to reconnoiter stopped their rowing. They let the pinnace drift. A swerve of current almost took them down on Tortuga. But they hardly noticed it. They stared at Hispaniola.

Some trees were tall shafts of flame color. Others were the coconut palms that afforded food, drink. The rest were such as Europeans believed to exist only in the fables of Cathay.

The men beached the boat. Thornbush and machineel and sea grape; they crashed through, and past the palmettos and palms and weirdly tangled mangroves of the shore. Now they were in the forest itself and they took their cutlasses and hacked aside the liana tangle, cut into the bark of the wood.

Mahogany and rosewood and satinwood and lignum vitae and pine and cedar and cottonwood, they came to call the stands. And logwood that stained the hands red, and mapou, and trees that hung with gourds which, when dry, chattered with the wind. Orchids grew in the moistness of the thickets beside the streams. The flowers in the savannahs and the creepers overhead were as bright as the iridescent butterflies among the shoulder-high ferns.

The pirates went back to the beach. They looked in vain for the people of the island. But the Tainos, a tribal part of the Arawaks, kept deep within the forest. They were the last survivors of the Spanish cruelty, and a bitter distrust dominated their lives.

They had been a simple and an innocent people, their existence without much distinct purpose. Before the arrival of the Spanish about a million of them lived in the islands. The men were quite tall, and supple in their movements, and smeared their yellow skins with *roucou,* a reddish vegetable dye that was a protection against the mosquitoes that bit like the smack of a whip. Men, boys and young girls went naked. Only the women wore a kirtlelike skirt from the navel to the knees. They bound the heads of the children at birth between planks, or the mothers pressed them flat between their hands, motivated by some obscure religious compulsion.

Crabs, gathered on the beach, fish, the little, brown-furred conies that burrowed in the ground, cassava flour made from the manioc root, maize johnny cakes were their food. The women made a maize wine, masticating the kernels, then spitting the stuff out to ferment. A hard, pointed stick was their plow, their hoe. The men built drums of logs, H-shaped apertures cut in the sides for added resonance. Men danced with men, women with women, and sometimes as the chief drummed, there was a sexual stimulation and couples danced opposed to each other. Beyond that was the satisfaction they got from the tobacco leaf they smoked.

They spread it, half green, over a loose, not very hot fire. Then, as the smoke from the leaf arose, they inserted bamboo rods in their noses and inhaled until they were in a state of ecstasy, which declined gradually into stupor. The chiefs' women with traditional acceptance carried them to their hammocks.

But there was also religion to occupy the thought when the tobacco bouts dulled. The northern region of Hispaniola was called Bohio. It meant, in the Arawak talk, the Great Country. To the south was Quisqueya, the Mother of Earth. Between them where the great mountain ranges ran was Haiti —the High Country. There were the sacred caverns that held the gods.

The gods were called *zemes* and were worshiped in the shape of crudely cut stone idols of grotesque human beings or animals. It was the Arawak concept that the sun and the moon emerged from Haiti to enlighten the world. Pilgrimages were

The Spanish Main

made to the sacred caverns. Fragments of meteor stone, carefully polished, were put before the idols, and ornaments, beaten into shape from the alluvial gold taken out of the mountain streams.

Gold betrayed the Arawaks. Lacking it, the Spaniards might have let them live. But within fifteen years of the discovery in the name of His Catholic Majesty, less than fifty thousand of them remained on Hispaniola and Cuba. Later, they became extinct.

But beyond Hispaniola for the pirates was the lure of the Windward Passage that opened out past the huge crablike claws of the island to Puerto Rico and Jamaica. Spanish *guarda costa* vessels patrolled it and had to be avoided in the bays, the coves and bights and river mouths. Then the short traverse was made across the Mona Passage south to Puerto Rico.

Puerto Rico, the Rich Port, was also mountainous, laced with rivers. The main town of San Juan had been very well fortified, though, and the garrison was one of the strongest on the Main. The pirate captain braced his yards fair to the wind and stood away to the westward.

The next island was Jamaica. It lifted from the sea much like Hispaniola, the peaks of the range on the southern shore a vast emerald scarp that caught the wind. Below them was a curiously shaped, long coral formation, curving to create a sheltered bay. The Spaniards called that Los Palisados and it deserved the name, for within the curve vessels of any draft could safely anchor.

Ashore was a verdant beauty to equal that of Hispaniola, but also the deadly orange-splotched coral snake which was unknown on the northern island. Small rivers in the interior were held by five- and six-foot-long alligators. Geese, ducks, which came from a much colder climate, appeared transitorily in the lagoons among the mangroves and after the wild rice. Behind the coastal range was a fantastic region of nightmare appearance: irregular holes and pits and crevasses worn by the rain in the soft limestone rock. The coastal settlements were without wealth, though, and the port protected by Los Palisados too difficult to attack.

The ship stood forth to sea. South again, and east, bucking the Gulf Stream push, yards hauled around to take every slant from the Trade. Once clear of the lee of Puerto Rico, there was island after island. The Virgins were sailed down— a sprinkling of more than a hundred in that group, some barren reefs and cays with just enough soil to support the swaying palmetto rows. Then the Saints—Bartholomew, Eustatius and Christopher—the last two volcanic, the slopes gentle to the sea, and at the peak of Christopher, in the thick forest, the only monkeys on the Main.

Then Nevis, where the landing party found hot mineral springs bubbling from the ground, and Antigua, low and violet-shaded under the summer rain, Monserrat and Guadeloupe, where there was a live volcano that the French buccaneers named La Soufriére. It sent up a grayish smoke plume like a signal flag flung widely to the sky. The mountains had the same quality as Hispaniola, the valleys lilac in shadow, mist wreathing fast along the ridges at night and spangled with sun at dawn.

Along to the southward were more of the volcanic chain, and Dominica, rugged and wild and inaccessible. This was Carib country. The Caribs were cannibals. High on their menu were Spaniards, although one captured priest given to the pot had made them very ill.* The landing party sent in from the pirate ship with the fresh-water casks were all dressed in rude cassocks and fervently crossed themselves.

Martinique, on beyond, held Pelé, and the mountain sputtered and fumed and from the crater the night was lit with a ruddy sheen. Men who went ashore on Martinique found great forests, and batteries of crickets that each dawn promptly at four thirty stopped their rasping chorus, and the most deadly

* Père Labat, *Journal*

The Spanish Main

snakes in the islands. These the French buccaneers named; they became the *fer-de-lance.*

The buccaneers came on eight varieties. A large number were dark gray, speckled with black, the exact shade of the tree roots where they hid. The head was triangular-shaped, the iris of the eye orange with a red flash through it that at night glowed like the embers of the Carib cedarwood fires or Pelé. Some of the rest were a banana yellow, and yellowish brown, wine-lees red, absolute black with a pink or yellow belly, and all the color gradations of jungle mold and decomposition. They mounted to the summits of coco palms, swam rivers, climbed walls, coiled in the thatch of roofs, bred everywhere in the dank underbrush. The Caribs were defenseless against them; they accepted them with the stoic fatality they refused to accord the Spanish.

The captain took his ship from the land and stood out again to the southward. Few ships were in these waters, and most of the islands were left to the Caribs. The one named St. Vincent was heavily wooded, the wild cotton blossoms sparkling along the shore, the scent of arrowroot on the wind. The Grenadines stretched in a slender cord towards Trinidad. This was big, occupied by a garrison, and Sir Walter Raleigh, in his time, had sacked it. But there were *guarda costas,* and the ship sailed east, out into the open board.

Barbados lay alone, rich only in sugar cane and a green so intense in color that in the midday sun it shone almost blue. The pirate captain came around on his course. He headed for Curaçao, low, flat, nothing except a cattle ranch for the Spaniards close across on the South American coast. Their ports there on the original Main were Borbaruta, Coro de Vela, and the pearl fisheries on Margarita and at Rio de la Hacha, then Cartagena de Indias.

If a man could get into Cartagena he could have a fortune, because Cartagena tapped the immense wealth of the Andean highlands behind it. But a fleet was needed to take the place, and even Maracaibo on the lake and the town of Gibraltar at the other end, in from the sea, were jealously guarded. They had been raided and raided, and the garrisons were big.

Along the Main, with the Gulf Stream push astern, the courses were laid off carefully, the lookouts doubled aloft day and night. Here the coast swung to the Isthmus of Panamá. The ports were Madre de Dios and Puerto Bello where each year, even in that stinking, fever-ridden town the Spaniards held their great annual fair. Merchants from Spain came to it with finished European goods and traded them for the gold and the silver bullion of Perú, the llama wool, the wax and drugs and dyewoods, even the hides that had been brought from as far away as the Rio de la Plata and Buenos Aires. Across the Isthmus was Panamá City where the loot was stored during the months before the fair.

But a man needed more than a single ship's company to raid Panamá. So the ship kept north, avoiding the *guarda costas*.

The Mosquito Coast was miserable in rain. There were prizes of hides and dyewood and some gold off Yucatan, then Campeche, from carracks that were considered too small to be given protection by the fleet escort. That fleet waited in San Juan de Ulúa below Vera Cruz for the treasure to be transported out of New Spain. It would join later at Havana with the other fleet from Puerto Bello. Together, under double guard, they would sail for Spain.

But the pirate captain remembered the Gulf Stream thrust. He traced in his mind the reefs, the shoals, the tortuous passages and the storm tracks the huge, deep-laden ships would meet before they were north of the Florida capes and squared away into the Atlantic. There would be stragglers. His was a lot always anxious for a prize. But he could afford to wait longer than the Spaniards. He and his crew held no orders to sail home.

The Spanish Main

The Points of War

"King James, who from his infancy had reigned in peace
with all nations, had no employment for those men of war
so that those that were rich rested with what they had;
those that were poor and had nothing but from hand to
mouth turned pirates; some because they became slighted
of those for whom they had got much wealth; some, for
that they could not get their due; some, that had lived
bravely, would not abase themselves to poverty; some
vainly, only to get a name; others for revenge, covetousness
or as ill."

CAPTAIN JOHN SMITH, in *Travels and Adventures*

The method of the chase for a pirate at work in the Caribbean
during the great age was of prime importance. While the confines of the sea aided him, and he could use its islands to mask
his actions and sail suddenly out into the narrows of the Florida
Strait or the Windward or the Mona Passage, danger might
rest with a guard ship, a heavily armed escort beyond his sight
at the time of the attack. So he sought to engage as much as
possible at dawn and at dusk, while the light was not clear
enough for him to become the pursued instead of the pursuer.

His vessel was almost invariably the smaller among those
to be engaged. He liked it that way. Speed, the ability to maneuver, a low silhouette and a shallow draft, to allow him to
escape into some back creek after the capture was made, were
distinctly to his advantage. The rig he preferred was a sloop
of from twenty to thirty tons.

52

The "sloop" of those days meant a single-decked vessel. It was much broader in beam and heavier in construction than the conventional present-day craft of the same name. In almost every case, she had been built originally as a cargo-carrier and the pirate had seized her as a prize. He cleared her decks of any roundhouse or other obstruction so that the crew could move fast from side to side. He raised her bulwarks to waist height to hide the attackers from sight until the last possible moment. His ordnance was small: a few light four-pounder cannon, the maximum number quite probably ten, fired in defense rather than assault.

The pirate trusted his ability to board, to fight hand to hand for his prize. His favorite weapons were the cutlass, pistols, the boarding axe and pike, grenades, stinkpots, and, occasionally, the musket or a swivel gun. The cutlass took its name from the curtal axe of the Middle Ages. The blade was approximately three feet long, slightly curved and thick, the brass guard round and protecting the hand and wrist of the man wielding it. Both thrust and cut were delivered with it, and a blow could sever a man's head or arm from his body. The pistols were flintlocks, the barrels of iron, sometimes of brass. Their customary caliber was .50 or .60 and they threw an ounce ball. Up to twenty yards, they were deadly, and beyond they could knock a man down with a crippling blow.

The
Points
of War

The Age of Piracy

Each pirate supplied his own cutlass and pistols. The cutlass was carried at the hip. The braces of pistols were held in loops on slings of leather or cloth worn across the shoulder. Often in action, once the pistols had been discharged, they were flung by their owners at the enemy or gripped by the barrel and the butt employed. The importance given to pistol work is shown by the fact that the pirate who first sighted a prize was, after victory, given his choice of the best brace of weapons taken.

The boarding axe was like a huge, long-handled hatchet; it was used to chop through enemy rigging, nets and bulwarks. The cruelly pointed pike was for assault over the side of the enemy ship before man reached man in handystrokes. Grenades were made from square-faced bottles filled with gunpowder and pistol shot or old iron. They were often extremely effective. Stinkpots were crockery jars loaded with sulphur. The musket was, if the pirate crew were lucky, the excellently made buccaneer weapon. Swivel guns or culverins or petereros, were long in the barrel, with a bulbous muzzle, and fired scattering shot and old spikes and nails, bits of crockery or glass. They were referred to by the English-speaking pirate as the "Murdering Pieces."

There are on record also accounts of successful attacks made from small, lateen-rigged yawls, even rowboats and Indian dugout canoes, and these against ships of three hundred to four hundred tons, armed with as many as thirty-six cannon. The pirate was able to sail much closer to the wind than his big, square-rigged adversary, and in the case of calm he and his mates rowed or paddled until alongside. Risk meant very little to the men who persisted in such an attempt. Yet behind the seemingly inordinate foolhardiness were coldly calculated logic, experience in action and profound sea knowledge.

It must be emphasized that the pirate crews of the seventeenth and early eighteenth centuries operating in the Caribbean were exceptionally fine physical specimens. They had surmounted practically every disease, every hazard and type of wound; the weaker men were long since dead. Existing on a diet of smoked, jerked meat, fish and sea turtle and a few yams; adjusted to the climate, hardened by exposure, and with an enormous personal pride in their use of weapons, they were a formidable enemy. While they did not look upon the Spaniards as cowards or fools, they considered themselves definitely superior in any encounter.

When the action was between a small craft and a ship, the attack in most cases was made from astern. The best helmsman among the pirate crew, a real "sea-artist," took the tiller if the boat was under sail. He kept his glance intently upon the canvas of the ship ahead and exactly followed her course.

This was according to careful plan. Should the ship tack and come about, she would be able to deliver a broadside that with a single blast would sink the pirate craft. But, held stern-to, she could only serve the pieces mounted in her aftercastle, usually no more than four. And each time the gun-ports were opened and the gunners stooped to train the guns, they received volleys of musket fire.

Former buccaneers, or men taught in their tradition, stood in the fore part of the pirate craft. A pitching boat, spray across the face, a dimly seen target, did not deflect aim. They peered into the obscurity of the gun-ports at the straining gunners, fired, reached around for a freshly loaded musket, fired, saw that their aim was true, and then that the ports were lowered, shut.

The men with the muskets moved aft in the boat. Others, specially trained, came to the bow. They had a sack filled with wide wooden wedges, and big mallets. The sea-artist at the tiller sailed right up on the ship, underneath the scrolled and fancifully decorated aftercastle overhang. Sail dropped in the

The
Points
of War

55

boat; way was off her. Sharp-fluked grapnel hooks with light lines attached to them were thrown up to catch along the aftercastle molding.

Musket and pistol fire came down from the taffrail at the boat. Swivel guns firing scatter shot were depressed, but not enough. The pirate lot with the wedges worked fast. The wedges were driven in by the mallets between the huge rudder and the sternpost. It jammed.

The ship lay without the control of her helm on the sea. Her sails whoomed as they jerked aback. Voices shouted orders on the aftercastle. A trumpeter sounded the call to repel boarders.

Now the pirates went up, barefoot and bare to the waist. They swarmed the grapnel lines and the first man aboard was promised an extra share of loot. Toes shoved against the scroll designs, found the ledges of the lead-framed windows of the main cabin. Glass broke under pistol butts. Men were in the cabin. Their mates kept on, jumped inboard from the taffrail or were killed or flung backwards down the steep side to the sea.

Along the deck at the foot of the aftercastle ladders and on the poop the fight was decided. It was all handystrokes: cutlass, sword, dirk, a blow from a pistol butt or barrel, a pike, a halberd. The end was usually sudden—a cry given by the surviving senior officer; perhaps the crew, weary of it and liking life, dropping their arms.

Mercy was accorded in some instances when a ship was taken. But if men of the pirate company had suffered previously under the Spaniards, none of the officers was spared. If the fight had cost a large number of casualties, and the pirates found liquor too soon, often the entire captured crew was killed.

The story about the prisoners being forced to walk the plank is almost complete fiction. Examination of the record gives only a single example. Men were thrown over the side, though, and strung up from the yards for musket practice,

The Age of Piracy

pistoled point-blank. Such a sadistic brute as L'Ollonais boasted that he never spared a prisoner's life. In each ship, with the temper of the victors or the severity of the defense, fortune varied.

When Spanish wealth declined in the eighteenth century and the ships of almost any nation were seized as prizes, more humane treatment was the rule. Men of a captured vessel were asked if they wished to join the pirates. Some pirate captains made it an established practice not to press into their crews a married man; there was the morale factor to be considered. Surgeons although in great demand were not forced to sign pirate articles. Specialists like gunners, bosuns, carpenters and sailmakers stood little chance of going free. Women when found were badly treated. Accounts exist of pirate gentleness and forebearance, but in the main they are to be doubted. A woman's lot in a seized ship was not an easy one.

The pirates, in the later days of the eighteenth century as they ranged out from the Caribbean, employed larger vessels. Engagements were begun quite invariably by the exchange of false signals. Either ship, or both, ran up the flag of whatever nationality the captain decided might serve his purpose best. The pirate ships had a broad variety, but in most cases the skull-and-bones flag, (white upon a black field), or the hourglass and flaming arrow, or the skeleton in some form, was shown by the pirates to create fear and bring about a quick surrender. Failing in that purpose, the big red battle banner was bent onto the halyards. The record states, too, that this battle banner was sometimes plain black, without device of any sort.

The opposing vessel at last ran up her national colors from the poop staff. Within hailing distance and finally sure that he was threatened by pirates, the captain called forth the name of his ship, her home port and his own name. The pirate answer was delayed while both vessels maneuvered to gain the weather gauge. Then, if the pirate got it, the bawled yell came: "From the Sea!"

Streamers and pennons were hung from the yardarms of the menaced ship during the tense lull before the first shot was fired. The spritsail was furled and the yard brought alongside so that the pirates in boarding could not get grapnel hold. The lower yards were slung with chain and the important ropes, sheets and braces doubled.

Bulkheads and wooden cabin walls were knocked away when possible. Those that were left were fortified with bedding and hammocks against splinter damage. The guns were cast loose, run out, prepared for action.

Boarding nets were strung above the bulwarks of the lowest deck, along the waist of the ship, to impede attack. Tarpaulins were secured in the same fashion to protect the men stationed on that deck from small arm fire. Movable bulkheads of stout timber and planks, called "close quarters" and designed as further protection for the crew, were thrust into place on the side where the pirates would attempt to enter the vessel.

Musketeers were sent to the roundtops on the masts with orders to direct their fire at the enemy wherever exposed, but, without fail, at the officers. Supplies of grenades were sent up, and stinkpots. Pikes were issued to the men behind the close quarters bulkheads.

A similar procedure was gone through on the pirate ship except for the precautions against boarding. Powder and cartridges were brought up in leather-covered "budge barrels" from the magazines and stowed well away from the cannon, either amidships or from the side that was not to be actively engaged. Tubs of water, blankets soaking in them, were placed between the guns, against the possibility of fire. Other tubs filled with vinegar water or urine were hauled beside the guns for sponging.

The Points of War

59

The Age of Piracy

The light sails were furled, sent down on deck as a fire hazard. The doors to the magazines were hung with wet blankets to fend off sparks. Shot was sent to the shot lockers on deck. Sand was sprinkled. The gunner and his mates checked: the lead plates were taken from the touchholes; the powder was poured to prime the cartridges within the guns; the tackles led free. The gunner lit his linstock, a long iron-plated pikestaff with a forked prong at the end which held a rope match.

Orders came from aft. The carpenter was ready. He had his sheets of lead and plugs of oakum for shot holes. The cookroom fire was out. The working sails still aloft were splashed with fire-preventive solution, and the extra tiller ropes of rawhide rigged.

When there was sufficient time, the people aboard the ship about to be attacked were given a ration of beer or spirits, biscuit and a bit of meat. Then the hatchway ladders were taken up so that no man could desert his station. The "musickers"—drums, fifes, fiddlers and trumpeters—received the order to sound. They played the "points of war" while from the pirate ship drums and trumpets rapped and shrilled.

The pirate gunner let go his bow piece, a warning shot clear of the other ship's bow. The pirate crew showed themselves from below their bulwarks, wild, yelling, waving their cutlasses. Erect beside the quartermaster at the tiller, the pirate captain conned his ship rapidly closer. Grapnels were whirled aloft.

This was action. The opening broadsides were delivered. They were answered. The ships shuddered. The pieces were served, hauled, reloaded and fired, and down on the powder-darkened gun decks the men could barely see. Guns kicked badly in treacherous, unaccountable recoil as the barrels overheated. Rammers were told by the gunners to stand away from the side exposed to the enemy.

But the men detailed to handle the wounded aboard the attacked ship were already busy. The surgeon in his cockpit

61

The Age
of
Piracy

had them stretched in rows on old sails. They died, most of them stoically, from loss of blood while they waited their turn with him. Up on deck the crepitation of small-arms fire was unbroken. Then there was the shock of hulls meeting. Bare feet thudded as the pirates leaped the side. Cutlass steel racked. The surgeon wiped his face and kept on at his work.

Your Head or Your Son's

"If I call for it and it is gone, I will take your head or
your son's."

CAPTAIN WILLIAM KIDD to John Gardiner

Kidd meant the chest of treasure he had left with Gardiner
on Gardiner's Island off the eastern end of Long Island. No
man is more famous than he for the amount of treasure he is
supposed to have left or buried. The stories about the Kidd
caches stretch from the Indian Ocean to Hispaniola to Nova
Scotia and a number of improbable sites in between.

But Kidd took treasure, great treasure, and of that there
is no doubt. He also established a tradition. The popular imagination holds firmly to the scene on the barren strand. Crab
grass is in the foreground and in center perspective on the
wind-swept, sunny ridge are three figures; in the background
surf, a ship's boat, a boat-tender or two, some palmettos; and
on the horizon, a ship with the Jolly Roger flag at the mizzen
gaff. A pair of the central figures are palpably pirate seamen,
for they wear bandanas, earrings, loose, flapping cotton
breeches; pistols are in their belts, cutlasses at their sides.
Above a freshly dug hole they hold a chest. It is big and
strapped with iron and secured with a great lock, and on it
are carved mysterious letters along with the skull-and-bones
design. Behind the pair holding the chest is the pirate captain,
and that and the contents are unquestionably his.

He stands the ridge astride, eyes somber under the sweep
of the tricorne. His dress is almost fancy, and slightly shabby.

The Age of Piracy

Lace is at his wrists, his throat; the coat he wears was not long ago magnificent and his boots are still fine. His pistol sash contains several weapons, the sword on which his hand rests is of Toledo manufacture, the hilt and guard bossed, the scabbard chased in silver.

Howard Pyle in his illustrations for his "Book of Pirates" did a very great deal to perpetuate the tradition and create the scene. Yet Pyle's work was essentially remote from the truth. Only a rare, small group of pirates, Kidd among them, ever left any treasure anywhere. They spent it in their lifetimes, as fast as they took it and could get back to port, or they were killed before they could amass much. The alehouse keepers of Port Royal in Jamaica, the trulls and doxies and pimps and go-betweens and agents, lastly and most importantly, the merchants of the coastal ports of England, France and colonial America who outfitted the pirates got the greatest share of the loot.

Prostitutes durable enough to accept the love-making of the buccaneers went home wealthy to Europe from the beach huts of Tortuga. There is a well-authenticated account of the Henry Morgan days in Jamaica in the latter half of the seventeenth century where a pirate was chased to sea by debt. He had extended his credit to the limit with a Port Royal alehouse keeper. Ship out, he was told, go on "the account" or he would be sold, according to law, into indenture to liquidate the sum owed.

Instead of being buried in chests on isolated tropical strands, "Arab gold" (*i.e.*, pirate loot brought back from the Red Sea and Indian Ocean regions) was common currency in New York in the 1670's and '80's and to the turn of the century. Then the East India Company, under orders from London and after threats of severe reprisal from the potentates who had been robbed, began to close down on the marauding activity. Before that, pirates in from a voyage frequented at their leisure the Manhattan pothouses along Dock and Great Queen

Streets and the Beaver Path, but with most of their share-out already in other hands.

Colonel Frederick Philipse, for twenty years a New York City Councillor, was broadly alleged to have sold pirates gunpowder, spirits, flour and all sorts of stores at enormous rates. Robert Livingston, a manor-lord and also a colonel of the New York militia, is said to have backed many Red Sea letter-of-marque ventures. Respectable merchants of Boston and Salem and Philadelphia and Charleston, even unto a number of governors* were in the trade. They set up clearinghouses for the loot. Some of them had factors or agents at Santa Cruz in the Danish West Indies, for a considerable period in the late seventeenth century a pirate rendezvous, and as far afield as Madagascar, right at the source of the seized wealth.

Still, the man who sailed perilously for such masters clung to an illusion. He held close the dream that he in his short time could become rich. The rum wouldn't stop him, or the fever, or the harpies and the smooth-talking dock folk. No, he'd get his, too.

There was reason for the dream. Men had drawn fantastic wealth from piracy. Among the illiterates of any pirate crew the great stories were known, told and retold.

Sir John Burgh, in 1592, had taken the fabulously rich-laden Portuguese carrack, *Madre de Dios*. That was twenty miles west of Flores Island in the Azores and near the position where Grenville fought his famous battle. Grenville had engaged five big Spanish galleons while five more stood by ready to relieve. He was dismasted, his crew decimated, his guns lost, the decks smashed out of the ship. She received eight hundred shot, but she burned three of the galleons and put a fourth ashore and killed a hundred Spaniards. His terms of surrender were accepted: the survivors of his crew were to be sent back to England. Then, grievously wounded, he was taken

* We will go into the governors' story in a later chapter.

Your Head or Your Son's

65

aboard the Spanish flagship. He lived for three days in intense agony and, out of his mind with it, crunched and swallowed a wineglass to "show his English spirit."

Burgh must have been imbued by Grenville's example. The *Madre de Dios* was of more than sixteen hundred tons and carried a crew of eight hundred men. Burgh fought her for sixteen hours, took her and sailed her into Dartmouth harbor on Queen Elizabeth's birthday. The ship was in from Malabar and the Spice Islands.

Her cabins were "lined with rich carpets of a thousand hues, sarcenet quilts, lengths of white silk, and cyprus." Her holds were charged with benjamin, cloves, nutmeg, civet, ambergris, frankincense. All told, she had aboard 530 tons of spices, and fifteen tons of ebony, and chests of sandalwood that held rubies, pearls, amber, porcelain, ivory, rock crystal, golden armlets, crystal forks and spoons set with rubies. There were planks of cinnamon, pots of musk, tapestries, satins. Her pepper cargo alone was estimated at 102,000 pounds sterling. Two huge gold crosses were found aboard her, and diamond pieces set with precious jewels.

The captains who had sailed with Sir John Burgh disputed his possession of the loot. A division of a kind was made on the dock in Dartmouth. The town went mad in a frenzy of cupidity. Fights broke out; thieves, jewellers, prospective buyers and officials whose duties should have kept them in London hurried down the Dartmouth Road. It was for several days a fantastic fair.

Sir Walter Raleigh was in the Tower of London under Elizabeth's dire disapproval. Yet she recognized that he was the one man who could put matters straight at Dartmouth, for most of the crews involved had been hired by him. He was released and sent to adjudicate. Along the way, he met officials who had hidden on their persons some of the crystal spoons and golden armlets, sacks of rubies, pearls. He cleaned them out and they went on sorrowing. For his share of the work in the port, when he had terminated the fair and settled all claims, was thirty-six thousand pounds. Elizabeth in addition restored to him his freedom.

Raleigh was never again so lucky, never got so much for so little ventured. But the common pirate had clearly in mind the fortune Thomas Cavendish had taken in his ship, *Desire,* while circumnavigating the world. Cavendish had caught up with the great, the eagerly sought Manila plate ship off the California coast and stripped her to the bilges. On his return home in September of 1588, because of the strained relations with Spain, the amount of the loot was kept secret, but by any account it was immense, and Cavendish was knighted.

Sir Francis Drake in his Nombre de Dios raid on the Isthmus of Panamá during his expedition of 1572–3 admitted to having seized more than twenty-thousand pounds in gold. But it was only his own share and the shares of his men; the largest part of the haul was split with his French pirate allies who had helped him attack the Spanish mule train that carried the treasure. Drake, who later took the famous Spanish ship, *Cacafuego,* and her wealthy cargo off the South American coast, was reticent about the details upon his return home. The fact was still known that he had paid off his backers to the tune of 1400 per cent on their investment.

Men woke up at night on the watch below to talk of that. They repeated to each other what was known about the *Cacafuego* wealth. Drake had made the share-out with his crew on a Peruvian island that buccaneers, out of due respect, had since renamed in his honor. The spoil was equally distributed. Each man of Drake's company was given sixteen bowlfuls of doubloons and pieces of eight.* That was right—sixteen bowlfuls.

When the Tortuga buccaneers who served under the French commander, the Sieur de Poincy, at the siege of Cartagena de Indias, in 1597, were told that their part of the loot

* Doubloons = $8.00; pieces of eight = $1.00.

The Age of Piracy

was only forty thousand gold ducats* they went back on their own account. They sacked the city with real thoroughness and came away with several million dollars in plunder.

Even the Englishman, John Oxenham, executed much too fast by the Spaniards, had done better than Drake on the Isthmus of Panamá. And when a man talked of Panamá, you couldn't get around Henry Morgan. He had been the greatest there. Morgan in the sack of Panamá City alone had captured loot worth at least a million and a half dollars.

Add to it his other prizes. Puerto Bello on the Isthmus must have brought eight hundred thousand. Puerto del Principe in Cuba a clean seven hundred thousand. Maracaibo and Gibraltar down along the coast of the Main, another four hundred thousand. Then there were the ordinary sea captures and smaller, incidental raids. They gave a quarter of a million. So, all counted, Morgan had piled up $3,560,000, no mean work for the space of a few years.

Nor should a man forget what the Dutch admiral, Piet Heyn, had done off Cape San Antonio to the westward of Cuba in September of 1628. Heyn waited for the entire Spanish treasure fleet to gather at Havana, then sail for the Florida Strait and home. He closed with the great galleons and with his squadron of thirty-one ships, seven hundred cannon and almost three thousand men drove them inshore. The Spaniards attempted a running fight, but they couldn't outsail the Dutch. They headed the galleons into the Matanzas River near Havana in the hope that the ships might be beached and some of the cargo saved. Heyn came right in after them. He seized the fleet.

The cargoes from it when sold in Amsterdam—the gold and silver and sugar and logwood and indigo—were assessed at fifteen million guilders.** The Dutch West Indies Company, upon whose orders Heyn operated, declared at once the un-

* Gold ducats = $2.15.
** Guilder = 40.2 cents.

precedented dividend of a flat fifty per cent to its stockholders. But the Spanish commander, a general named Don Juan de Benavides, was looked upon with some disfavor for his loss of the fleet. He was returned from Cuba to Spain and put in prison, then he was beheaded.

The English captain and circumnavigator, Woodes Rogers, on his voyage around the world in 1708–11 fetched up with the "Acapulco ship" after he had sacked Guayaquil on the Chilean coast and taken other Spanish prizes. She was out of Manila and richly laden. The contents of her holds brought his total spoil to a value of approximately 800,000 pounds.

There were a number of prizes just about as great as the plate ship Rogers took. But their value was hard to calculate, for the wealth had been spilled from many hands. Captain "Red Legs" Graves, for instance, had sacked the Spanish island of Margarita off the coast of Venezuela in the 1660's and scooped up the wealth of the famous pearl fisheries and a huge amount of gold, too. Around the same time, the Sieur de Grammont came up with and captured a Dutch ship near Martinique in the Antilles. She was in a cargo worth four-hundred thousand pounds. Captain Jean David Nau, known better as Francis L'Ollonais, after a raid, in 1667 into the Gulf of Venezuela that included the sack of the town of Maracaibo divided with his men 260,000 pieces of eight. That meant every member of the crew drew more than a hundred pieces of eight and further got his share of jewels and bullion and silk.

Captain Ben Johnson at the end of his career as a renegade and Red Sea rover reached Constantinople with only a part of the booty he had won. It amounted to eight hundred thousand pounds. Before him, fifty years earlier, in 1695, another Englishman, turned pirate and operating in the Red Sea and Indian Ocean, the infamous Captain John Avery, seized the Great Mogul's own ship. He took out of her one

Your Head or Your Son's

69

The Age of Piracy

hundred thousand pieces of eight and one hundred thousand chequins* and a lot of other immensely valuable spoils.

The record was long, and complicated by half-remembered fact and falsehood. But out of it a man who sailed in secret desperation on "the account" could derive hope. Big hauls had been made; they would be made again. The failures, of course, were nearly forgotten. There were too many of those, and they were not to be mentioned while the rum lasted.

Beyond the pirate dream was the reality of the loot. It was of any conceivable kind and form, and over the centuries of the great age, in the ports where it was delivered or the seas in which it was seized, had vastly differing value. Spices, silks and perfumes from the East were close to the top of the list, though; and not far behind them in expanding commercial England, the indigo, cochineal, logwood to be used in the dyes for cloth. For the Spaniards and for the Dutch and French and Portuguese they were just as valuable. Then there were precious woods, and sugar, and later, tobacco and hides, and from the Spanish dependencies in South America, the superb and soft llama wool.

Sometimes, cruising to the northward in the summer months of extreme heat and fever in the West Indies, pirates struck among the cod fleet on the Grand Banks. Southward-bound again in the fall, they would meet up with a Spanish ship on the course for Puerto Bello. Then the cargo might well be bales of damask and striped and raw silks for the colonial ladies, bolts of uniform cloth, pieces of velvet by the thousands, bolts of sheer linen, bales of laces, hundreds of stands of arms, fowling pieces and pistols inlaid and damascened with silver and gold. Also, for colonial satisfaction, were cask upon cask of fine wines in the lower holds, and East Indian spices, and—more carefully stowed—candlesticks, religious statues, copes, chalices, miters, missals and patens.

The wines went down the pirate gullets at sea. The rest of

* Chequin = approximately $1.75.

70

the goods was sold at public auction at Port Royal or Santa Cruz or on the beach at Tortuga. The alehouses were jammed, and the harpies busy. A week, ten days, two weeks and the share-out was gone. Sober, hungry, hardly any wiser, the pirates began to look for another ship.

The gold they sought and so rarely found in great quantity came from the Mexican highlands of New Spain, from Guatemala, New Grenada and the South American mines of the interior. Fortunes in pearls were raised by Carib and Negro slave divers off the Venezuelan coast at Margarita and Rio de la Hacha and Rancheras; but the pearl fisheries, like the gold mines, were severely depleted within the space of a century after the Spanish conquest.

It was the incredible richness of Perú that maintained Spain. Potósi, "The Mountains of Silver" were in the province of Charcas, high, far in *Alto Perú*. The Indians had at last shown their Spanish masters how to use the Inca fire pots. Those were clay jars with air holes let into the sides. Charcoal fires were started in the bottoms of the jars, the silver ore piled on top, and the jars lined the ridges by the thousands to catch the wind. At night, the ridges glowed weirdly and the Indians stooped in stark relief to pull loose the molten silver.

Then, when the stuff was stamped into bars or ingots and the King's seal affixed and the King's inspectors had made sure His Majesty received his fifth, it was packed for transport. Mule and llama trains took it in hide-covered loads down the precipitous trails to the coast. Small ships picked them up there, along with cargoes of gold and wax and wool dyewoods and crude drugs, and stopping at each coastal port for further consignments, hauled them North to Panamá. They were stored in huge King's warehouses. Muletrains guarded by strong military complements took them later across the Isthmus to be loaded for the final voyage to Spain.

Two fleets of great size and under extensive escort sailed once a year from Spain to the colonies. One went to Cartagena

Your Head or Your Son's

71

The Age of Piracy

de Indias to pick up the gold and pearls and other cargo of that coast, then on to Puerto Bello for the Panamanian shipments. The other went to San Juan de Ulua, the port for Vera Cruz and eastern Mexico. At San Juan de Ulua were loaded the Mexican consignments and the cargo brought by the annual plate ship from Manila and the Philippines to Acapulco, then carried by mule train across the breadth of the continent to the east coast.

The fleet arrived in the fall, usually laid up for the winter. They outfitted and loaded in the early spring, took their cargoes aboard and sailed in May to meet at Havana. The final preparations for the voyage home and probable pirate attack were made in Cuba. Fast frigates were sent out to scout the Florida Strait. The passage called clear of danger, the fleets set sail out past El Morro and rounded clumsily and anxiously onto the northerly tack. When they were into the open Atlantic, and the coral reefs, the narrow waters and sudden storms were astern, they no longer need fear the pirates.

It was the lasting pirate hope to catch one of these ships, a straggler fallen out of the fleet, a prize that would take hard fighting, yet could be won. Sometimes there was success. Again, the attacks were beaten off, and the pirate vessel, riddled, half-awash, most of her crew dead, was forced to beach on the nearest cay.

So the practice became more and more common to go for any vessel that showed over the horizon. Stories are told in the old records of a pirate ship that, north of Jamaica and after a long chase, hauled up on what looked like a fine prize. But the gear was all foul aboard her, and the sails backed and gybed, were not trimmed to the wind.

The pirate crew boarded her. She was from the Guinea coast, in from the Middle Passage, and her cargo of slaves had broken loose from the holds and killed the crew. But among the slaves was no man who was a sailor. The pirates by signs explained the basics of sail handling, then left her to her fate.

72

Another unwanted prize was a ship loaded with horses being sent to Cuba. The pirates contented themselves with a few wild rides around the deck. Then, when one of their number had been thrown, they abandoned the ship to what was left of her crew.

After a long and savage fight off Jamaica, a heavily armed ship was seized, her crew subdued. The tarpaulins were thrown back, the hatch boards heaved out. Below the coamings were hundreds of felons bound from England to indenture slavery on the Jamaican sugar plantations. The pirates again gave sailing directions and set the ship on a course that would put her ashore around Montego Bay. It was country where the felons might hide, disperse and escape. Anyhow, let the Governor of Jamaica settle the rest of the problem. By the gesture, the pirates taunted him and expressed their feeling for the felons. Neither the felons or themselves, the pirates knew, would ever be fully free.

Your Head or Your Son's

73

Night of Great Miserie

John Hawkins was eight years older than his cousin, Francis Drake. He had made voyages down the West African coast, to the West Indies and the Spanish Main before Drake started to sea. But they were very much alike, of exceptional spirit, hard to the point of ruthlessness, in their way gallant and to the very last intrepid. The Spaniards declared them as pirates; that was justified in many ways. Further, the cousins were among the small original group of Englishmen to engage wholesale in the capture, transfer and barter—often by force—of Negro slaves.

Yet to them such conduct did not deserve reproach, violated no code which they had been taught to respect. Devonshire-born and Devonshire-bred, they had learned more from the sea than from any schoolmaster. It was the waves upon the cliffs seen through the study window that drew their fancy, and the way the tucks of a splice were finished in a piece of rope, how masts were set up and tackle rigged, and a cutlass whetted, a pistol primed. They knew the smugglers' trails around Tavistock village, and they knew the smugglers. Not long after they were able to swim the difference between high and low tide, they were sailing offshore in any sort of craft.

The word "pirate" in their vocabulary was something to be batted around for sport, like the ball used in the game of tennis played by the London gentlemen. England was a small and poor country and must expand or be crushed under the lopping weight of Spain. There, right past the headland, was the sea that led to other seas, and they were free and from them fortune could be taken if a man was sailor enough, owned the intelligence to handle the Spaniards.

In both families, the sea was heritage. John Hawkins's grandfather had served in the navy of Henry the Eighth. His father, William, had created, in 1530, the first English trade with Brazil. A chaplain in the Royal Navy with twelve children, Francis Drake's father wrote reflectively, "And as it pleased God to give most of them a living on the water, so the greatest part of them died at sea." *

When John Hawkins made his third voyage in 1567, he took his cousin with him. Drake sailed as captain of the fifty-ton bark, *Judith*. The expedition had Queen Elizabeth's blessing and two of its ships were owned by her. Reports from London at sailing time said that Elizabeth had been forced to lie most skillfully to the Spanish ambassador. But on the previous voyage Hawkins had returned with "a great store" ** of gold, silver, pearls and other jewels. The Queen was in keen need of what might be brought home.

Hawkins, who had served his apprenticeship in slavers, was in favor of a rather complicated method of gathering fortune. It was his fashion to sail to the Sierra Leone coast, anchor and go ashore by small boat. The coast was notoriously dangerous, fever-ridden, claimed to be the possession of the Portuguese who killed any interlopers they caught, raided by the Spanish and the Dutch, and populated by tribes that fought each other, turning without warning on the white men who came among them in the expectation of trade.

Hawkins had fought or bought in the past, depending on the circumstances. On his first voyage, in 1562, with three ships, he had procured three hundred slaves and, with a Spanish pilot aboard, squared away for the West Indies. Labor was in great demand on the Spanish plantations in the islands. He sold

* Walter Raleigh, *The English Voyages of the XVI Century.*
** Richard Hakluyt, *Principall Navigations, Voiages, and Discoveries of the English Nation.*

his lot for a fine profit in Hispaniola, paid off his pilot and headed home. Although the Queen was gratified by his success, he was informed at court that more discretion must be necessary. A decree had been made public at Madrid; it forebade all English trade in the West Indies.

His second voyage was in 1564. He had five ships, one of which, the *Jesus of Lubeck,* was owned very privately by the Queen. A larger number of slaves than before was taken. It meant fighting with tribe against tribe to get them, but once at sea the cargo was quite tractable. Hawkins put in at the island of Dominica, in the outer fringe of the West Indies. His purpose was to collect fresh water for the slaves. They were served with "such as fell from the hilles, and remained as a puddle in the dale." *

The course from Dominica was south, to the Spanish Main. It was new territory for Hawkins, and he had worked out a new idea. He closed with the mainland at Borburata, a small port near present Puerto Cabello in Venezuela. The Governor, he was convinced, might be persuaded to buy part of the cargo.

So that the Governor would share his conviction, Hawkins landed a hundred men on the beach. They were "well-armed with bowes, arrowes, harquebuzes and pikes." ** The governor lacked any such force. He agreed to what Hawkins considered a fair purchase price. The gratings over the main hatches in the ships were lifted; men went below and loosened the fetters. Staggering, blinking, sour in their own filth and weak with hunger and fever, the slaves were led to the sides, shunted into the boats and rowed ashore.

Hawkins counted carefully what the Governor had paid. Then he passed the order for the ships to proceed. He still had more cargo for sale. His next port of call was Rio de la Hacha, wealthy and famous as the center of the Spanish pearl fisheries. But here the man in command was the King's Treasurer; he respected fully the decree that barred trade with the English.

* Hakluyt, *Navigations.*   ** *Ibid.*

Hawkins put his one hundred troops on the beach. He sent with them two "falcons," small, light cannon. Those were trained on the Spaniards the King's Treasurer had mustered. They were fired; the Treasurer capitulated and bought, and Hawkins cleaned out his holds, sat once more in his cabin and estimated the total loot. Contented as he was, he did not know that on his return home he would be greeted quite openly as a hero.

An enthusiastic chronicler had written of him, "His name be praised for evermore. Amen." * But on this third voyage, in 1567, the luck was not the same. There were rough and costly fights with the tribes on the African coast, and Francis Drake at twenty-two was a veteran of repeated handystrokes combats. Then, along the Main, the Spanish officials were much more obdurate. Hawkins was forced to take Rio de la Hacha by assault while offshore Drake ran down and captured a dispatch boat that would spread the news of their arrival to all the coast.

They sold their more than four hundred slaves, yet only after great trouble. The officials of almost every port along the Main were afraid to violate the Royal decree. Trade was arranged and carried out at night. Cartagena de Indias, the wealthiest, the biggest town, was left because Hawkins decided that the haggling was unworthy of any forthcoming profit.

Hurricane season was about to break. His ships were slow and foul-bottomed and cranky. He headed them north with the aid of the Gulf Stream current to avoid the storm sweep. However, on the twelfth of August, 1568, between the western end of Cuba and the Florida coast, they were struck by wind of enormous velocity. The *Jesus of Lubeck* was pounded until her "higher buildings" had to be cut down. Her rudder was "sore shaken"; she was in "so extreme a leak" ** that the crew were told to be ready to abandon.

She rode through it with the other ships and held north

* Raleigh, *English Voyages.*
** Hakluyt, *op. cit.*

Night of Great Miserie

77

The Age of Piracy

again towards Florida. An even greater storm overtook them. Hawkins did what he could; his captains exerted the same fine seamanship. But they could not claw off and keep to seaward. They were driven down on the Mexican coast and the short, tight roadstead at San Juan de Ulua. Aware that they were fortunate to be alive, they offered thanks to God as was their daily custom and put their vessels into it, set down anchors bow and stern.

A flat and sandy, small island was between the roadstead and the inner harbor. It formed a lee for twelve Spanish ships that were at anchor there. This Hawkins saw swiftly as a boat was rowed off to greet him; he had been mistaken, he realized, as part of a fleet that was due in from Spain. He was aware that the port served the town of Vera Cruz beyond on the alluvial river, and that from Vera Cruz the *Camino Real,* the royal road, climbed into the highlands to Mexico City. There that connected with the road to Acapulco on the West Coast. All Spanish treasure came finally to San Juan de Uluá for shipment home.

Hawkins employed some of the shrewdness that had been to his advantage in Sierra Leone and on the Main. He kept two of the principal officials of the welcome party as hostages. But he sent off a conciliatory message to the Royal Viceroy at Mexico City pleading the effects of bad weather and hinting at the chance of trade and mutual understanding. The message would take some few days in transmission. Meantime, Hawkins kept his crews at a sharp lookout and held them at their stations. The youngest pageboy among them could sense that the circumstance was very precarious.

On the second day, over the palmettos that lined the shore, the topmasts of large vessels were sighted. Thirteen ships, each heavily armed and massive, came in single file through the roadstead. It was the expected Spanish fleet; aboard it was the new Viceroy to relieve the incumbent at Mexico City. The ships went to anchor alongside the English, and swung bumping with the offshore wind. Hawkins stood as if calmly on the quarter-deck and planned how best to meet the new Viceroy.

The man's name was Don Martin Henriques. He treated with Hawkins quite pleasantly, received him in the great cabin of his flagship. Terms were arranged. Supplies that were sorely needed by the English were to be brought from the town and paid for at established rates. The English were to have license to sell as much of their cargo as they wished. A dozen gentlemen from each side were to be exchanged, held as hostages.

Still, Hawkins was not content. He looked out a cabin window of the huge galleon at the island. It was no more than three feet above water at high tide. The length of it was a bowshot. Only two bowshots separated it from shore. Of course, he had owned the foresight while the galleons came into the roadstead to set up eleven of his brass cannon on the island; the advantage was clearly his. At any time, he could open fire, put salvos into the *flota* before a vessel was able to move.

Hawkins continued his conversation with Don Martin. He asked further concessions. The English were to keep possession of the island; no Spaniard was to be allowed there while armed; the number of hostages would be reduced to ten apiece. Thus only the truce could rest assured.

Don Martin agreed. A document was drawn that cited all of the conditions, and affixed with the great viceregal seal, and signed by both parties. Hawkins bowed and went back aboard the *Jesus of Lubeck*. A trumpet blast was sounded in his honor, and to celebrate the truce. The Spanish ships hauled up anchor and warped around the English, stood in past them to the inner harbor while each fleet saluted the other with ceremonial cannon discharges.

Almost three full days passed in a semblance of peace. Men in the three small, sea-battered English ships unremittingly watched the ships that so greatly outnumbered them. The gunners who manned the cannon emplaced on the island stayed close beside their pieces. Hawkins was suspicious. There

Night of Great Miserie

The Age of Piracy

were several signs that the Spaniards were about to violate the solemnly given word.

Hawkins called the sailing master of the *Jesus of Lubeck* to him. The master could speak Spanish, and Hawkins ordered that he board the Spanish flagship, protest to Don Martin. Boatloads of men were being carried out from the town to the Spanish fleet, as many as a thousand. Guns were being slewed around and trained on the English, or sent over into closer-lying ships.

The master saluted Hawkins, took a boat to the Spanish flagship. He was welcomed at the side, Hawkins saw, but that was all. A Spanish trumpeter on the flagship's poop let go the shrill, quick notes of the call to arms; it was answered by each Spanish ship and from inshore and the town. Gunners bent at once to the touchholes with the linstock flames and the gunports were up and the broadsides delivered like one enormous salvo.

Hawkins had calculated that three hundred Spaniards had gone into the ship alongside the *Minion*. She was much larger than *Minion,* her guns double-tiered. They hammered her from bowsprit pole to stern. Then her other batteries flung shot at the Englishmen on the island. Those men were killed where they stood or knelt or tried to run and swim. A very few of them managed to crawl into the *Jesus*.

The *Jesus* was under concerted fire. She got it from the Spanish ships around her and from the seized guns on the island. Hawkins blinked to keep the wood splinters from his eyes; he cried hoarsely for the bow anchor cable to be cut, the stern cable hauled in and every gun served. There was wind. The *Jesus* caromed from her berth and bent on sail and came about and ran down on the Spanish Vice-admiral's galleon and let go a broadside and another. The galleon began to stream flame; banners of it flaunted up the masts and shrouds to the furled sails.

Hawkins nodded, called an order for his helmsman. He

80

ran down tight aboard the next Spanish ship, served her as he had done the Vice-admiral. She exploded with the solid shot she took, then listed and sank. Hawkins veered past her survivors; he wanted to get to the landward side of the *Minion* and protect her. She was under way, her cable cut, and with what sail was left to her proceeding to sea. Hawkins thought about his cousin in the smallest ship of all.

Francis Drake had the *Judith* bound out for open water. The little bark had had her canvas lacerated, her hull punctured, still Drake could navigate. He beat to windward along the channel with swerving, eel-like tacks and evaded the brunt of the Spanish fire. Hawkins gave his attention back to the other two ships.

The *Jesus* had had her yards, her masts and shrouds chopped out of her by the intense cross salvos while she protected the *Minion*. She was a ruined hulk and could not be taken to sea. Now the Spaniards floated a pair of fire ships down-wind on her. Hawkins passed the order to abandon.

He managed to make his way into the *Minion,* and a boat filled with his men followed. But there were still some of the crew aboard the *Jesus,* and for them nothing could be done. Hawkins committed them silently to very dubious Spanish mercy and occupied himself with taking the *Minion* to sea.

She succeeded, threaded through the channel, reached the bar and there felt the fury of the northerly gale that still blew. Men jammed her decks in every available space; laden as she was and leaking so badly, she would never survive the night outside. Her last pair of anchors were hove and held. They kept in the ground during the night of "great miserie"* within two bowshots of the Spanish. Lookouts discovered no evidence of the *Judith,* and it was reckoned that she had sailed on her own course for home.

Dawn eased the sea. The *Minion* clawed offshore and reached into the Gulf of Mexico, clear from the Spaniards.

* Hakluyt, *Voyages.*

Night of Great Miserie

"So thus with many sorowful hearts we wandered in an unknown sea by the space of 14 dayes, till hunger inforced us to seek the land, for hides were thought very good meat, rats, cats, mice and dogs, none escaped that might be gotten, parrats and monkeyes that were had in great price, were thought profitable if they served the turne of one dinner."*

On October the eighth the decision was made to divide the crew. The ship, even under maximum sailing condition, would be unable to carry such a large company home. Hawkins drew the men up on the beach, listened to each in turn. There were two hundred, and one half of them, many no more than teen-age boys, elected to try the jungle and the Indians, test the quality of Spanish mercy. The rest were for the voyage home.

That was frightful. The ship was still overcrowded, rations almost at a famine basis. Men died daily in the higher, colder latitudes and spoke longingly of their mates left behind on the warm Mexican shore. Hawkins drove to the northeastward, saying little, dour and withdrawn, lines deep around the clamped mouth. A great deal of his thought, he admitted later, was for the men he had been forced to put on the beach.

Wind took the ship past England. She fetched up on the European mainland, made her landfall at Ponte Vedra near Vigo. It was the Spanish homeland, and Hawkins was completely conscious of both the irony and the danger involved. Out of sheer necessity, a boat was sent in for supplies; any attempts at capture were evaded and she came back out with a supply of meat. It was most likely tainted, or the weakened men's stomachs weren't ready for it. But a number of them, once they had eaten, sickened violently and died.

Hawkins persisted. He laid his course up the coast to Vigo, took aboard there twelve English seamen to aid the remnants of the crew. Those men worked the ship on the final homeward run. January 20, 1568, she made Cornwall and Mounts

* *Ibid.*

Bay, entered and anchored. The voyage was at an end, and soon Hawkins was told that Drake was also safely home in the *Judith*.

Hawkins remained an embittered man for the rest of his life. He tried through devious, adroit representations to gain back from the Spanish crown what he considered to be his just losses. Madrid rebuffed him, and the majority of men who had gone from the *Minion* on the beach in Mexico were either subjected to the Inquisition, burned at the stake, condemned to years in the prison galleys or killed by savage Indian tribes. Hawkins wrote for his nation to understand:

> If all the miseries and troublesome affaires of this sorowful voyage should be perfectly and thoroughly written, there should need a paineful man with his pen, and as great a time as he had that wrote the lives and deathes of the Martyres.*

Hawkins elected to stay shoreside. He interested himself more and more in the growth of the Elizabethan navy. There is no sure evidence of bad feeling, but he and Drake were never as close again as they had been before the night of "great miserie" off San Juan de Uluá. The younger man seemed less dismayed by the experience; he was determined to return to the Main.

As his own commander, in the ship *Dragon* with a small, thoughtfully chosen company, Drake reached it in 1572. His principal purpose was to discover a shore base, raid from that against the Spaniards. He coasted South of Panamá among the shallows and reefs of the Gulf of Darien. When chased by a Spanish ship, he simply entered shoal water where the bigger vessel could not sail. The hidden, deep-water cove that pleased his fancy he named Port Pheasant. He had aboard *Dragon* four pinnaces fashioned to his specific design in England and stowed unbuilt in the hold.

* Hakluyt *Navigations.*

Night of Great Miserie

The Age of Piracy

Dragon was towed far into the cove, her topmasts struck, her guns and ballast shifted, and then she was careened, camouflaged with a lattice of tree branches. The pinnaces were put on the beach and assembled by the ship's carpenter and his mates. Drake went inland to hold conversation with the Cimaroons, the part Negro, part Indian people who had revolted from Spanish rule.

The Cimaroons were friendly with any enemies of Spain. The chiefs told Drake in detail of the best possibilities for loot. There was the port town of Nombre de Dios up the coast on the Isthmus of Panamá, lightly held because of the prevalence of fever, and yet the gold trains that crossed the Isthmus from Panamá City brought their wealth to the place. Drake studied his charts; he talked with his officers and further with the chiefs. The sea approach, an attack upon Nombre de Dios seemed the best. He spent long hours planning the assault in each detail.

Then the expedition pushed off in the pinnaces accompanied by Cimaroon guides. The town, Drake understood, was on a sandy bay that lay unprotected to seaward and was considered dangerous to the Spanish shipmasters ordered to discharge or load cargo there. A powerful fort guarded it on the east and dominated the harbor, and inshore were salt marshes that almost surrounded it. The buildings of the town were about thirty in number, made of wood, easily inflammable; the citizens were sluggish, the garrison weak.

Drake timed his arrival with care, came into the outer bay after darkness. His first point of attack was the fort. He had one hundred and fifty men, and he sent them up into it on the double under strict orders to make no noise. Sentries were seized, choked, subdued. The guardroom was taken, and the officer of the watch, then the entire garrison without a shot or injury.

This to Drake promised very well. He left seventy men

84

and a trumpeter to hold the fort and went down from it to the town. The place seemed full asleep in the misty night; shutters were closed on the houses around the plaza; the streets were empty. But Drake was able to discover the building that was the King's storehouse. The door to it was heavily barred. He ordered the bar broken.

The men working at the thick iron made noise. A shutter was raised in a house window, and a sleepy voice called. Drake stood tense. The town was eerie. It seemed incredible that there was no patrol through the streets. Perhaps, he thought, he had led his force into an ambush. He motioned to his trumpeter and the men who formed loose rank behind him.

They were armed with calivers, short-barreled muskets that gave a loud report. The trumpeter released his blast above the caliver roar and the wooden houses took up the echo. Now doors were open. People ran, barefoot and in nightdress. Their direction was away from the plaza, towards the marshes outside town. Drake smiled and looked up at the fort.

The signal had been prearranged by him. A trumpet blast answered the one from the plaza, and a caliver volley was fired from the ramparts. The citizens of His Catholic Majesty should be profoundly frightened. But at the far end of the plaza was a group that didn't run, and it was armed. Drake made out fourteen or fifteen Spaniards who wore cuirasses and helmets, carried arquebuses. Shot racked into the Englishmen.

Drake was wounded, caught in the thigh by an arquebus ball and knocked nearly off balance. He disregarded the wound while he formed his men. Then he led them in the charge. Part way across the plaza the pain and loss of blood stopped him and he slipped and fell, lay useless, his rapier in his hand.

It was enough for the men. They wanted no more of Nombre de Dios. Now was the time to go. Drake's wound was bound up and he was assisted, slack and weak, out of the plaza and through the blank dimness of the streets to the beach. The de-

Night of Great Miserie

85

tachment from the fort was already there. Drake lacked the strength to protest; he was put aboard a pinnace; the men crowded in and a course was set for Port Pheasant. Astern, as the boats breasted the offshore swell, the town appeared once more locked in sleep.

Drake lay and recouped for some weeks at Port Pheasant. But he held lengthy conversations with the Cimaroon chiefs. He was told by them in further detail about the treasure trains that traversed the isthmus. Fifty, sometimes sixty mules transported the rawhide-covered gold and silver bullion. The stuff was sent from the vast King's storehouse in Panamá City to Nombre de Dios for shipment aboard the fleet that came annually to take it to Spain. No attack had ever been made upon the trains; they were guarded by only a few cavalry who rode with the muleteers.

Drake began to plan, envisioning the terrain, computing the distances to be marched through the jungle and over the mountains of the Darien range, the chance of success returning under the load of loot. He didn't look forward to another failure like that at Nombre de Dios. Without loot, the best of his men would gradually defect from him.

But out at the entrance to the cove the lookout that kept watch at the top of a tall cottonwood tree gave a hail. There was a ship standing in from sea. She sailed as if these waters were known to her, and her gun-ports were triced and her pieces ready. Drake hurried to examine her in his long-glass.

She rounded up and her anchor splashed. A boat was sweated over the side, lowered, put in the water and rowed to the beach with only a small number of men aboard. Drake heard French spoken among them. He relaxed. These newcomers could be his allies.

The French captain called himself Tetu and said without preliminary that by trade he was a buccaneer. Port Pheasant was known to him; he had made use of it in the past for his own depredations on the Spanish. He expressed admiration for Drake's choice of site, asked in a friendly fashion what might be the English captain's next objective.

Drake did not hesitate. It was obvious to him that Tetu was of his own kind. He explained the idea for the mule train raid, and also cited the difficulties and dangers. Tetu was as decisive. He said that he would join in the raid with a picked detachment of his men if Drake would accept them as equal partners. Drake pondered that briefly, then approved of it. He and Tetu studied Drake's maps and came to the conclusion that they would take no more than a hundred men with them, sail north by pinnace before they started the march inland to bisect the route followed by the trains.

Drake was secretly quite pleased. He would much rather have the hard-bitten French captain as an ally than an enemy. The *Dragon,* careened and with the guns out of her, was defenseless. All Tetu had to do in the case of any disagreement here was to go back aboard his ship and order a broadside and the English force was finished. The buccaneers, too, had the reputation on the Main as being highly skilled at shore work, ambush and jungle combat. Drake's own English lot were brave enough, but not many of them had a real feeling for such, he knew. It was good fortune; he and Tetu should do well together. Drake called for his musickers to play and said that a pipe of claret needed broaching.

It was a long and a galling and anxious march after they left the pinnaces with a small crew of boat-keepers up the coast at the mouth of a river. The men struggled painfully through the bush. Mosquitoes pestered them; chiggers burrowed under toe nails, gorged, swelled and burst, spreading infection. There were poisonous snakes to be avoided, and what the Cimaroons called *tigres* (really jaguars), and long-tusked wild hogs that would kill if encountered suddenly, and boa constrictors that looped loosely, swinging from tree limbs.

Drake kept his men going with visions of the loot to be taken. Each would be wealthy, he promised. Never another

Night of Great Miserie

voyage. This was just about the last of it, lads. Then in darkness they were at the rudely marked trail and prepared to
meet the train.

While they crouched among the ferns and bamboos beside the trail, the Cimaroons explained to Drake the need for
absolute silence until the final moment of attack. The lead
mules of the trains were belled. A train could be heard as it
advanced along the trail. Just when it was opposite the point
of ambush was the time when the men should leap forward.

Drake passed the explanation on to his detachment. A
translation was given by Tetu to the Frenchmen. Weapons
were checked again, and the last slap at a mosquito permitted,
the canteens gulped dry of their supply of rum. Along the
black channel of the trail fireflies danced; monkeys chirruped
in sleep in the trees, and an orchid fell and softly burst and
men jumped at the sound.

Off in the jungle, just a thin tracery of vibration that
hardly reached the eardrums, a mule bell jingled. Man nudged
man. Hoofs thudded on mud. Rawhide that covered pack-
loads was scraped past cactus, rustled ferns, made bamboos
creak. There was a faster hoof thud: a Spanish officer rode a
jennet at point in front of the column. This was not yet the
time; Drake held back the shout to attack.

But across the trail one of the anxious young Englishmen
jumped upright and his white shirt showed among the ferns
before a Cimaroon could yank him back. The Spanish officer
halted his mount several yards further along the trail, then
turned, trotted to rejoin the column. It advanced, and yet
slowly, as if prepared for ambush.

The same officer led again. He stopped near where the
sailor had sprung up and called, *"Que gente?"*

"Englishmen!" Drake bawled. Waiting was of no more
worth.

The fight was short and confused in the narrow trail.
Pike, cutlass, dirk and pistol butt were used before the Span-

iards broke. Drake gathered his command, dared enough to light a torch and examine the treasure dumped from the mules. He cursed; this stuff was silver, and bulky, heavy. They had missed the gold train, quite probably because of the sailor's stupidity. The officer had been given time to warn the others, send the less valuable load ahead.

But Captain Tetu was wounded, and several more Frenchmen, some Englishmen. Take what you can carry and get out, Drake ordered. Follow me and head towards Las Cruces. That was a village farther inland where in the rainy season the muleteers passed the night before going on to Nombre de Dios. By chance, he might pick up more plunder there.

Las Cruces was a collection of palm-thatch hovels graced by a storehouse with His Catholic Majesty's seal on the door. It held no wealth, though, except in bolts of cloth and clumsy pieces of merchandise. Drake was furious; he was afraid that his escape route to the sea was cut off; the keen-eared Cimaroons told him they were able to hear the blat of Spanish trumpets. Fire the place, Drake said. A torch was thrown into the storehouse and the men swung from the deserted village into the bush.

The march was too much for the wounded. They dropped out along the way, and the more desperate among the rest of the men hid their loot in the shallow river bottoms where they forded. It was impossible to carry the stuff any longer, they said, as Drake remonstrated with them; once the Spaniards were shaken off, they would come back.

Drake kept on towards the coast. He marched with instinctive stubbornness, hearing from the rear, where the wounded had fallen, torture screams, the baying of blood hounds. From the crest of a ridge, he looked back in broad daylight and saw the gleam of cuirasses. Spanish cavalry, as many as three hundred. He looked around for Tetu. Tetu was gone, lost on some winding of the trail. But a man could not wait. There was the coast to be reached, and the pinnaces. The

Night of Great Miserie

89

The Age
of
Piracy

Spanish would put the whole lot to the torture if they were caught.

Drake lifted up his loot yoke-style on a sapling across his shoulders and marched. The men lunged, tripped, panted and wept behind him. He no longer looked back. His thought was on the pinnaces that should be waiting at the river mouth.

There were no boats to be seen on the dun spread of water where the river met the sea. Drake slipped out from under his load. He was so fatigued that he was numb. But he took a cutlass from a sailor and cut palmetto logs to make a raft, lashed it with lianas, ripped off a mangrove branch for a paddle. Alone, kneeling waist-deep as he came to the open sea and the raft was swept, he went forth to find the pinnaces.

They must be found. He had his duty to his men, and a not inconsiderable sum of treasure.

A severe squall had sent the pinnaces offshore. He sighted them once he was over the horizon curve, and their lookouts made out his naked body above the waves. The helmsmen headed in; he was picked up, and his breath back, talked fast. Every man on the beach and each sack of silver ingots were put aboard before the bloodhounds began to bell the alarm.

The little flotilla was well to seaward when the Spanish cavalry came to the water's edge. Drake estimated that he had outdistanced them by about half an hour. It was grievous about Tetu and the rest, but on the Main any man's life was within range of forfeit. Death, either way, was the price of the prize.

Drake remembered when the pinnaces returned to Port Pheasant. He apportioned the share-out with meticulous fairness, and the survivors of the French contingent received theirs in gratitude. The major part went to them. Drake and his men, the *Dragon* recommissioned and ready for the voyage home, shared an amount in excess of twenty thousand pounds. Port Pheasant had served them most happily.

Back in England, Drake was recognized as a figure soon to become a national hero. Merchants were eager to outfit any fleet that he'd take to sea; he was high in the Queen's favor and had far eclipsed his cousin, now content with dockyard life and an appointment as Treasurer and Comptroller of the Navy. "He was in many ways the perfect Elizabethan of tradition, short with a ruddy beard, utterly self-confident, quick to suspect enmity, a man of the boldest courses and courageous phrasing. He had a quick pictorial imagination. 'The wind commands me away.'" *

The urge was too great, and he was outward-bound from Plymouth once more November 15, 1557. He commanded a fleet of five ships and a company of 164 "men, gentlemen and

* David Mathew, *British Seamen.*

Night of Great Miserie

sailers." * The pretended and announced port of call was Alexandria at the foot of the Mediterranean, but his definite plan was the circumnavigation of the world.

He took the fleet south, holding for the Cape Verdes. Then canvas was set, braces and sheets trimmed for the long traverse haul. It was fifty-four days without sight of land to Brazil. One of the company, Edward Cliffe, who sailed in the ship commanded by Captain John Winter, left a vivid description** of the traverse and the cruise along the Brazilian coast:

The Age of Piracy

> Wee came to anker under the West part of this island (Mayo) the 28 day of Januarie, and stayed there untill the 30 of the same. During which time, our General appointed M. John Winter and M. Thomas Doughtie, to goe over to the East part of the island with 70 men, to get some fresh victuals. And as wee marched through the island, about the middest thereof, we found one house having a garden belonging to it, in wich wee found ripe grapes, also ripe gourds and melons, in the most dead time of our Winter. We found also a tree which beareth the fruite Cocos, which is bigger than a man's head, having within the utter (outer) coate, which is about 3 inches thicke, a certaine nut as bigge as two fists, and hath within a white substance, cleaving fast to the shell, which is halfe an inch thick, very pleasant to the taste, and within that a certaine hollownesse or voyde place, wherein is contained a pure and pleasant water in taste, and as some think, marveilous comfortable. As we passed through this island the inhabitants fledde into the mountaines, so that we could have no talke with them." †

Steering a South-southwest course, the fleet came to

. . . the isle of Fogo, so called, because it casteth contin-

* Hakluyt, *Navigations.*
** *Ibid.*   † Hakluyt, *Voyages.*

ually flames of fire and smoake out of the top thereof;
all the whole island being one high mountaine. Two
leagues West from the isle of Fogo, is another island called
Brava, where the sea is above 120 fathoms deepe neere to
the shore, so that we could not anker for the depth of the
sea, by reason whereof we were constrained to depart
without water.

Drake could recognize some of the further dangers ahead
of him. He proposed to push his small, poorly furnished ships
into one of the most inaccessible regions known to seamen, one
very vaguely described on any chart owned by him. So he decided to get rid of the Portuguese he had kept aboard as prisoners. But he kept in his ship a man named Nunez de Silva, an
experienced navigator who would serve him as pilot. He gave
the others at the Isla Brava a pinnace in which to make their
way, and wine, and bread, and fish from his short supplies.
Then he proceeded south.

The 17 day (of February, 1578) wee were right under
the line, which is the most fervent place of the burnt Zone:
where in the middest of February we susteined such heat,
with often thunders and lightninings, that wee did sweat
for the most part continually, as though wee had bene in
a stove, or hote-house. Here wee saw flying fishes in great
abundance, some a foote long, some lesse. Their fynnes
wherewith they fly be as long as their bodies. They be
greatly pursued by the Dolphine and Bonitoes, whom as
soon as the flying fishes espie, immediately they mount out
of the sea in great numbers, and fly as long as their fynnes
continue moyste: and when they bee dry, they fall downe
into the sea againe. And here is to be noted, that after we
came within 4 degrees of the Equinoctial, untill we were
so much past it, no day did pass without great store of
raine.*

* Hakluyt, *Navigations*.

Night
of Great
Miserie

The fleet met heavy weather, fog along with the rain, and the ships were separated. When it reformed, Drake put into shore for badly needed supplies.

The Age of Piracy

In the meane while there came about 30 of the countrey people downe to the sea side: and when they were within 100 pases of our men, they set themselves in array very orderly casting their companie into the forme of a ring, every man having his bow and arrowes: who (when they had pight (put) a staffe on the ground, with certeine glasses, beades, and other trifles) returned backe. Then the countrey people came and tooke them and afterward approached neerer to our men, shewing themselves very pleasant, insomuch that M. Winter daunced with them. They were exceedingly delighted with the sound of the trumpet, and the vialles. They be of a meane stature, wel limmed, and of a duskish, tawnie, or browne colour. Some of them having their faces spotted with divers colours, as red, white and blacke. Their apparel is a certeine skinne (wherein they wrap themselves) not reaching so low as to cover their privy members, all the rest of their bodies are naked, saving that they wear certeine roules upon their heads, whose ends hang over their shoulders. Every one beareth his bow, being an ell in length, and arrowes made of reeds, having heads, framed very strangely & cunningly of a flint stone. They be much given to mirth and jollity, and are very sly, and ready to steale anything that comes within their reach: for one of them snatched our Generals cap from his head (as he stouped) being of skarlet with a gold band: yet he would suffer no man to hurt any of them. They eate rawe flesh, for we found seales bones, the raw flesh whereof they had gnawen with their teeth like dogs. In this bay we watered, and victualed with seales: for there is such plentie that we slew above 200 in the space of one houre upon a litle island.*

* *Ibid.*

94

Then, in the drear, gray reaches of Patagonia, close to the Straits of Magellan, tragedy caught up with the fleet. The men went ashore, and

> . . . we found a gybbet on an hil, whereupon they were executed that did conspire against Magellan, and certaine bones also of their dead bodies. The 22 of this moneth (June) our Generall going to shore upon the maine with 7 or 8 of his men, met with 3 of the Patagons, having bowes and arrowes, who came neere to our men making them signs to depart. Whereupon a gentleman being there present, and having a bowe and arrowes, made a shot to the end to shew them the force of our bowes, with the which shot his string broke: whereupon the Patagons presumed to encounter them, directing their arrowes first at our M. Gunner, who had a caliver (musket) ready bent to shot at them but it would not take fire: and as he levelled his peece one of them shot him through the brest, and out at the backe, wherewith he fell down starke dead. Also the gentleman that shot the arrow was so wounded that hee dyed the 2 day after and with the other was buryed in a litle island lying in the said port. Our men left the slaine man on shore till night, and then fetched him in a boat. In the meane time the Patagons had stript him of all his clothes, and viewed his body laying his clothes under his head, and so left him untouched, saving that they had stuck the English arrow in his left eye. These men be of no such stature as the Spaniardes report, being but of the height of English men: for I have seene men in England taller then I could see any of them. But peradventure the Spaniards did not thinke that any English men would have come thither so soone to have disproved them in this & divers other of their notorious lies: wherefore they presumed more boldly to abuse the world.*

Drake must have gone to stand in contemplation before

* *Ibid.*

Night of Great Miserie

the gibbet that Magellan had reared for the execution of his mutineers. There was very strong suspicion in Drake's mind that Captain Thomas Doughty, one of his closest friends and a hitherto trustworthy officer, was guilty of at least disloyal talk against him.

In this Port our Generall began to enquire diligently of the actions of M. Thomas Doughtie, and found them not to be such as he looked for, but tending rather to contention or mutinie, or some other disorder, whereby (without redresse) the successe of the voyage might greatly have bene hazarded: whereupon the company was called together and made acquainted with the particulars of the cause, which were found partly by master Doughties owne confession, and partly by the evidence of the fact, to be true: which when our Generall saw, although his private feeling to M. Doughtie (as hee then in the presence of us all sacredly protested) was great, yet the care he had of the state of the voyage, of the expectation of her Majestie, and of the honour of his countrey did more touch him (as indeede it ought) than the private respect of one man: so that the cause being thoroughly heard, and all things being done in good order, as neere as might be to the course of our lawes in England, it was concluded that M. Doughtie should receive punishment according to the qualitie of the offence: and he seeing no remedie but patience for himselfe, desired before his death to receive the Communion, which he did at the hands of M. Fletcher our Minister, and our Generall himselfe accompanied him in that holy action: which being done, and the place of execution made ready, hee having embraced our Generall and taken leave of all the companie, with prayer for the Queenes majestie and our realme, in quiet sort laid his head to the blocke, where he ended his life. This being done, our Generall made divers speaches to the whole company, perswading us to unitie, obedience, love, and regard of our voyage; and for the better confirmation thereof, willed every man the next Sunday following to prepare himself to receive the Communion, as Christian brethren and friends ought to doe, which was done in very reverent sort, and so with good contentment every man went about his business.*

This peculiar, almost incredible scene took place July 2, 1578. A grave for Captain Doughty was dug on the same small island where the other dead were buried and the body solemnly interred. The men stayed on for two months in the bay which Magellan had called Port St. Julian. Then, their ships loaded with stores, fuel and fresh water and trimmed for sea, they sailed on August 17 to make the dangerous passage.

And the 20 of the said moneth we seazed (cleared) Cape Victorie, by the which Cape is the way into the South sea, called The streights of Magellan, the first discoverer thereof.**

Drake brought the ships west and north, up along the South American coast that was all but completely unknown to English navigators. He picked up an Indian who fished from a canoe, used the fisherman as pilot to lead the fleet into the small Chilean port of Santiago. A landing party went ashore into the town that had been very recently and rapidly evacuated by the inhabitants.

There was nothing like the extraordinary wealth for which Drake had hoped. The best available was taken from the town's chapel. It consisted of "a silver chalice, two cruets, and one altar cloth, the spoyle where of our Generall gave to M. Fletcher his minister." † With the religious endowment, Drake put to sea again on a continued Northerly course.

Luck was better on the upper coast. A Spanish ship was met with and taken and in her were twenty-five thousand gold ducats. She was also loaded with a quantity of Chilean wine

*Ibid.   **Ibid.   †Ibid.

Night of Great Miserie

The Age of Piracy

that the Englishmen declared very much to their taste. So fortified and encouraged, more raids were made against the local towns. "From hence we went to a certaine port called Tarapaza, where being landed, we found by the Sea side a Spaniard lying asleepe, who had lying by him 13 barres of silver, which weighed 4000 ducats Spanish; we tooke the silver, and left the man." *

Three small barks were seized at Arica. Out of one of them came "57 wedges of silver, each of them weighing about 20 pounds weight, and every one of these wedges were of the fassion and bigness of a brickbat." **

The major town of Callao, port for the capital city of Lima, was struck on February 13, 1578. All the ships in the roadstead were systematically rifled. One held "a chest full of royals of plate, and good stores of silks and linnen cloth." †
But, more importantly, there were men among the captured Spanish crews who would talk. They told of the enormous plate ship, the *Cacafuego,* which had just left the port bound for Paita.

Drake ordered the cables of the Callo ships cut so they would drift down on the beach and wreck themselves, then he bent on sail after the *Cacafuego.* He missed her to the northward at Paita and held course along the coast. If he didn't overhaul her soon, he knew, she would be safe with the rest of her sister ships under the guns of the forts at Panamá.

Drake promised that

> . . . whosoever could first descrie her, should have his chaine of gold for his good newes. It fortuned that John Drake going up into the top, descried her about three of the clocke, and about six of the clocke we came to her and boorded her, and shotte at her three pieces or ordinance, and strake down her Misen, and being entered, we found in her great riches, as jewels and precious stones, thirteene chests full of royals of plate, foure score pound

* *Ibid.*   ** *Ibid.*   † *Ibid.*

weight of gold, and six and twenty tunne of silver. The place where we took this prize, was called Cape de San Francisco, about 150 leagues from Panamá.

The pilots name of this Shippe was Francisco, and amongst other plate that our Generall found in this ship, he found two very fair guilt bowles of silver, which were the Pilots: to whom our Generall sayd: Senior Pilot, you have here two silver cups, but I must needs have one of them: which the pilot because he could not otherwise chuse, yeelded unto, and gave the other to the steward of our Generals ships.

When this Pilot departed from us, his boy said thus unto our Generall: Captaine, our ship shall be called no more the *Cacafuego,* but the *Cacaplata:* which prettie speech of the Pilots boy ministred matter of laughter to us, both then and long after.*

Drake's great good fortune continued. He met other Spanish ships along the coast and forced them into surrender and looted them. There wasn't another as richly charged as the *Cacafuego,* but he had already made himself wealthy; would, he hoped, be looked upon with favor by the Queen, and had brought his crews a share-out beyond their imagining. When it was rendered to them on a coastal island where the fleet cleaned, graved and overhauled, each man was given as his portion sixteen bowlfuls of pieces of eight.

The rest of the voyage has about it the quality of Homeric legend, although it is well and soberly recorded. Drake held to the northward for purposes of exploration, put into what is from the evidence the California coast around San Francisco. The Indians of the region were a curiosity to the English, but no source of wealth. Drake laid off the course for the Pacific traverse. He was becoming homesick.

For the most part in fair weather, with favorable winds, through days and nights that sparkled and glistened, the fleet

Ibid.

Night of Great Miserie

The Age of Piracy

steered west. The men were in splendid shape. They were the survivors of battle and storm and fever and Cape Horn cold; they were tanned and tough, keenly alive, and none of them was past his middle forties. Drake entertained his officers at dinner in his great cabin and musickers played while the meal was served on crested Spanish plate; the Chilean wine was drunk out of gold-lined goblets; jewels shone on the hands, at the throats of the officers; the cabin was radiant with the sunlight reflected from the embroidered tapestries hung upon the bulkheads. Here this company enjoyed with unabashed pleasure the spoils of victory.

David Mathew, in his *British Seamen,* gives a clear individual portrait of Drake. He depicts him seated at his cabin table "while his ship moved through the ice calm waters of the South Pacific, drawing new charts of the Americas and painting them with their proper colors, a mixture of heraldry, hydrography and bestiary." Drake had in no wise forgotten his responsibilities as a loyal servant of the Queen.

It is worthy of note that he never thought of further loot, although at times a profusion of wealth was close at hand. There was an occasion when he sent some of his officers to make a formal call upon the King of the Moluccas on the island of Ternate.

The King being yet absent, there sate in their places 60 grave personages, all which were said to be of the kings Counsel. There were besides 4 grave persons, apparelled all in red, downe to the ground, and attired on their heads like the Turkes, and these were said to be Romanes, and Ligiers there to keepe continual trafficke with the people of Ternate. There were also 2 Turks Ligiers in this place, and one Italian. The king at last came in guarded with 12 launces covered over with a rich canopy, with embossed gold. Our men accompanied with one of their Captaines called Moro, rising to meete him, he graciously did welcome, and intertaine them. He was attired after the manner of the Countrey, but more sumptuously than the rest. From his waste downe to the ground, was all cloth of golde, and the same very rich: his legs were bare, but on his feete were a pair of shooes, made of Cordovan skinne. In the attire of his head were finely wreathed hooped rings of gold, and about his necke he had a chaine of perfect golde, the linkes whereof were great, and one folde double. On his fingers hee had sixe very faire jewels, and sitting in his chaire of estate, at his right hand stood a page with a fanne in his hand, breathing and gathering the ayre to the King. The fanne was in length two foote, and in bredth one foote, set with 8 saphyres, richly imbrodered, and knit to a staffe 3 foote in length, by the which the Page did hold, and moove it. Our Gentlemen having delivered their message, and received order accordingly, were licensed to depart, being safely conducted backe againe by one of the kings Counsell.*

Night of Great Miserie

From the Moluccas to Java, and then Drake sailed for the Cape of Good Hope. "This Cape is a most stately thing, and the fairest Cape we saw in the whole circumference of the earth, and we passed by it the 18 of June." But he returned to an England that offered him dubious welcome.

He had to wait long, tense months while the Queen decided whether she was to declare him hero or have him beheaded as pirate. Her mind made up, she boarded the *Golden Hind* and knighted Drake and threatened the Spanish ambassador with jail when he protested. Elizabeth recognized that war was inevitable. Sooner or later, England must fight Spain. In that fatal struggle, men like Francis Drake should assuredly be among her admirals.

Sailing under royal commission from Elizabeth, Drake gave full value to her confidence. He sacked and burned Vigo, and in 1585 went again to the West Indies and plundered Santo Domingo City and Cartagena de Indias and Santiago and St.

* *Ibid.*

101

Augustine. *El Draque* became a curseword to the Spanish. He burned to the water's edge or destroyed with cannon a number of their ships in the harbor of Cadiz in 1587, and as a vice-admiral in command of one of the English fleet divisions took his share of glory against the Armada. He battered the Spanish ships from Gravelines onward, hung with those that remained after the Channel action until they were north of Scotland. Then, in an expedition against Coruna in 1589, he and Sir John Norris wrecked another Spanish fleet.

Drake was in his early fifties. He had sailed and fought and won enough to satisfy most any ambition. Elizabeth had further appeal to make to him, and his vanity responded. Philip II of Spain was once more threatening England. Invasion was planned; Spanish troops were massed across the Channel in Brittany. Raids were to be expected on the English coasts. So Elizabeth sought to stop Philip II for all time, sever his war sinews at the source. That meant that Panamá be taken and held, the flow of Peruvian gold pass into English hands, not Spanish.

Drake was fired by the idea. It was the sort of conception that aroused his grandiose fancy. He would ready to leave almost at once, he told the Queen. Let him immediately muster the crews, assemble the ships for the venture. Panamá would be easily his.

But there were cooler heads at court, and more deliberate natures, and Elizabeth was advised that it would be well if Sir John Hawkins, now in his sixties but still sturdy and resolute, accompany his eager if valiant cousin as joint commander. Hawkins had become a man who after years of service as a dockyard admiral was renowned for caution.

Elizabeth was in agreement. The two cousins were issued commissions of joint command, both instructed to raise their own crews, equip and provision the vessels equally. There was delay, though, and bickering at court, then hesitation that had behind it alarm. The Spanish coastal raids at Mousehole and

Newlyn and Penzance in Cornwall while the fleet prepared in the summer of 1595 were not to be disregarded. If a Spanish force could so readily attack England, what would happen when Philip set forth with the full Spanish army in assault?

The Drake-Hawkins expedition was held in port at Plymouth to meet Philip. Weeks dragged. Elizabeth was in one of her famous moods of indecision. It was all that Drake could do to restrain himself before his officers. His impatience caused him to be careless about the details of the voyage; he was aware that Hawkins in his vessels allocated space to the crews on the basis of a man to a ton.* That to Drake seemed excessive; after all, the total complement, about half of them soldiers, would not number three thousand. Let the men cram in where they could, and the victuallers figure out the ration lists. He was for the Main and action, the contents of those huge King's storehouses at Panamá.

He talked with Hawkins, imparted some of his fire to the older man. They proposed to Elizabeth that the expedition could reach Panamá, take possession, leave a sufficient garrison and be home again within six months. The plan was quite obviously near to impossible, though, and it was abandoned. Then an English letter-of-marque ship came into Plymouth with Spanish prisoners aboard. The entire Spanish plate fleet was home from the Main, the prisoners said, except for the flagship. She had been badly injured in a storm in the Bahama Strait, lost her mainmast. Leaking, her hull planks punctured, she had reached San Juan de Puerto Rico and now rested on the bottom mud, a practically defenseless hulk. At least two million ducats in gold were in her holds.

Drake and Hawkins took the word to the Queen. They pleaded that this was a venture which could be accomplished well within six months' time. Their single, simple objective would be the seizure of the flagship loot at San Juan de Puerto Rico, and thus they could return to the home station before

* Ton in this sense, a unit of space.

Phillip had his invasion fleet in readiness. Elizabeth acceded; war, she had been recently reminded, kept a nation poor.

The fleet sailed from Plymouth on August 28, 1595. Hawkins was in the *Garland,* Drake aboard the *Defiance.* Both were new, post-Armada galleons, and of powerful armament. Twenty-seven ships formed the fleet. It had the appearance, finally, of an auspicious voyage.

They had been at sea for only a few days, though, when a bitter dispute started between the cousins. During a conversation held at a fleet rendezvous, Hawkins accused Drake of bad judgment when Drake admitted that he lacked supplies for three hundred of his men. Hawkins went further; he refused Drake's request to make a landing in the Grand Canaries and attack to pick up stores. It was Hawkins's contention that such action would give warning to the Spanish, expose the purpose of the voyage. Drake answered that then he would take his division and attack alone. The troop commander, Sir Thomas Baskerville, backed him up and said that he could take Las Palmas, the main town, in four hours, collect the stores inside four days.

This proved to be grossly mistaken. The Spanish garrison at Las Palmas was entrenched, in a full state of defense against attack. A heavy surf was running, and the troop-laden English boats were unable to land. The orders for the boats were changed; they were sent around the island to take aboard fresh water. Those that got to the beach were captured, and there was nothing for the fleet to do but sail the Puerto Rican course. Drake did not need his cousin to tell him that now, certainly, a strong Spanish force would follow them.

Neither of the men knew, however, that Philip had already dispatched five *gallibrazas,* fast "running ships" used ordinarily as treasure-carriers, and that the Governor of the Canaries had also sent a fast caravel on the same mission of warning to Puerto Rico. The English fleet made a slow crossing. It was October twenty-eighth or twenty-ninth when the rendezvous was kept off Guadeloupe.

Some of the lesser ships were stragglers, had fallen back from the fleet. These the outward-bound *gallibrazas* from Spain picked up at sea short of the rendezvous point. Among them was the small bark, *Francis*. The captain of the *Francis* had written orders that gave the intention of the expedition; he failed to destroy them. Men in his crew under the threat of torture stated the size of the English force. But the consort of the *Francis,* almost too insignificant for Spanish notice, got away and reached the rendezvous. Hawkins and Drake were informed that Don Pedro Tello de Guzman was in command of the *gallibrazas* and bound straight for Puerto Rico.

Drake wanted to pursue the Spanish ships despite their headstart against the fleet. Hawkins refused. He cited the instance when, in 1591, an English fleet under Lord Thomas Howard and Sir Richard Grenville had been trapped in similar circumstances by the Spanish. First, he said, he must have time "to trim his ships, mount his ordnance, take in water, set by some new pinnaces, and to make things in that same readiness that he cared not to meet with the King's whole fleet.*

But even as he spoke Hawkins realized that the expedition was a failure. Hesitation had led to rashness, incompetence had been aggravated by bad luck, and no amount of daring could bring success. Drake expostulated with the usual ardor, then at last left his cousin's ship for his own. Hawkins saw him off and almost at once fell ill. This was October thirty-first, and he went to his cabin and lay down, and two days later he was so weak that he was incapable of moving from it. His malady had no name that the surgeons knew, still on November twelfth, with the fleet at anchor off San Juan, he died. He dictated to Captain Troughton at the end a codicil to his will in which he gave to Queen Elizabeth two thousand pounds, "to make Your

* Walter Raleigh, *The English Voyages of the XVI Century.*

Majesty the best amends his poor ability could then stretch unto." *

Drake was not yet daunted. He went ahead and attacked San Juan, attempted to take the strongly fortified harbor that was protected by an alert and large number of Spanish troops. The English were beaten off with heavy losses and the fleet stood away to sea. Drake, in the awakening of his anguish, called to the men from his quarter-deck, "I will bring you to twenty places far more wealthy and easily gotten." **

The promise turned out to be tragic bombast. Some loot was taken at Rio de la Hacha, but none at Santa Marta, and Cartagena de Indias was too powerful for the fleet. Drake pointed towards Panamá, landed Baskerville and the troops. They were repulsed and back in four days, asking to be received aboard. The road to Panamá was much more jealously guarded than when Drake had made his march to seize the mule train.

A great deal of fever was in the fleet. While the ships sailed the swampy mangrove coast off Nombre de Dios, Drake sickened of it and died. This happened on the night of January 27, 1596. On the next day he was given full honors and his body committed to the sea. Baskerville, a soldier, ordered the ships on the course for home.

* *Ibid.*
**J. A. Williamson, *The Age of Drake.*

And Greatly Daring

John Oxenham was an ambitious young Plymouth man who had served as one of Drake's lieutenants in the raid upon the mule train and in 1575 returned with his own expedition to Darien. He had a company of seventy, a ship of 140 tons and an original idea. Rather than base on the Caribbean coast he planned to strike overland, carrying the necessary arms and equipment, and upon the Pacific side of the isthmus, build a sailing pinnace and with it raid against Spanish shipping at will.

He warped his ship well up into Drake's hidden Port Pheasant, careened her, covered her with a lattice of branches until she was invisible, then dug pits for her heavy cannon and masked them, and prepared for his march. He had already procured Cimaroon guides, who were to lead them across the isthmus, and the expedition moved out with two swivel guns that were to be mounted aboard the pinnace, the men's calivers, cutlasses and pistols, and a good supply of stores and sails, axes, saws and other tools.

After a march of about fifty miles, the Cimaroons put them on the Santa Maria River that would take them down from the isthmus spine to the Pacific. They followed the river in canoes until they came to a site that Oxenham judged was suitable for the construction and launching of the pinnace. The men turned to and felled the needed trees for timber, and the ship's carpenter and his mates fashioned out a sturdy craft with a forty-five-foot keel length. The swivel guns were mounted aboard, powder and shot were stowed, the mast and the hauls and the shrouds and sails checked. Then with six Cimaroon guides the company pushed off down the winding stream for the Pacific.

They made their entrance into the ocean wholly unknown to the Spaniards, and the expedition's future looked very bright. Still unseen, they ran out from shore to the Islas de Perlas, an island group West of Panamá and right on the Perú-Panamá ship route commonly used by the Spanish. Oxenham concealed the pinnace among the islands and waited for a prize.

He waited ten days. Then a small coastwise bark was sighted by the lookouts. The pinnace put out and after a fight that involved no serious casualties seized her. She had a cargo from Quito; in it was sixty thousand pesos in gold. Oxenham showed an almost exuberant chivalry towards his prisoners. He did no more than confine them aboard their ship and hold the ship with his own at the Islas de Perlas. The people there were Cimaroons, of the same stock as his trusted guides, and he doubted that they would communicate his presence to the Spanish. He and his men were gay, relaxed while they waited for another prize.

She was again a coastwise bark, out of Callao. They boarded her from the pinnace without much trouble and found in her one hundred thousand pesos in silver bars. But Oxenham was not content. He let himself be convinced that there was still time for him before Spanish pursuit began. He secured the people of the second ship as he had the first, below-decks in their own vessel, and left both vessels at an anchorage in the Islas de Perlas. Then he sailed the pinnace around the islands looking for pearls, and even found a few.

It was only after he had finished the pearl hunt that he thought of escape. He headed the pinnace across the Gulf of Panamá and sought out the river that was to take the expedition to safety. But the Cimaroons in the islands had several times before suffered the wrath of enraged officials at Panamá. The night Oxenham left, some of them went in their canoes to Panamá City and reported to the Governor.

The Governor was two days in recruiting a force to find the pirates. He got hold of a veteran officer, Captain Juan de Ortega, and he gave him one hundred men and four *barcas longas*. These *barcas* were lugsail-rigged small craft very similar to Oxenham's pinnace, but also manned by skilled oarsmen and carrying in addition to swivel pieces a long-bore cannon at the bow. Captain de Ortega set out at once for the islands after he had received his orders.

He came upon no evidence of the Englishmen around the Islas de Perlas, but out to sea he met the two ships that had been captured by Oxenham. The crews, released by their former captors, were voluble. They had seen with no strain of vision the course the pinnace had steered; it was right there, for the river that debouched into the sea on the mainland.

Captain de Ortega put all possible way on his *barcas* and closed with the mainland coast. The Englishmen had been almost insanely negligent in their lack of concealment, yet they still held a considerable handicap, must be already some days inland up the river. Ortega scanned the narrow, dusky river mouths, lined with mangroves, reeds, bamboos, ferns, wild banana plants and stub palmettos. There were three mouths; the pirates might have gone up any one of them.

Ortega hesitated. He was reluctant to make a choice, and he feared ambush. But he remembered his orders, and knowing he must go on, started the boats up the main stream. Then, in another boat, a man called; he indicated one of the lesser river mouths. On the dark current of the river carried fanwise out to sea was a wide spread of varicolored pheasant feathers. Up that stream, somewhere, Oxenham's men had committed the final carelessness and when they had cleaned the fowls after the day's hunt had dropped the pluckings into the river instead of upon the bank.

Ortega did not delay any further. He entered that stream and ascended it, his men poling their boats and hauling them, scouts ahead in the bush. The fourth day, where the bank

And Greatly Daring

109

sloped down to the water, they found the English pinnace. She was beached and guarded by six men and, briefly, until one of them was killed, the six fought. The other five were quick to escape into the jungle.

The Spaniards examined the pinnace. She held nothing in her of value. Ortega detached twenty men to guard her and led the rest of his force inland as skirmishers. They had gone no more than a mile or so when in a clearing they came to a palm-frond hut. It contained all the Englishmen's spare gear and all the loot taken from both ships.

It was difficult for Ortega to believe that he was so lucky, and his enemy so flagrantly negligent. He gave the order for the loot to be packed back from the hut to where the *barcas* were moored. But he deployed his men around the clearing in anticipation of an attack by the pirates. He recalled the members of the pinnace guard who had fled after the attack.

Oxenham and all his men and two hundred Cimaroons arrived within three days. There was a fierce fight for possession of the loot. The Spanish, for once using jungle tactics with skill, won it. They hid behind trees, protected themselves and killed eleven Englishmen and five Cimaroons and took seven English-men prisoner, among them Oxenham. The Spanish commander sat down and talked with Oxenham. He asked him bluntly why he had wasted his fifteen days' headstart that, if spent correctly, would have put him far beyond capture.

Oxenham made no attempt to evade the fact that the major blame for the failure belonged to him. But he said that his men had argued bitterly about carrying the loot from where Ortega had found it. They had wasted days in dispute. So he had been forced to leave them in the vicinity of the hut and go inland and persuade Cimaroon tribesmen to act as porters for the loads. Then, while returning with the Cimaroons, he had met the main body of his company with the survivors of the pinnace guard, learned of the Spanish arrival. He had promised his men and the Cimaroons half the treasure if they would re-win it, but obviously the incentive had not been enough.

Captain de Ortega took his prisoners and treasure to Panamá under tight guard. The Governor, after Ortega had reported, sent word to the Governor of Nombre de Dios on the Caribbean coast. A vessel was dispatched to Port Pheasant, discovered Oxenham's camouflaged ship, seized her. The Viceroy of Perú, when the word reached him, issued orders to one of his captains, Diego de Frees, to take care of the fifty Englishmen still loose in the hinterland of Darien, also their Cimaroon allies.

The Spanish patrols under de Frees ran the pirates down methodically, caught some who in desperation built dugout canoes on the rivers, others who were sick, immobile with the fever, and a few more who were betrayed or sold at last by the Cimaroons when the tribesmen were put under frightful pressure. Those who lived were brought to Panamá City to join John Oxenham and the rest already in prison.

> And the Justice of Panamá asked the English captaine whether hee had the Queenes licence, or the licence of any other Prince or Lord for his attempt. And he answered he had none, whereupon he and all his company were condemned to dye, and so were all executed, saving the Captaine, the Master, the Pilot, and five boyes, which were caried to Lima, and there the Captaine was executed with the other two, but the boyes yet be living.*

* Hakluyt, *Voyages.*

*And
Greatly
Daring*

So Many of Us as Lived

"And such as were willing to land I put them apart, and such as were desirous to goe homewardes, I put apart, so that they were indifferently parted a hundred on one side and a hundred of the other side: these hundred men we set a land with all diligence in this little place beforesaid, which being landed, we determined there to take in fresh water, and so with our little remaine of victuals to take the sea."

Captain John Hawkins, in his account of the events
subsequent to the battle of San Juan de Uluá,
as reported in HAKLUYT's *Voyages*

Job Hortop was one of those who elected to try their luck ashore. He came back finally to England after twenty-three years of Spanish imprisonment. His story, recited in his own terms, maintains a blunt lack of adornment that thrusts aside time. The reader is there with him; the reader knows that what the old veteran had to say was true. Hortop experienced this, he persisted, and being a man of great courage and tenacity, he survived.

He was born in the town of Bourne, in Lincolnshire, and apprenticed at the age of twelve to Francis Lee of Redriffe, near London, who was the Queen Majesty's Powdermaker. He worked with Lee for some years and until at the request of Captain Hawkins he joined the *Jesus of Lubeck* as a gunner. There is no description of him that is left to us, but he must have been a man of powerful build, and observant and hardheaded, and for his time, well-educated, in every sense the best type of chief petty officer.

After the night of "great miserie" that followed the battle at San Juan de Uluá, the sorely overloaded ship that Hawkins commanded put into the Gulf of Mexico coast in the region of the Rio Panuco. All hands were aware that she could not proceed to sea and towards home as she was. Hortop made his decision, and he was calm, able to record in his mind the tragic scene. He related it graphically years later in his account:

> He (Captain Hawkins) asked them who would go on shore, and who would tarry on ship-board, and those who would goe on shore, he willed to goe on foremast, and those that would tarrie, on baft mast: fourescore and sixteene of us were willing to depart. Our Generall gave unto every one of us six yards of Roane cloth, and money to them who demanded it. When we were landed, he came unto us, where friendly imbracing every one of us, he was greatly grieved that he was forced to leave us behind him, he counselled us to serve God, and to love another, and thus courteously he gave us a sorowful farewell, and promised if God sent him safe home, he would do what he could, that so many of us as lived should by some means be brought into England, & so he did.*

There was trouble for the party right the next day. They were met by Indians in a savannah near the Rio Panuco. Their six yards apiece of cloth, their money and the facility of some in Spanish did them no good. They were robbed to the skin and one of them was shot dead by an archer. Marching onward numbly, wreathed in branches and leaves against the penetrant sun and the gnats and mosquitoes and blue-bottle flies, they were harried by the Indians.

It was impossible to fight back. They lacked weapons, and the best they could do was to stay together. Eight were killed,

* Hakluyt, *Voyages.*

So Many of Us as Lived

many more wounded. But they reached the river and a pair of Spaniards across it saw them and came out in a canoe and inspected them. The pair summoned a force of one hundred cavalrymen, who drew up in formation on the opposite bank and the Englishmen were ferried over in canoes and made prisoner. They were taken to the town of Panuco, questioned, kept over night and sent on to Mexico City. That was a march of ninety leagues and they struggled along on foot under heavy guard.

> And thus we came to Mexico, which is seven or eight miles about, seated in a great fen, invironed with 4 hils, it hath but two wayes of entrance, and it is full of creeks, in the which in their Canowes they passe from place to place, & to the Islands there within.*

Priests interrogated them in Mexico City after the military and civilian authorities were done. The Englishmen were asked, were they good Christians, and they said that they were, and as proof some recited prayers in Latin. This satisfied their interrogators for the moment and they were quartered in a tanner's house and brought clothing and food. The wounded, the sick were taken to hospitals "where many were cured, and many died." **

Through the fluctuations of religious-political affairs, the rest were able to keep going. But the Viceroy held their leader and senior officer, Robert Barrett, a personal prisoner in his palace until the plate fleet would sail for Spain.

> "The rest of us he sent to a towne seven leagues from Mexico called Tescusco, to card wooll among the Indian slaves, which drudgery we disdained, and concluded to beat our masters, and so we did: wherefore they sent to the viceroy, desiring him for Gods sake and our Ladies, to send for us, for they would not keepe us any longer, they said that we were devils and no men." †

* *Ibid.*   ** *Ibid.*   † *Ibid.*

114

The Englishmen were enormously daring when they attacked their masters. They were all of them put down already in the colonial records as pirates and heretics, and they had been subjected to the preparatory, milder phases of the Inquisition, knew enough about it to realize what lay beyond. But nothing was done to them except that they were removed from Tescusco and the wool business, and Hortop along with Robert Barrett and some others were kept in Mexico City for two more years. Their companions were sent back to Spain when the annual fleet sailed.

Then the group to which Hortop belonged was ordered down to the coast. They entered from Vera Cruz into San Juan de Uluá and as they stood in their fetters on the boat-quay they could look out across the shallow harbor at the little sandspit island where their ships had been anchored and where the Spaniards had opened simultaneous broadside fire upon them in that cruel battle. It aroused intense, harsh memories and the men were somber when they were brought aboard the flagship of the plate fleet.

The fleet was about to sail. It was commanded in fulsome Spanish style by an Admiral-General, whose name was Don Juan de Velasco de Varrc. He gave an order for the guards to assemble Barrett and the rest of the prisoners in his cabin. Then he asked the group if they would fight against their compatriots if they met them at sea. They said, no, they would not, "but if we met with any other, we would do what we were able." *

Don Juan considered the statement. His reply to it was, "That if we had said otherwise he would not have believed us, and for that we should be the better used, and have allowance as other men had: and he gave a charge to every one of us, according to our knowledge." **

Robert Barrett, a highly qualified officer, was stationed with the pilot. Hortop went with the gunners, and William

Ibid.   ** *Ibid.*

Cawse with the bosun. John Beare was assigned to join the quartermasters, and Edward Rider and Geoffrey Giles were bunked with the sailors. "Richard the masters boy attended him (Barrett) and the pilote." *

The fleet cleared from San Juan de Uluá and after a slow sixteen days' passage stood into Havana. It took supplies aboard there while it waited for the second fleet to arrive from Nombre de Dios. This came in under the command of another Admiral-General, Don Diego Flores de Valdes. The Englishmen learned as the combined fleet prepared for sea that protocol assumed such proportions that the Admiral-Generals split the command between them; each of them assumed it for a period of fifteen days.

Don Juan de Velasco de Varre, in whose ship the Englishmen sailed, was the commander when the fleet got under way and left Havana for the Bahama Strait. The vast, cumbrous galleons were protected by long screens of escort vessels, but they had to tend to their own navigation through the Bahama Strait. They kept sailing at night, a bad time for such clumsy, balky craft, and they jammed one after the other in single column, lookouts in the tops and in the bow chains, the big lanthorns on the scrolled gilt poops of the galleons giving a steering mark for the ships astern.

Hortop was among the watch on deck aboard Don Juan's ship, which led the main fleet. The pilot in charge took her well off course. He almost ran her down on the Florida coast.

> His pilote had like to have cast away all the fleet upon the Cape called Cannaveral, which was prevented by me, Job Hortop, & and our master Robert Barret: for I being in the second watch escried land, and called to Robert Barret, bidding him to look over boord, for I saw land under the lee-bow of the ship: he called to the boat-swaine, & bid him let flie the fore saile sheat, and lay the

* *Ibid.*

116

helm upon the lee, and cast the ship about. When we were cast about, we were in but seven fathome water: we shot off a piece giving advice to the fleet to cast about, and so they did.*

Hortop's simple recital evokes an unforgettable and most unusual scene: The vast and dark ships with their mounds of canvas white in the starlight, lumbering blindly down on the shore where the coral heads would rip the bottoms out of them like a knife. Then the shout in English from the heretic pirate prisoner as he saw close aboard the shadowy land. Barrett, who had been sailing master of the *Jesus of Lubeck,* must have been on the quarter-deck, and with him in such a difficult passage, the pilot. But according to Hortop, Barrett did not even consult the pilot. He gave his own order in Spanish to the bosun, in direct charge of the watch down on the main deck. And without hesitation the bosun obeyed him.

The ships must have been on the starboard tack, with the wind probably southeast or south-southeast. The bosun in his turn with Hortop and a couple of half-comprehending sailors to help them jumped for the windward sheet that controlled the big foresail whose draw could swing the ship in either direction. He and Hortop and the sailors threw the sheet rope clear of the belaying pin that held it, and the mass of canvas tumbled, fluttered and spilled her wind as the leeward sheet was let go, too, and the ship's head eased. The helmsman, aft in the steerage, peering out to see what little he could of this sudden danger, put the helm down at Barrett's order, and slowly, the long, heavy yard came around as the bosun and Hortop and the men hauled on the braces that trimmed it; the mainsail went over also, the men in a concerted scramble to reach the capstan and haul tight to the new course.

Then the ship stood off on the port tack and into safe water. Down in his cabin as she lurched and came about to

* *Ibid.*

So *Many*
of Us
as Lived

The Age of Piracy

her right heading, the Admiral-General heard the gear slam, the rumble and squeal of blocks, the canvas snap, jerk, murmur, and he wondered about his pilot as he sprinted in his small clothes or his nightshirt from his bunk to the quarter-deck companionway.

When he gained the quarter-deck, the warning cannon for the other ships piling along astern had just been fired. The Admiral-General gazed at them as they hauled over in answer to the signal, and he peered at Cape Canaveral, still near enough to make his stomach muscles twitch, and he listened to the leadsmen report the shallowness of the water. Right after that, Don Juan certainly engaged in some acrimonious and pointed conversation with his pilot.

Hortop tells the story very well:

> For this we (Barrett and Hortop) were beloved of the Generall, and all the fleet. The Generall was in a great rage, and swore by the king, that he would hang his pilote: for he said, that twice before he had almost cast away the Admirall. When it was day, he commanded a piece to be shot off, to call to councill: the other Admirall in his ship came up to him, and asked what the matter was, he said, that his pilote had cast away his ship and all the fleet, had it not bene for two of the Englishmen, and therefore he would hang him. The other Admirall with many faire words perswaded him to the contrary.*

The pilot sharpened up his navigation and the fleet stood to the eastward in good weather across the Atlantic. The course was by way of Fayal, in the Azores, and with the island astern the Spaniards gave themselves fervently to the celebration of their great *fiesta,* St. James' Day. There were bright fireworks; the crew pranced around the deck with pinwheels and rachets and the Englishmen, their proven shipmates, joined

* *Ibid.*

with them. But Robert Barrett was conscious of what lay ahead at the completion of the voyage; he and his companions were sure to be summoned before the Inquisition.

Barrett approached the other Englishmen singly, impressing upon them the necessity of action. The fleet was closing in towards the island of Terceira, still among the Azores group. Their ship was the only one that towed a pinnace. The pinnace was their sole chance of escape. Morsels at a time, the men filled a bag with bread. They procured a *botija,* a large water jug, and hid it with the bread. Barrett talked quietly and persuasively with the master gunner, and borrowed from him a small hand compass. The group was ready to swarm down the painter at night, cast off and sail out from the fleet in the pinnace to Terceira, make a try from there for England.

The master gunner, though, went quietly to see Don Juan in his cabin. He told of the compass loan, and Don Juan took instant action. Barrett was seized, put in the stocks and a great pair of iron ballast bars set on his legs. The rest of the Englishmen were placed in leg stocks beside him. A signal cannon was fired and the pinnace sent to pick up the other Admiral-General and all of the captains and masters and pilots in the fleet for a council.

They boarded Don Juan's ship. He had the main yard lowered to deck and blocks set up for hanging purposes. He informed his brother officers that the Englishmen had plotted against him; they had planned to blow up the ship by powder trains to the magazine, shove off in the pinnace while she sank. But Don Diego Flores de Valdes, who had pleaded for the pilot's life off Cape Canaveral, now, perhaps not strangely, made a plea of clemency for the Englishmen. He told Don Juan;

> I nor the Captaines, Masters, and Pilotes will not set
> our hands to that, for hee said, if he had been prisoner as

So Many of Us as Lived

119

we were, he would have done the like himselfe. He coun-
selled him to keepe us fast in prison, till he came into
Spaine, & there send us to the Contratation house in Sivil,
where if we had deserved death the law would pass on us,
for hee would not have it said that in such a fleete as that
was, sixe men and a boye should take the pinnesse, and
goe away, and he returned to his ship againe.*

The attempt to take the pinnace had ended any possibility
of trust between the Spaniards and the Englishmen. The
prisoners were held in close confinement until the fleet crossed
the bar at San Lucar in Spain. Then they were sent, still in the
stocks, into the pinnace which brought them to the Casa de
Contratacíon in Seville. Here they were held for a year, after
which they broke out, some of them, and escaped.

Details are not complete. Hortop tells the story most
baldly, but there were influential Englishmen, Catholic mer-
chants with very strong connections at court, who had lived in
Seville for generations. True to his word also, back in England,
their former commander, Captain Hawkins, now a Royal Navy
Admiral, did his best in an oblique fashion to save his men.
Hortop and Barrett, John Emery and Humphrey Roberts and
John Gilbert were caught, though.

They were returned to the Casa de Contratacíon "where
we remained in the stocks till twelfe tide was past." ** This in-
dicates that they were kept in miserable underground dungeons,
close enough to the Guadalquivir River that flows past Seville
so that they could mark the passage of the tides. Then they were
shifted to the main prison of Seville, and from there to the ill-
favored incarceration cells of the Inquisition at Triana.

It was for them a slowly lost struggle, which hope alone
kept alive. At the end of the year they were released from the
incarceration cells and assembled in a procession. Here was the
beginning of the descent towards actual doom; the devious
minds of their inquisitors had been resolved.

* *Ibid.*   ** *Ibid.*

120

Every one of us having a candle in his hand, and the coate with S. Andrewes crosse (the dread *san benito* garment) on our backs: they brought us up on an high scaffold, that was set up in the place of S. Francis, which is the chiefe street of Sivill: there they set us downe upon benches, every one in his degree, and against us on another scaffold sate all the Judges, and the Clergy on their benches: the people wondered, and gazed on us, some pitying our cases, others said, burne those heretikes. When we had sit there two houres, we had a sermon made to us; after which one called Bresinia, secretarie to the Inquisition, went up into the pulpit with the processe, and called Robert Barret and John Gilbert, whom two familiars of the Inquisition brought from the scaffold before the Judges, where the secretarie read the sentence, which was that they should be burnt, and so they were returned to the scaffold, and were burnt.*

Robert Barrett, still in the full strength of his years, consistently brave, looked forth as the smoke rose and the flame spurted. He could see more in the keen Andalusian sunlight than his shipmates, his judges and the fear-rigid crowd. The plaza in which he and the other condemned Englishman died dissolved before his eyes; the crackling of the flames, the awful heat about his body were momentarily gone.

He was no longer in Seville. His spirit took him from the tight red and yellow and dun city where the pigeons stirred in fright from the sparks; he was far away and gone out of Andalusia and the plains along the river which each year received the plate fleet that had cost so many men their lives.

This was New Spain, Mexico. He was in the port of San Juan de Ulúa. His commander, sensing Spanish treachery, had sent him because of his rank and his knowledge of the language to treat with the Viceroy who had given his solemn written word to keep the peace. But as he boarded the Viceroy's

So Many of Us as Lived

* *Ibid.*

ship, it was already too late. His arms were pinned behind him; he was overpowered, and a prisoner, he saw the uneven battle.

Then he was in Mexico City, and confined, kept despite any protest. He met there the survivors from among his General's men, and with gladness recognized Hortop and the others, the sturdy, the lucky. In his way, he was able to help them and ease a bit their suffering. But a friar in the service of the Inquisition insisted that he translate a sermon to them.* He added some remarks out his bitterness; he said that the friar was not to be believed, and was really a Jewish knave. Perhaps later in the daze of an Inquisition process some prisoner told that. Not that it mattered, not now.

Or did the night off Cape Canaveral when he and Job Hortop saved the fleet have meaning. Barrett looked for the gunner's face through the smoke and could not find it. Flame seared him. His hair had started to burn like the pinwheels aboard the flagship at the *fiesta*. He had been happy then; he had been able to forget. Now, too, he must forget, because the flame hurt cruelly and he could not cry out.

Job Hortop sat motionless while Barrett burned and died and Gilbert sagged in final agony in his chains. He did not know what his own fate would be.

Then I Job Hortop and John Bone were called, and brought to the place, as before, where we heard our sentence, which was that we should go to the Gallies, and there rowe at the oares end ten yeares, and then to be brought backe to the Inquisition house to have the coat with S. Andrewes crosse put on our backs, and from there to go to the everlasting prison remedilesse, and so we were returned from the scaffold from whence we came. Thomas Marks & Thomas Ellis were called, and had sentence to serve in the Galleys eight yeeres, and Humphrey Roberts, and John Emery to serve five yeeres, & so were returned

* Henry Charles Lea, *The Inquisition in the Spanish Dependencies.*

122

to the benches on the scaffold, where we sate till foure of clocke in the afternoone. Then we were lead againe to the Inquisition house, from whence we were brought.*

The next day, Bresinia, the secretary of the Inquisition, put in each man's hand a formal copy of his sentence. Then they were sent to the galleys. They were chained four-and-four to a sweep. Their daily food allowance was twenty-six ounces of "course blacket bisket and water." ** The clothing issued them annually was two shirts and two pairs of breeches of rough canvas, a red, loose surcoat of little practical use and a "gowne of haire with a friars hood." † They slept on the galley thwarts or the floorboards in all weathers. Once a month, their beards and heads were shaven. "Hunger, thirst, cold, and stripes we lacked none, til our several times expired." ††

Hortop served an additional two years over his sentence, possibly for mutinous action, although he does not say. Then, with twelve years completed, he was allowed to leave the galleys and return to Seville. He wore the shameful *san benito* coat and was remanded "remedilesse" to everlasting prison. But outside forces prevailed for him; he was not forgotten at home. After he had worn the *san benito* for four years and after "great suit" in court and the payment of fifty ducats, he was able to take it off. He mentions very briefly that he was lent the sum by Hernando de Soria, the treasurer of the King's mint, for whom he had worked "as a drudge for 7 yeres." * Still the fact that he got the money, and from a man of such caliber, signified a great deal.

Then in October, 1590 he was at last in a position where he could leave. He went down the river from Seville to San Lucar on the coast and there made contact with some Flemish seamen who were married to Spanish women and in Spanish service. They had a flie-boat, a fast coaster, and a cargo

So Many of Us as Lived

* Hakluyt, *Voyages.*   † *Ibid.*
** *Ibid.*   †† *Ibid.*

of wines and salt. Out to sea, they kept rendezvous with an English galleon, the *Dudley*, and Hortop went aboard with the contraband cargo.

The *Dudley* took him to Portsmouth and he landed December 2, 1590. He was received by the King's Lieutenant, who sent him on to the Earl of Sussex at London. Sussex commanded his secretary "to take my name and examination, how long I had bene out of England, and with whom I went, which he did. And on Christmas even I took my leave of his honor, and came to Redriffe." *

Hortop was home. He wrote in conclusion: "Thus having truely set downe unto to you my travels, misery and dangers, endured the space of 23 yeeres, I end." *

* *Ibid.*

The Age of Piracy

The Iron Maiden

During the closing years of the sixteenth century the Spanish colonial authorities began to use the Inquisition actively as a means for the repression of piracy. The judges of the Lima tribunal wrote in 1578 to Juan Constantino, its commissioner at Panamá, that it understood that English pirates who appeared there were heretics and should be treated as such. The Englishmen were reported to have robbed the commissioner and left him in his shirt, broken a chalice and patina, thrown an altar and missal into the sea. The bishop of Santo Domingo requested, in 1594, that a tribunal be established on the island to take care of the increased number of buccaneers who entered the mountain regions from Tortuga, and in 1606 a similar request was made because of the influx of "heretic traders and sailors with their books." *

But before this, on February 28, 1575, a great *auto-da-fé* had taken place in Mexico City. The victims were the survivors of Captain John Hawkins's company who had stayed on in the country. Six years had passed since the San Juan de Uluá battle, the terrible march to the Rio Panuco and the march into High Mexico. For most of that time the main group of Englishmen had been quite fairly treated by the masters to whom they had been assigned. Some were youngsters still in their teens and the rest were just as eager to live; all of them had done their best to adjust to colonial conditions.

They had discovered that in New Spain no Spaniard, no matter how low in rank or poor upon arrival, was willing to serve another of his nationality in any sort of subordinate,

* Lea, *Inquisition*.

The Age of Piracy

menial capacity. Each immigrant from the mother country considered himself a *caballero,* and his sons, in the fashion he set, were to be gentlemen, perform nothing that resembled labor. So the English prisoners formed a new class; they served their masters as table servants and butlers, chamberlains, and as they grew accustomed to the country and learned the language, they progressed to further trust.

A good many were sent out of Mexico City to the silver mines their masters owned. They worked as overseers in charge of the Negroes, the Indians, and they began to prosper. Sympathetic in their treatment of the slaves, they were able to increase production substantially. Their masters paid them three hundred pesos a year, which came to sixty pounds sterling, and on Saturday afternoons, during their free time, as a sign of gratitude, the slaves worked silver for them. This they were allowed to keep with their masters' knowledge, and it reached a sizable amount. Men started to think of permanent acceptance of their status, of marriage and settling down in this country.

Then, for the first time in the colonies, the Inquisition was established and trials begun. There was a good deal of protest against it, even among the clergy, for the organization was dreaded, mistrusted. But the two chief Inquisitors, Don Pedro Moya de Contreras and Fernandez de Bonilla, turned to the Englishmen. These were an easy target, and practically defenseless.

A proclamation was issued that all Englishmen in the country should be assembled in Mexico City. Any person who harbored them was threatened with the loss of his property, and excommunication. The four-year period of grace the men had enjoyed since their initial imprisonment was at an end. Their masters relinquished them; they were brought to Mexico City, and whatever they owned was taken from them; then they were placed in dungeons so dark that they could not see except by candle light. No more than two of them were allowed to stay in the same dungeon, to keep them from conversation and common council.

A number were held so for a year and a half. They were led singly before the Inquisitors. Their faith was severely examined; they were forced to recite the Pater Noster, the Ave Maria and the Creed in Latin. They stood for hours at a time in front of their judges. Behind the dais where the judges sat in the audience chamber was a life-sized image of Christ. The image's head was moved in various fashions by a hidden familiar of the Inquisition to confuse and appall the accused. Most of the men were illiterate, and no match for their judges in logic or points of law; they were never given the exact charges against them, were refused the opportunity to confront those who had given the information on which the charges were based. The trials lasted as long as two years.

The stubborn, or those who seemed to be lying, were submitted to torture. They were introduced to the *cordeles,* the rawhide cords that were tightened around the skull to summon truth; and the *jarras de agua* treatment, wherein the contents of water jars were poured down the accused's throat on strips of cotton. As many as three jugs were sometimes expended before the prisoner started to confess as his judges thought he should. Then there was the *mancuerda,* "the crippler," and the *trampazo,* which was the last, awful twist of the torture cord, and the *garrucha,* a pulley arrangement that dislocated bones, and the pillory where a man was locked to be scourged. Some scourges were of sharp-pointed steel-wire chains, and other tools were netted, pointed wire to fit the wrists, waists, legs, arms; and thumb screws were applied.

Peculiar, devious distinctions were made by the judges as they dug into the roots of the prisoners' minds to explore what was, in their estimation, truth. If the accused were young, he might miss the worst of the torture because he was able to plead that he had done no more than accept the religion of his country. Those of teen-age who had been small children when

The
Iron
Maiden

127

Queen Elizabeth came to the throne, and who, therefore, had never had any Catholic instruction, were treated with reasonable lack of severity because of ignorance. But for the older men there was the repeated, dragging examination, punctuated by hours upon the rack; and they were asked the sly and involved, lengthy questions in multifold forms.

Did they believe in the Sacrament, and did they believe in the wine and bread, and were those the very true and perfect body and blood of the Savior Christ? Answer, yea or no. What had been the beliefs of their families? Then instruction was given them to inform upon their companions, their shipmates and friends, the men whose screams could be heard from the torture chamber.

Men broke. They falsely confessed, and others, a number of them quite likely part crazy, informed. But it came to an end after all the mature prisoners had been submitted to the rack. The Inquisitors had concluded that they were in possession of enough testimony to proceed in judgment. Time was taken to build a large scaffold and grandstands for the clergy, the viceregal and military and municipal officers and their favored guests in the market place. A trumpeter sounded; drummers went through the city and a public announcement was made that sentence was finally to be given, and the people should gather to be witness.

The night before the execution of judgment the prisoners were taken out of their dungeons and led to the courtyard of the Inquisition house. There they were dressed in the *san benitos,* the yellow cotton coats that bore front and back the red St. Andrew's cross. Then they were drilled all night long in the formation they would take to the scaffold. Weak from the torture or crippled by it, sleepless, they were given at dawn a cup of wine a man and a piece of bread fried in honey. About eight o'clock they were marched forth to the market place.

The prisoners went up stairs onto the high scaffold. They sat down each in his place on benches and they faced the Viceroy and the chief judges, who were shielded from the sun beneath an embroidered canopy. Friars of various orders assembled, and silence was called for, and the sentencing begun.

The first man to receive his sentence was Roger Armar, who had been the chief armorer in the *Jesus of Lubeck*. His punishment was three hundred lashes, to be given to him while on horseback, then he was to go to the galleys for a term of ten years. After him were John Gray, and John Browne, and John Rider, John Moone, and James Collier, and Thomas Browne. Their punishment was two hundred lashes on horseback, and eight years in the galleys.

In all, sixty-eight were sentenced, but for the younger ones relative mercy was shown. Miles Phillips, who had been only fourteen at the time of his capture, was sentenced to serve for five years in a monastery, was ordered to wear the *san benito*, and received no stripes of the lash. After him were called others who were saved from the severe forms of punishment because of their youth: John Story, Richard Williams, David Alexander, Robert Cooke, and Thomas Hull and Paul Horsewell. It was known to the Spanish that Horsewell was Captain Hawkins's nephew, and he was entered in the records as "Pablo Haquines," and special note was made of him. He, along with Phillips and the rest of the younger men, were given sentences to monasteries, some for three years, some for four, and ordered to wear the *san benito*.

It was almost dusk. Sentence had been passed on every prisoner, and the executioners got ready to burn the three who had been condemned to the flame. John Martin of Cork, known to the Inquisitors as "Cornelius the Irishman," and George Ribley, and Peter Momfries, both Englishmen, were led down from the scaffold and taken to the stakes.

Those were close, and their shipmates were able to watch as the fires were set. But the temper of the people was such that the condemned were not submitted straight to the flame as was the fashion in Spain. First, they were garrotted, and

The
Iron
Maiden

129

then the fire consumed them until their bodies crumbled into ash.

The prisoners were marched back to their dungeons, and spent a night of tense, sleepless waiting. The next day was Good Friday; the Inquisition took them forth into the courtyard and the sixty men who were to receive the lash were mounted on horses. They were bared to their waists and then exhibited through the main streets and plazas of the city. Criers went before them and called out to the people, "Behold these English dogs, Lutherans, enemies of God!" *

Executioners with long whips doled the blows to the half-naked men who reeled upon the shivering horses.

> And all the way as they went there were some of the Inquisitors themselves, and of the familiars of that rakehel order, that cried to the executioners, Strike, lay on those English heretiks, Gods enemies: and so this horrible spectacle being shewed round about the cities, they returned to the Inquisitors house, with their backes all gore blood, and swollen with great bumps, and were then taken from their horses, & carried againe to prison, where they remained until they were sent into Spaine to the gallies, there to receive the rest of their martirdome: and I (Miles Phillips) and the 6 other with me which had judgement, and were condemned amongst the rest to serve an apprentiship in the monastery, were taken presently and sent to certaine religious houses appointed for the purpose." **

Phillips and his companions were extremely conscious of their good fortune. They cherished it, and among the friars in whose care they had been put, they encountered a subdued abhorrence of the Inquisition and all its works. Phillips was assigned as overseer in charge of the Indian slave laborers who built a new church for the Black Friars. Another young Eng-

* Hakluyt, *Voyages.*
** *Ibid.*

lishman, William Lowe, was with him, and his duty was to help the cook in the kitchen. The rest had various similar duties, except that Paul Horsewell became the personal servant of the secretary of the order.

> We must needs confesse that the Friers did use us very courteously: for every one of us had his chamber with bedding & diet, and all things clean and neat: yea many of the Spaniards and Friers themselves do utterly abhorre and mislike of that cruell Inquisition, and would as they durst bewaile our miseries, and comfort us the best they could, although they stood in such feare of that divelish Inquisition, that they durst not let the left hande know what the right doth.*

At Lima, the second great viceregal seat, the Inquisition also sought out its form of justice for pirates. John Oxenham, whose carelessness at Darien had trapped him and his men, was brought to trial in 1581. Tried with him were Thomas Harvey, his sailing master, John Butler, his pilot, and Butler's younger brother, Henry. The three officers were found guilty and hanged, but Henry escaped with his life.

The Lima tribunal was extremely busy with piratical heretics in 1587. Among its noteworthy victims was John Drake, a cousin of the famous Francis Drake. He had been shipwrecked in the Rio Plate on the Argentinian coast during the course of a voyage, and with one of his officers, Richard Farrel, he was brought overland to stand trial. After the tremendous journey, the wearying, galling examinations, they were sentenced at an *auto da fé,* held on November thirtieth, where both confessed conversion. Drake's punishment was reclusion for three years in a monastery and perpetual residence in Perú. The judges must have found Farrel more recalcitrant, for he was sent to the rack, condemned to four years in the galleys and then irredeemable prison.

* *Ibid.*

The Iron Maiden

Three men who had been members of Captain Thomas Cavendish's expedition were also tried in the same year. They along with nine others had formed a wood and water party that had gone ashore in a small boat near Santiago, on the West Coast, and been captured as a result. Taken to Santiago, nine were hanged at once "to the great benefit of their souls, for they professed conversion." * The trio who survived them were William Stephens, Thomas Lucas and William Hilles.

The Inquisitors ordered them brought to Lima, then took three years to try them. Stephens protested in the audience chamber that both his parents were devout Catholics. He stated further that his mother had died in prison for the possession of holy beads and images. Yes, he had "taken the religion of his country," ** but he assured his judges that he was at heart a Catholic. For such testimony, he was let off with four years of prison and the wearing of the *san benito*. Lucas had a Protestant father, but a Catholic mother. He informed the tribunal that while he had "always been a Protestant," he was "now a Catholic." † This won him reconciliation at the price of four years in the galleys, six in prison, the *san benito,* and then he was to remain perpetually in Lima. The third prisoner, Hilles, was seventeen years old, and he used the same dialectical defense as his shipmates to evade the noose, the flame. He also made known to the tribunal that, while he had been born a Protestant, he was now a most devout Catholic. His reconciliation was six years in the galleys, irredeemable prison and the *san benito*.

The same tribunal decided to try another group of Englishmen, who for five years had lain in the Lima dungeons. This lot had been captured at Puna Island, below Guayaquil, and they were in pitiful shape when they appeared for the *auto-da-fé.* Walter and Edward Tillert, brothers, weakened at the last moment, although they had clung hard to their faith,

* Lea, *Inquisition.*   ** *Ibid.*   † *Ibid.*

132

and they were garrotted before being burned. Henry Axli (Oxley) retained his courage; he was burned alive. The fourth of their number, Andrew Marle (Morley), was eighteen years old, and like Hilles, he professed conversion, was reconciled with two years of reclusion among the Jesuits for instruction.

The next *auto-da-fé* to concern itself with pirates took place at Lima on December 15, 1595. Its victims were the members of Captain Richard Hawkins's expedition which had sailed from Plymouth two years before. Hawkins, a younger brother of the renowned captain, operating in the family tradition, had dropped anchor off Valparaiso on the West Coast in April, 1594. He seized and then released four small craft he found in the roadstead and kept a bigger ship for ransom, which was paid. But when he left port and sailed north, the *corregidor*** manned one of the abandoned small craft, a bark, with a good crew. They sailed her into Callao in fifteen days and the Viceroy, Hurtado de Mendoza, was informed of Hawkins's presence on the coast. The Viceroy had time to fit out a squadron which he sent to sea under the command of his nephew, Beltran de Castro.

De Castro caught Hawkins in Atacames Bay, beyond Quito, on July second, and there was a desperate fight. Hawkins, forced into surrender, had yet conducted the action so bravely that De Castro promised him and his men treatment as prisoners of war and not as pirates. But, once ashore, sixty-two men were sent at once in irons to Cartagena de Indias, a huge distance away, to serve in the galleys. The rest, thirteen, were dispatched to Lima and the Inquisition. They entered the secret prison December 4, 1594. They were tried with what was for the Inquisition unusual speed.

At the *auto-da-fé* held for them December 15, 1595, there were also sentenced seven other Englishmen captured at La Yaquana in Santo Domingo and, incredibly, "forwarded" to Lima. No martyrs could be discovered in either group, and

* Administrative officer.

The Iron Maiden

The Age of Piracy

they were sentenced to various terms of reclusion except for William Leigh, who received six years in the galleys, then irredeemable prison.

Captain Hawkins was very ill, and his trial was held separately. It ended July 17, 1595, but illness kept him from appearance at the *auto-da-fé,* and he was transferred from his dungeon to the Jesuit College. He had made an excellent impression upon the judges, and finally, through the intercession of two viceroys, Cânete and Velasco, he was able to arrange that all of his men who had been captured in 1594 should be sent to Spain.

But it had taken him until May 21, 1607, to achieve this, and he, himself, was not released. Captain John Ellis was also kept, and Hugh Carnix (Charnock) and Richard Davis. They were "experienced seamen and Davis was useful in the position assigned to him." * The group waited patiently, and at last their time came and they were allowed to sail with the homeward-bound plate fleet, their case given over to the *Casa de Contratacíon* at Seville. When Hawkins reached England, he was knighted.

Dreams of home had sustained Miles Phillips for years in Mexico. Unlike his fellow prisoners, Phillips had been unwilling to marry a local woman in accordance with the instruction of the Inquisition. But David Alexander and Robert Cooke, who served in the chief Inquisitor's household, had married Negro women who were domestics there. Richard Williams had married "a rich widow of Biskay with 4000 Pezos." ** Paul Horsewell of the Hawkins family had taken a *mestiza,* a part-Spanish, part-Indian woman as his wife, and she was said to be the descendant of one of the original *conquistadores* who had entered Mexico with Hernando Cortez. She brought Horsewell a dowry of four thousand pesos and a good house, and his branch of the family was traceable in Mexican records for a full century after his marriage.

* Lea, *Inquisition.*   ** Hakluyt, *Voyages.*

John Story also married a local Negro woman, and with the consent of the Inquisition and the other authorities, William Lowe had been given permission to go to Spain and marry. But Phillips remained obdurate in his monogamous state. He understood that by their insistence upon marriage the Inquisitors meant to keep the prisoners within reach and really under secret bondage for life. He described his feelings in the account he put down:

> For mine owne part I could never throughly settle my selfe to marry in that countrey, although many faire offers were made unto me of such as were of great abilitie and wealth, but I could have no such liking to live in that place, where I must ever see and know such horrible idolatrie committed, and durst not once for my life speake against it: and therefore I had alwayes a longing and desire to this my native countrey.*

Phillips kept as far as he could from the Inquisition spics. He paid 150 pesos to become apprenticed to a silk weaver, learned how to make taffeta and grosgraine, saved his money and carefully planned how he would get home. But he was sought out by the Viceroy and closely questioned with some of his compatriots about the Drake family. Word had just reached Mexico City that Francis Drake was on the West Coast and there was great alarm. Phillips was sent to serve as an interpreter with a ship's company that sailed down the West Coast in search of Drake, and he had intense hope that he would meet him. He foresaw defeat for the company with which he was, victory for Drake, and a happy passage home.

Drake was gone from the coast, though, and Phillips returned to the weaver's trade. He began again to plan escape. It was at best very difficult. The Viceroy had ordered that he was not to leave Mexico City, and within an hour's warning

* Hakluyt, *Voyages.*

The

Iron

Maiden

135

he was to be at his master's house. There was on the East Coast just the one principal port of San Juan de Uluá where annually the plate fleet touched to discharge, load and sail for Spain. Even should he succeed in getting to the port and aboard some ship, there were all the further dangers of detection while at sea or upon arrival in Spain, for he proposed to pass himself off as a Spanish soldier. If his luck lasted that far, he had to land in Spain, maintain his false identity and by some means leave the country and return to England.

Phillips had enough courage to try it. His master had business at Mecameca, a town eighteen leagues from Mexico City, and he received permission for Phillips to make the trip. Phillips stayed at Mecameca until he had made certain that the fleet was ready to sail. He was three days' journey from San Juan de Uluá, well-dressed and well-mounted. He set out for the port on a moonlit night.

Riding almost constantly for two days and two nights, he came to Vera Cruz, within a few miles of San Juan de Uluá. But he was stopped, taken to the jail and questioned; he had not been recognized, he discovered to his relief; still his situation was bad. A wealthy Spaniard's son had run away from home, and the local police thought that Phillips was the prodigal.

He stayed in jail under strong protest, then was revealed through chance as an Englishman. Orders were given for him to be returned to Mexico City in the wagon train that carried cargo from the fleet at San Juan de Uluá. While aware of the imminent danger, Phillips persisted in his hope of escape. A friendly fellow prisoner in the Vera Cruz jail had helped to supply him with a combination knife and file.

Phillips put it to work during the wagon journey back up the *Camino Real*. The wagon train had come to a hill so steep that several mule teams were needed to move a wagon. The team harnessed to Phillips's wagon was unhitched and the muleteers went with it. Phillips was ready; he had sawed through the leg fetters and the bolts of the manacles, and it was dark. He left the wagon with the ironware, a few biscuits and two small cheeses. Through the night, he hid in the nearby woods.

He took a bearing on the sun at dawn and kept on in the woods, still wearing his cumbersome iron collar and holding onto the cheeses. That morning he met on a mountainside Indians who hunted deer. He knew their language, and he counted upon their hatred of the Spanish. They agreed to file off his collar for him, rejoiced at his escape, gave him a man of their number as guide, and in an Indian town he was able to buy a horse.

The horse was of immense aid. Phillips rode him into Guatemala, spending thriftily the gold coin which, back in Mexico City, he had quilted in his doublet. Various Indians guided him along the way, and once he met a Gray Friar whom he had known and who might well betray him. But the friar had little good to say of the Inquisition, and Phillips traveled in his company for three days.

When they parted, the friar advised him as to the right route to be taken. Phillips followed it, and passing safely through Guatemala City, he entered rugged jungle country. This he traversed with his faithful horse, and came out at the small port of Cavallos, on the East Coast.

Ships loaded mainly with Canary wine were at anchor; Phillips talked to the master of one and persuaded him that he, like the master, was a native of Grenada. Then, with the payment of sixty pesos, he bought passage in the man's ship. He sold his horse in the port, supplied himself with chickens and bread to sustain him during the voyage and went aboard.

The ship's first port of call was Havana. Phillips went boldly and volunteered as a soldier, was accepted and assigned to serve aboard the Admiral-General's flagship. Havana har-

The Iron Maiden

bor was filled with the assembled plate fleet, and the new recruit spent his time off duty watching the transfer of troops and
ordnance.

Don Pedro de Guzman was in command of the fleet of
thirty-seven ships. He took them successfully to Spain through
bad weather, and Phillips, wisely, went over the side as soon
as he could at San Lucar. He stole the ship's boat, got ashore
and lit out on foot for Seville. When he was in the city he
wasted no time; he apprenticed himself immediately to a silk
weaver and did not leave the weaver's house for three months.

He asked for his wages then and ventured out into the
streets despite the repeated talk about the heretic Englishman
who had come back with the fleet. He bought new clothes,
eased along to the coast and finally found a shipmaster willing to take him to England. He was a West Country captain,
and the ship was named the *Landret*. Phillips landed from her
in Poole in February, 1582. He had been gone from home sixteen years.

The pirate abhorrence of anything to do with the Inquisition lasted for more than another century. When the French
force of buccaneers commanded by the Sieur de Pointis took
Cartagena de Indias in 1697, the Boca Chica fortress was
stormed first. The buccaneers found in the dungeons nine men,
Spaniards, accused by the Inquisition of having committed bigamy. In joy, eight of the prisoners instantly joined the buccaneers. But the ninth, whose name was Pablo Sarmiento, bolted
most inexplicably and ran off to the village of Mompox. This
was still held by the Spanish, and with the troops were known
to be the officials of the Inquisition.

Cartagena de Indias capitulated on May sixth, and the
buccaneers as they entered went to the Inquisition house. They
took out from it the officials' vestments and the *san benitos* and
the miters worn by the penitents. Then they held a mock *auto-
da-fé* in the plaza, and issued enormous, horrendous sentences,
parodied the solemn rituals. Piracy might at times appear even

to them as some form of crime. But bigamy was always a joke.

With the gradual draining away of the Inca wealth and the diminution of the colonies as a center of strength for the home country, the Inquisition's power in the New World was reduced. Resentment against the body broadened in Spain, and as more liberal feeling became prevalent, the Inquisitors lost their all-but-invulnerable power. Tribunals were no longer maintained at Lima and Mexico City.

The judges did not have pirates or heretics to supply the *auto-da-fés,* and the public was not awed by the arraignment of bigamists. Like piracy itself, the Inquisition in the colonies dwindled, then expired. The latter-day pirates who sailed West Indian waters could worship God in any random form they chose; the Inquisitors were not in waiting to correct, maim, hang and burn them.

The Iron Maiden

Manila Galleon

Another expedition which intended to circumnavigate the world and hoped to seize the Acapulco plate ship outfitted at Plymouth in 1586. It sailed July twenty-first under the command of Captain Thomas Cavendish. He was twenty-six years of age, a Suffolk man born in Trimley, and he had a fleet of three ships. They were the *Desire,* of 140 tons; the *Content,* of 60 tons; and the *Hugh Gallant,* a bark, of 40 tons. The expedition muster on sailing day was 123 men, and the ships carried supplies believed to be sufficient for two years.

An account of the voyage was kept by Francis Pretty, a Suffolk man from Eye. The usual southeasterly course before the Trade Wind was followed, and the coast of Brazil raised. There was very little untoward incident until the ships reached the region of the Straits of Magellan. Shore parties that went on the beach met a Spaniard named Hernando. He told the Englishmen that he and twenty-three others were the survivors of the garrison left three years before by Magellan to guard the passage.

The garrison had originally been four hundred men. The rest had died from famine, and Hernando and his companions, living on limpets and mussels, were in very bad shape. After the Englishmen had examined Magellan's fort, now abandoned, and his gibbet, they took Hernando as an eager recruit along with them and started to navigate the straits.

Drenching rain, head winds, fog and poor charts put them into danger. They entered strange bays, anchored in the mouths of rivers where on the banks savage Indians who were stark naked and, according to Hernando, cannibals, threatened death. The vessels evaded shipwreck, the crews kept from becoming an item of Indian diet, and the expedition emerged to sail the Pacific.

The course took them north to the Spanish settlements on the West Coast. Parties were sent ashore for wood and water, and in the Bay of Quintero one was caught. This was on April 1, 1587, and twelve men were flanked by almost two hundred Spanish cavalry, killed or captured. Cavendish was not dismayed; he had expected losses.

Further up the coast, he raided the town of Paita, then Puna Island, but without much profit. On Puna Island he was attacked by a large Spanish force and was lucky to be able to withdraw. He lost a number more men killed and three others who were taken prisoner. Back at sea, he proceeded in search of Spanish vessels that would repay him.

North of Panamá he closed with, fought and seized a ship of 120 tons. Her cargo was not of great worth, but she had aboard a Provencal born in Marseilles and named Michael Sancius. He was a pilot, decided to throw in his lot with the Englishmen, was the first to tell them of the real prize, the plate ship, *Santa Anna*. She was supposed to be inward-bound to Acapulco from the Philippines, and they went after her.

While they sought her, they engaged in routine raids upon the coastal towns. They sacked, ravaged, burned, and found only enough to make them realize they must take the *Santa Anna* or go home poor. Off the California coast on November fourth, beyond Mazatlan, the trumpeter aboard the *Desire* went aloft to the main top to stand lookout. He sighted a huge spread of sail to seaward and hailed the quarter-deck and brought several men to the top to confirm his report. That was the *Santa Anna*.

She was a ship of seven hundred tons; she fought hard against the much smaller, lighter-armed English vessels. But they hung in alongside her and riddled her with broadsides.

Manila Galleon

They whipped musketry and culverin fire through her gun-ports and then went up to board. Loads of stones were dumped on their heads and they were met by javelins and rapiers and men who fired arquebuses and pistols from behind shields.

The Englishmen were driven back from boarding twice. Cavendish exhorted his crews. He had the trumpeters sound, the musicians play. Then the third attempt was made. The battle had been going on for over five hours, and the English fire had taken severe effect; the gun deck of the *Santa Anna* was awash; she was almost in sinking condition. Her captain, an admiral, who had fought her very bravely, decided to surrender. The Spanish flag came off the stern pole, the white flag went up, and truce was asked.

Merchants on their way home from the Philippines were aboard the *Santa Anna*. Their representative came aboard Cavendish's ship. He prostrated himself, wanted to kiss Cavendish's feet. He was told to get up and go back aboard the *Santa Anna;* truce would be observed if her cargo were turned over without trouble to the English. The *Santa Anna* dropped her sails, and her boat brought the admiral and her pilot to the *Desire*. Cavendish promised the Spanish their lives and good treatment. He then asked what the *Santa Anna* had as cargo.

It was twenty-two thousand pesos in gold, silks, satins, damasks and musk; a tremendous quantity of general merchandise, along with conserves and delicate, valuable wines. Cavendish ordered the admiral and pilot to stay aboard the *Desire*. He took the ships into Puerto Seguro on the California coast on November sixth and put the Spanish complement, 190 people, women among them, ashore near a fresh-water river. The prisoners were given supplies, the sails of their ships for tents, spare planks to build a boat.

The Englishmen went about the hoisting out of the *Santa Anna* cargo into their own vessels, then the division of the treasure. The almost-inevitable attempt at mutiny took place at the share-out. Men in the crew of the *Content* led some of the others in the avowal that they wanted more than Cavendish had allotted them. But he took care of the mutineers and felt secure enough to celebrate the Queen's Coronation on November seventeenth with a display of ordnance.

It lasted during the day, and at night there were fireworks which drew applause from the Spaniards. They said that they had never seen such a sight before. Cavendish was pleased, and he went among them and took from their number two young men native to Japan and three youths born in the Philippine Islands. They had been on their way to Spain to be exhibited at court, then educated, and Cavendish believed that they would be better off in England and of interest to Queen Elizabeth. He also supplied himself with a pair of pilots, bearing in mind the rest of the voyage. November nineteenth, Cavendish passed the order, and the *Santa Anna* was burned to the water's edge. A salute was fired for the Spanish on the beach; with a fair wind, the English ships stood to sea on the Pacific traverse.

The fair wind held for almost the entire passage to Guam, a period of forty-five days. Then the fleet coasted down through the Philippines, skirmished with the natives, was saved from a plot that involved one of the impressed pilots, who was hanged. From the outer, western rim of the great island group, Cavendish sailed for Java, reached it and went to anchor. He was entertained by Javanese royalty, and was able to repair his ships, take fresh stores aboard and think of home.

Java astern, the ships trimmed sail for the African coast and the Cape of Good Hope. After that it was St. Helena on a bow-and-beam bearing, and the crews went ashore to stretch their sea legs. They stayed to take in wood and water, and grave the ships, then stood away on a course that Cavendish calculated would send them near the Azores.

It proved to be a long, hard beat with heavy gales, but the Azores were raised, and on August twenty-third the islands of Flores and Corvo were identified. On September third, the fleet

Manila Galleon

143

The Age of Piracy

met, as they stood on the final homeward course, a Flemish ship out of Lisbon. Her crew told the Englishmen of the defeat of the Armada, which brought great rejoicing among the victors over the *Santa Anna*. They persisted through another tempest which destroyed most of their sails, then on September 9, 1588, they put into their home port of Plymouth. Their voyage, while not as monetarily successful as Francis Drake's, had been just as daring and accomplished with equal skill. It, too, became part of English naval history and was long remembered by the Spanish.

Even Such Is Time

Through all Raleigh's life, it had seemed that he must engage in hazard. This was more than personal impulse, he believed; it was the nature, perhaps the necessity of the entire Elizabethan age. He had done so when he left Oxford and went early to serve in the Huguenot army in the Lowlands, while he had spent the harshly savage years against the Irish of the Munster plantation, and in England during the fantastic, glorious span when he was the Queen's favorite and yet had dared to fall in love with and marry his own Elizabeth Throgmorton.

There were, too, the Virginia venture, and the Guiana expedition, in 1595, which had promised so much, brought him great fame but little monetary award. Then the Cadiz affair where, strangely, he had fought beside Essex and won, and the quirk of circumstance that after his marriage and his first confinement in the Tower had forced the Queen to allow him freedom to halt the furious thieving of the crews in the fleet that, under Sir John Burgh, had taken immense wealth from the Spaniards off the Azores and brought it to Dover. Most of those crews were in his hire; he was the one man to make them turn back the loot they had seized out of their own ships.

That had given him, the former, still-despised favorite, considerable fortune, and he had been permitted to keep his freedom. The times were now changed; Good Queen Bess, whatever her virtues or her faults, was dead; James, the canny and slow and cruel-minded Scot, ruled. Essex was also dead and by Bess's decree. There the peculiarities of chance were clearly evident. Raleigh was able to recall with absolute detail

The Age of Piracy

standing near in his fine orange silk uniform of Captain of the Guard while the headsman poised, hefted, swung, and Essex's head dropped. Essex, stretched to the block and in the last moment remembering the Queen's smiles, could very well have shared his belief, Raleigh thought.

But other memory was not so sharp. Raleigh was grateful for the book. He had written it when his imagination had been greatly fired, and he had difficulty to distinguish what was fact, and what part fiction. The printed words helped. While he waited out the dull, bleak imprisonment in the Tower and tried to calculate the new form of cunning that King James's mind might take, he reread them. They told of the venture back twenty-one years ago, and of the river.

The river was named the Orinoco. It led south from the Caribbean into the Guiana jungle and across and up towards the buff and purple mountains. Among those was fabulous Manao, the El Dorado which was supposed to hold wealth beyond anything possessed by the Grand Khan. Upon the page:

> I never saw a more beautiful country, nor more lovely prospects. . . . The river winding into divers branches, the plains adjoining without stubble, all fair green grass, the ground of hard sand and easy to march on, the deer crossing on every path, the birds towards the evening singing on every tree with a thousand several tunes, cranes and herons of white and crimson, the air fresh with a gentle Easterly wind, and every stone that we stooped to take up promised either gold or silver by his complexion.

The barrier of the years was broken, of course, each time he read. He was again in front of the smoky magnificence of the Orinoco falls and he could feel the flick of the spray on his face and he was young, he was powerful and already the Indians had brought him small bits of the gold. The book had been written in 1596, the year after the expedition to the Orinoco. He had called it *The Discovery of the Empyre of Guiana*. The region

146

*Even
Such Is
Time*

still belonged to him, he insisted in the secret recesses of his mind. He would go and claim that. The failures, the disillusionments of twenty-one years—even anything that James might do—were not strong enough to keep him away.

The old skill to organize returned. He forged dream slowly into fact. Through friends, men who were close to guileful James but still had faith in Walter Raleigh's destiny, he pushed aside the load of debt that oppressed him, established credit sufficient to buy ships, outfit them and recruit crews. The Stuart cupidity overcame fear; King James was finally favorable to the idea, Raleigh was told. James had the conviction that Raleigh should be let go from the Tower and despatched to find his El Dorado. A vast amount of any wealth discovered must by agreement accrue to the crown.

James laid down condition upon condition governing the expedition. They became a complex and dangerous maze into which a man like Raleigh who had been so long in the King's disfavor would be foolhardy to venture. The friends who came to the Tower to visit Raleigh gave serious warning. James and the Spanish ambassador, Don Diego Sarmiento de Acuna, Count Godamar, were very close these days. The ambassador was in constant contact with Madrid. Not only was Don Diego aware of all that went on at the Court of St. James; he was acting as marriage broker. James wished fervently to marry his son, Charles, to the daughter of Philip III and thus strengthen the Stuart line.

It was a trap that James, with the help of Don Diego, conceived for Raleigh. There was no doubt that the two schemed together. James was very much beholden to Don Diego, and Raleigh was hated and feared in Spain, considered to be a principal enemy by Philip. Stay in England, remain content with a simple pardon that freed him from the Tower and seek no more, Raleigh's friends advised him.

But Raleigh hardly listened. It was coming on spring. Flowers were in bud along the Tower walks below his window.

The hoarse, bawdy cries of the Thames boatmen as they rowed the river in the sunlight stirred him. When the wind was fresh and from the east and bore the scent of the sea, he paced the apartment for hours on end.

He was obsessed by his vision. El Dorado glistened in his mind. Some of his friends lost their patience outright with him. Francis Bacon was one. Bacon was wily, sagacious, and served the court as Attorney-General. He understood full well, he protested to Raleigh, just what the King and Don Diego planned; it was Raleigh's destruction. James had promised Don Diego that no harm would befall Spain from Raleigh's venture, and should there be any, Raleigh would pay for it with his life. There was also the possibility that El Dorado did not exist. If that were true, Raleigh, coming home empty-handed, would be immediate prey for James.

But he would not return so, Raleigh said. In the event that El Dorado was only myth, he'd take his ships and raid the Spanish plate fleet, or the Mexican ports. He had no fear of lack of wealth. Such action, Bacon said, was known as common piracy, and piracy was punishable by death.

Raleigh was sixty-four years of age. The hair above the long-browed face was white. There were white streaks through the big black beard; the shoulders were slightly stooped. He smiled with ease, though, as he answered Bacon. "Did you ever know of any that were pirates for millions? They only that work for small things are pirates."

He took pen in hand after Bacon was gone. He wrote out rapidly his appeal for recruits to join his ships. The dream was brilliant:

> The common soldier shall there fight for gold and pay himself, instead of pence, with plates a half-foot broad, whereas he beareth his bones in other wars for poverty and penury. Those commanders and chieftains who shoot at honour and abundance, shall find there more rich and

Even Such Is Time

149

beautiful cities, more temples adorned with golden images, more sepulchers filled with treasure, than either Cortez found in Mexico or Pizarro in Peru, and the shining glory of this conquest will eclipse all these so far extended beams of the Spanish nation.

The Age of Piracy

On March 16, 1616, the King's warrant was issued to the Lieutenant of the Tower. It permitted "Sir Walter Raleigh to go abroad to make preparation for his voyage."

Raleigh sailed a few weeks later. He was in command of thirteen ships and a thousand men. His beloved wife, Elizabeth, who had aroused such jealousy in the other Bess and shared his imprisonment with him as a consequence, saw him off at the dock. He had in his company his son, Walter, and his nephew, George. The name of his ship was *Destiny*. The bulkheads of the cabin he occupied aboard her were lined with book shelves, decorated by pictures; rich rugs were on the floor.

The fleet stood to the southward in good formation and fair weather, raised the Canaries and sent boats ashore for fresh stores, water and firewood. Then, three days later, on the open Atlantic traverse, fever broke out among the crews. Fifty men aboard *Destiny* were declared incapable of duty. In the fleet, two captains and the provost marshal died; and the surgeon, and Fowler, who was to have assayed the gold; and John Piggott, whose assignment was command of the shore forces; and John Talbot, who had been Raleigh's companion in the Tower; and Francis, Raleigh's cook; and Crab, Raleigh's servant.

Head winds buffeted the clumsy, high-built ships. They became hurricane. The *Destiny* wallowed; she lay on her beam ends and took solid seas aboard. Nothing was dry in the ship; the cooking fires were extinguished. The crew in their miserable quarters, when allowed relief from pumping, huddled soaked and silent. Forty-two men of her complement died.

Raleigh had never been a rough-weather sailor. He suffered acutely from seasickness. His condition was such that he could not get up out of his chair. He was carried around in it from his cabin to various vantages on the quarter-deck. Young pages, tight-faced and nervous, were in constant attendance; he had repeated need of their care.

But the fleet made good the course. The ships came up on the West Indies, held towards Trinidad and the loom of the South American coast. The news gained in the islands was very bad. Raleigh learned that Don Diego de Palomeque, His Catholic Majesty's Governor of Guiana, El Dorado and Trinidad, had been informed of the expedition, and also the Bishop of Puerto Rico. The maze of treachery must reach, then, from its source in London through Madrid to the furthermost Spanish outpost.

Raleigh was late. There was, though, he decided, no reason to turn back. The gold would still be the answer for James. Enough of that, and any amount of treachery was futile. Raleigh passed the order for the ships that were to make the direct attempt at the Orinoco.

He sent five, with a complement of 250 men, under the command of Captain Lawrence Keymis. Keymis had been in the original expedition on this coast in '95, and up the river an Indian chieftain had shown him the site of a gold mine. There had been no opportunity at the time for Keymis to explore it, still he was certain of the location of the site, assured Raleigh he could return there.

Raleigh's nephew went as second in command to Keymis. Raleigh's strapping young son, who not only bore his name but very much resembled him, asked to be allowed to go. Raleigh was proud and pleased; he'd been no older when he left Oriel College and gone to fight the Lowland wars.

The five ships hauled anchor, set sail for the mainland coast. Raleigh kept the rest of the fleet off Punto Gallo and Trinidad; he wanted the rear well covered. There should be no

*Even
Such Is
Time*

151

possibility that any Spanish might enter the river after the force. It was a weary vigil, more exhausting than the years spent in the Tower.

Raleigh paced the deck in the thick, humid nights. He slapped the mosquitoes away and in remembrance saw the muddy river, heard the red howler monkeys high on the mangrove branches, the parrots screech and the thud of an alligator turning ponderously through the mud. Then his oversensitized mind offered other images:

He walked Friday Street with a linksman ahead to the Mermaid Tavern. Shakespeare was there, and Donne, and Fletcher, Selden, Beaumont. The laughter leaped and the wine tankards were shuttled down the long table; Will had a new verse for them, and they were suddenly grave, the laughter stopped. . . . Then he was at court, still "our trusty and beloved servant, Walter Raleigh," and a patron of philosophers and musicians and poets, accepted by them as a peer because of his own literary work.

He wore a pearl hat band that was worth a handful of gold pieces, and the jewels on his shoes were worth a great deal more. His clothing was of damask, his stockings silk. Fur trimmed his collar. His armor was silver. At the end of the hall, somewhat in shadow, Elizabeth, the Queen, waited for him. Sunlight from a recessed window touched the bulging forehead, the distended eyes and the powerful, beaked nose, the mouth that he would soon kiss.

Raleigh swung back across the quarter-deck of *Destiny*. The junior officer of the watch was beside the binnacle. He turned the hourglass and scratched upon the tally slate. Raleigh counted, but not hours, days. The expedition had been gone for sixteen. The men and the ships were due to be here. Time was short.

But he had only been exposed to one weak attack. He was safe. So should Keymis be. There was no real reason to worry, none. But the lookouts were shouting. Sails were on the horizon to the southward. Raleigh took the long-glass from a page and stared and smiled. They numbered five, and they were the ships that Keymis had taken to the river.

Keymis sat awkwardly in the great cabin as he made his report. His brown, rough hands clasped and unclasped on his knees. He spoke in a voice that was so low and choked by repressed emotion that it was hard for Raleigh to hear.

There had been ambush on the river. The Spaniards had been prepared for them. Young Walter Raleigh was dead. He had died of his wounds, Keymis said, after leading the pikemen in attack at the village of San Tomas. In retaliation for what the Spaniards had done, Keymis had given the order to sack and burn the place. This was on New Year's Day, 1618, and in the morning, Keymis said. Not much of worth had been found in the village. It was a paltry place at the meeting of the Orinoco and Caroni. He had kept on from there and marched to within eight miles of the gold mine.

The men were no longer in fit shape, though, and he was uncertain about the location of the mine. Spaniards might attack him again. Delayed, weighted down with gold, the men would have small chance of regaining their ships. He had told them to withdraw.

Raleigh's control snapped. Under the lash of his despair and grief he ranted at Keymis until the captain rose and went from the cabin. Raleigh sat solitary. Words came to his mind like a forgotten childhood dream. But they were his own; he had them to say over now, and they had to do with the El Dorado who as a man was complete figment. "All the vessels of his house and table and kitchen were of gold and silver. . . . He had also ropes, budgets, chests and troughs of gold and silver, heaps of billets of gold. . . . Flowers of gold and silver. . . ."

Keymis was back in the great cabin. Raleigh saw him vaguely; the derisive figure of El Dorado was in between. But

Even Such Is Time

153

The Age of Piracy

Keymis had written a letter of self-defense. He had written it to Lord Arundel of the Council, and he insisted that Raleigh accept it, forward it.

Raleigh refused. No defense could be made, he told Keymis. The entire affair upon the river was a ghastly and irremediable blunder. The killing of Spaniards, the sack and burning of San Tomas were in flagrant violation of the agreement King James had made with Count Godamar.

Keymis, the letter in his hand, left the cabin. Raleigh sat in the chair still, listening to the water sounds along the hull, seeing the butterflies, as big as a man's hand and brighter than jewels, that flitted through the stern windows. Then there was a shot.

An officer came to inform Raleigh that Captain Keymis had attempted suicide in his quarters. No response was given by Raleigh; he stared at the butterflies and at the sunlight. Proceed upon the sunbeams and a man would fetch up with El Dorado. That was the only way. The officers bowed to him and turned; there was a confusion of voices out on deck.

The pistol shot that Keymis had fired had broken a rib. But a long knife was in his cabin. He thrust it under the short ribs up to the handle. He was dead. Raleigh made a sign that he understood; for hours, while the sunlight faded and darkness crossed the cabin, he remained motionless in the chair. Then he went to the quarter-deck and dull-voiced told the captains that the ships were to get ready to sail.

He took them north through the winding green island chain to St. Christopher. Most of the captains still had hope, and the crews were willing to make a try at the Spanish plate fleet. But Raleigh had no heart for that. There was a letter which Keymis had found when the English force sacked the village at San Tomas. It was written to Palomeque, the Spanish Governor, and had been sent from Madrid before the expedition left the Thames. To Raleigh, the perfidy of King James

154

was very plain. It was clear, too, that his own ruin was complete.

Aboard *Destiny,* he wrote a letter to his wife and sent it
home from St. Christopher by another vessel. He said in it:

> I protest before the majestie of God that as Sir Francis
> Drake and Sir John Hawkins died heartbroken when
> they failed of their enterprise, I could willingly do the
> like, did I not contend against sorrow for your sake, in
> hope to provide somewhat for you; and to comfort and re-
> lieve you.

He ordered the fleet home by the northern route. His resolve was to return to his true Elizabeth, confront James. But
that dream failed, although Elizabeth and what friends remained did all they could. The pressure was too inexorable,
and in final desperation Raleigh tried to leave London by boat,
get across the Channel; but he was caught before he was below
Greenwich.

There was no more, he knew. He had come to the end of
hazarding. Essex had met the headsman. His turn, then, after
Essex. She'd smile, Bess, the Queen would, if she could be told.

He left his Bible at the Gate-house at Westminster the last
night of his life. It was found there the day after his execution,
October 29, 1618. He had written in it: "Even such is time."

Even
Such Is
Time

The Better Shares

"The fewer we are the better shares we shall have in the
spoils."

HENRY MORGAN *to his men*

There was a certain inevitable quality about it which must
have impressed Henry Morgan: he was pre-eminently a man
to take up piracy, the West Indies was the place where he
would flourish, and the time was almost perfect for his purpose.
He was born on the estate of Llanrhymney in Glamorganshire
in 1635. The oldest son of Robert Morgan, a prosperous farmer,
he came from a famous family of professional soldiers. School-
ing was no more for him than for Hawkins or Drake. He was
soon on his way to the West Indies.

Some historians have written that he came out under indenture to Barbados, but there is little substantiation for this.
Morgan had two uncles, one of them a colonel, before him in
the islands. He was very likely able to pay his own way as a
free man.

Fighting was going on in an intermittent fashion between
the English and the Spanish. The rather vaguely conceived design of Cromwell to seize Caribbean territory was defeated in
Hispaniola but succeeded in Jamaica. Morgan, barely twenty-
one, enlisted as a common soldier and served in both expeditions under Admiral Venables. Many officers died of the fever
after Jamaica was taken, and Morgan's uncle with the rank of
colonel was present to push him along. He was sent on missions
against the Spanish where he not only profited from the loot

156

taken but learned the finer points of guerrilla warfare from the buccaneers recruited for the English force.

The buccaneers occupied bases at St. Ann's Bay and Cagua on the north coast of Jamaica and lived in reasonable amity with their neighbors, retired English soldiers given to the pursuit of wild hogs. The hunting method was much the same as on Hispaniola, and an estimated hundred thousand pounds of meat a month was brought in by the veterans, who enjoyed a good market. But they were often willing to put to sea again and shoot Spaniards instead of swine.

Morgan raided Santiago in Cuba with them. He was in raiding parties that struck the Yucatan coast and the town of Campeche and many more. After seven years of service, in 1664, he was given command of a small privateer vessel. Then as a token of his ability he was asked to join the expedition led by Captains Jackman and Morris and which had William Dampier as a volunteer.

These were illustrious men among the buccaneer elite, and they were possessed of great daring. It was their plan to leave the gulf coast near Campeche and go inland as far as they could, sack and loot wherever possible. They took Villa de Mosa and Truxillo, and with friendly Indians guiding them, crossed Nicaragua despite any Spanish opposition and captured the wealthy town of Granada.

It contained a cathedral, seven churches and a number of colleges and monasteries. The buccaneers looted it thoroughly and retired. They kept on through this rich and beautiful region without serious damage to their force, sailing lakes and rivers, hiding from the Spanish pursuers in the jungle and holding steadfastly to their plunder. When they returned in safety to Jamaica they had been gone nearly three years and performed an almost incredible feat.

Morgan, at the age of thirty, was ready to assume important command; offers were made at once to him. But he was also ready for marriage. He discovered that during his ab-

The

Better

Shares

157

The Age
of
Piracy

sence his uncle, Edward Morgan, who had been serving the island as Deputy Governor, had died. Edward Morgan's second daughter was named Mary Elizabeth and she was heiress to her father's interest in the ancestral estate of Llanrhymney at home in Wales. Dark and lean Henry Morgan gave thought to his cousin, proposed and was accepted. He settled down, content to become a planter.

The contentment did not last long. He was asked by Modyford, the Governor, to sail as Vice-admiral, second in command to Captain Edward Mansvelt. This was no small honor, and one Morgan was unable to refuse. Captain Mansvelt was a rough but happy-natured old Dutchman born on the island of Curaçao. He was intensely admired by the buccaneers, very popular among them, and acknowledged to be incomparable as a leader. Under Mansvelt's direction and Modyford's urging, a fleet of fifteen ships and five hundred men were assembled at Bluefields Bay in Jamaica in November, 1665. The crews were all seasoned buccaneers, mainly English and French, yet with half a dozen other nationalities on the muster lists.

Mansvelt had as his objective the seizure of Curaçao, well to the southward of Jamaica, and used by the Spanish as a huge slave-pen. His intention, though, did not hinder him from heading north for an attack on Cuba. At the time, England and Spain were at peace, and the colonial Spanish were not prepared for the visit. Mansvelt landed his men, marched forty miles inland, seized rich booty in the town of Sancti Spiritus, marched back to the coast again and sailed.

But Curaçao was still left unattacked. With supreme daring, Mansvelt sent the fleet in assault upon Old Providence Island, which the Spanish had heavily fortified and then made into a penal colony. The assault was successful, and Mansvelt showed true humanity; although Old Providence was very near to the major Spanish ports of Puerto Bello and Nombre de Dios and in the vicinity of Spanish guard ships, the prisoners were taken to the mainland and released there.

Mansvelt held a conference with Morgan after the liberated men were on the beach. They discussed the amount of plunder to be found in Campeche province and beyond. Curaçao was once more dropped as a port of call. The fleet stood away for the Gulf of Campeche; the ships were left with a skeleton force to guard them and the San Juan River was mounted. As Morgan had done with Jackman and Morris, the river towns were swept of anything valuable and the expedition went on through Nicaragua to the capital at Granada and sacked that.

Back at the ships with their spoil, Mansvelt ordered the crews to attack the Costa Rican coast to the south. The fleet landing parties pillaged farms and plantations. They hacked fruit trees to the ground in a lust of destruction. Church images were smashed; cows and mules hamstrung. The buccaneer work was tragically wasteful, yet thorough. The Span-

The Better Shares

159

ish, in futile rage, fled into the interior, hid until the ships were gone.

Mansvelt brought the fleet into Port Royal, reported to Modyford and was no more than gently reproached for his actions against a peaceful nation. Jamaica, the Governor reasoned aloud, was a growing colony, and such enterprise helped it grow. Morgan, with his part of the loot well accounted for, went home to his wife and plantation. But the old buccaneer chief, new visions before him, sailed to Tortuga to enlist a French force, collapsed and died.

The drowsy, quite feudal plantation life pleased Morgan for some time. It was good to be with his wife, sit on the gallery during a late afternoon while the shadows stretched purple from the mountains and listen to the creaking of the oxcart wheels as loads of freshly cut cane passed to the mill, swirl the rum of his own manufacture slowly in the glass in his hand. He reflected often, though, upon the proclamation issued by the insular council, in 1666, under Modyford's direction.

What was behind it became more apparent to Morgan every day. He remembered that the publicly proclaimed resolution had been given the unanimous vote of the Council. The members' reasons were simple. Regular English troops of the garrison and the local naval complement had been so reduced that in fact the "privateers" mentioned in the document ran the island.

The resolution read:

> Resolved that it is in the interest of the island to have letters of marque granted against the Spaniard.
>
> 1. Because it furnished the island with many commodities at easy rates.
> 2. It replenishes the island with coin, bullion, cocoa, logwood, hides, tallow, indigo, cochineal and many other commodities, whereby the men of New England are invited to bring their provisions and many merchants to reside at Port Royal.

The Age of Piracy

160

3. It helps the poorer planters by selling provisions to the men-of-war.

4. It hath and will enable many to buy slaves and settle plantations, as Harmeson, Brinicain, and many others, who have considerable plantations.

5. It draws down yearly from the Windward Islands many a hundred of English, French and Dutch, many of whom turn planters.

6. It is the only means to keep the buccaneers on Hispaniola, Tortuga, and the South and North Quays of Cuba from being their enemies and infesting their plantations.

7. It is a great security to the island that the men-of-war often intercept Spanish advices and give intelligence to the Governour, which they often did in Colonel D'Oyley's time and since.

8. The said men-of-war bring no small benefit to His Majesty and His Royal Highness by the fifteenths and tenths.

9. They keep many able artificers at work in Port Royal and elsewhere at Extraordinary wages.

10. Whatsoever they get the soberer part bestow in strengthening their old ships, which in time will grow formidable.

11. They are of great reputation to this island and of terror to the Spaniards and keep up a high military spirit in all the inhabitants.

12. It seems to be the only means to force the Spaniards in time to a free trade, all ways of kindness producing nothing of good neighborhood, for though all old commissions have been called in and no new ones granted, and many of their ships restored, yet they continue all acts of hostility, taking our ships and murdering our people, making them work at their fortifications and sending them into Spain, and very lately they denied an English fleet, bound for the Dutch colonies, wood, water or provisions. For which reasons it was unanimously concluded

The

Better

Shares

that the granting of said commissions did extraordinarily conduce to the strengthening, preservation, enriching, and advancing the settlement of this island.*

The Age of Piracy

Whatever Morgan thought of Modyford as an official, he was inclined to agree with the major statements of the resolution. Port Royal was all but openly the largest buccaneer base in the islands. It was kept free from molestation, as was the rest of Jamaica, only because the captains of the English ships were jealous of their French counterparts to the north at Tortuga. Modyford had been driven to his decision, and stood justified. The French in January of 1667 had declared war on England. Jamaica was in momentary danger of attack.

Word that Morgan had from old friends told of the new French Governor at Tortuga. He was Bertrand d'Ogeron, born in Anjou and a veteran officer in the *"troupes de la marine."* His more recent service as a privateer captain had given him a friendly understanding of buccaneers and their problems. Out of his own pocket, no interest money asked, he had extended loans to men who wished to establish themselves in homes ashore, and further furnished them with Portuguese letters of marque so that they would be able to make a living and repay the loans. Portugal was, of course, technically at peace with France, but d'Ogeron was far from Lisbon, and only in very tenuous contact with the seats of authority. If he made a mistake or so, the Portuguese government would have some difficulty in correcting the error.

Morgan came to the belief that he should go back to the more active life. Not only would his return to service prove a patriotic gesture; his own considerable interests might be lost in a night of French buccaneer looting and burning. He accepted the rank of colonel in the colonial militia from Modyford in 1668 and went about the collection of a fleet and crews.

He mustered ten ships and put aboard them, slightly to

* E. A. Cruikshank, *The Life of Sir Henry Morgan.*

Modyford's dismay, a force of about five hundred men recruited at random from among retired English soldiers living in Jamaica, French buccaneers who slipped down from Tortuga for the occasion, and polyglot veteran privateersmen. Setting to sea, he made no effort to attack d'Ogeron, but instead took the fleet to a rendezvous at the Isle of Pines off Cuba. Then the force started inland from the Cuban coast for the town of Santa Maria de Puerto Principe.* The place was the second largest on the island, and known to be wealthy. It took Morgan's lot twenty-four hours of steady marching to reach it. The sack accomplished, Morgan herded the stragglers onto the coastal trail, led the column back to where the ships waited hidden by the south-shore cays.

Most of the men were satisfied with what Santa Maria had supplied them. Morgan was not; he set the fleet course for Puerto Bello. That was the most important port in all of Central America, and he was certain that it could be captured. He recognized that Drake had been defied by it, but the fact did not deter him. He would have his try, and he would better Drake.

His crews lacked enthusiasm for the attempt. They could recall the Drake story, and they knew Puerto Bello as a strongly fortified pesthole, the harbor only three thousand yards long and fifteen hundred to eighteen hundred yards wide, and the marshes along the shore side so pestilential that the Spanish garrison was relieved every three months. Morgan listened without patience to what his officers told him of the men's sentiment. He was planning the assault, working over charts, evaluating all his profound knowledge of the area. The men were well fed; a good store of smoked meat had been put aboard before the fleet sailed from Cuba. Let them eat and sleep, grumble, drink and gamble. That was common buccaneer style. But, off Puerto Bello, they must make up their minds to fight.

* Present-day Camaguey.

The
Better
Shares

163

*The Age
of
Piracy*

Some, mostly the Frenchmen, refused him when, one hundred miles north of the objective, his canny sense of campaign warned not to continue any further by ship, but to make the rest of the distance by dugout canoe. The French buccaneers took a ship and sailed for Tortuga. The others listened to Morgan's statement about "the fewer we are the better shares we shall have" and embarked in the canoes and set out for Puerto Bello.

There were about four hundred men, and it was cramped, painful work alongshore through the coastal rollers. But they landed safely in darkness outside the town, marched rapidly towards the place. Their guide was an Englishman who had been a captive in it, knew it well. "This fellow had Abundance of Courage and was fit for the greatest Attempts. Besides, he was pushed on with the Desire for Revenge; for the bad Usage he had met with from the Spaniards had inflamed his mind to such a degree that he listed for a Pyrate with no other View than to be revenged." *

The former captive took three other volunteers and went ahead to secure the first sentry. They flattened him, snatched his musket, gagged him and brought him back to Morgan. A brief conversation persuaded the Spaniard to talk; he "told in what situation the Castle and the Garrison were, and everything else which they demanded. On the welcome intelligence he gave them, they instantly marched, carrying the captive Spaniard along, and having got close to the Castle, intirely surrounded it; and by this means effectually prevented any from going in or out." **

Prompted, the captive called upon the commander of the castle to surrender. His answer was a cannon blast that gave the alarm to the town. Morgan chose to leave the castle until later, preferring the much easier assault upon the town. The inhabitants were in great disorder although the Governor tried

* A. O. Exquemeling, *The History of the Buccaneers of America.*
** *Ibid.*

164

to rally them, and in fact caused severe damage among Morgan's ranks, separated part of his force. Then the Governor and a number of the leading citizens, who lugged their most valuable possessions with them, retreated to another castlelike fort, one of the three guarding the place.

Morgan smarted under the loss of his men, and the feeling of hurt increased when the churches and houses were searched and found to be almost empty of anything valuable. He gave the order for an assault upon the fort into which the Governor and the citizens had retreated. Expert marksmen with the long buccaneer muskets killed many of the Spanish gunners at the embrasures, but the assault was beaten back.

Fireballs were prepared to be used upon the gates while the force crouched on the slope below. The men went up with their flaming burdens and were met by huge stones, flasks of powder that smashed and killed. Survivors came away beneath a screen of musketry, and Morgan knew that his losses were extremely serious. He had strength for one more attack, but it was dubious if he could succeed in that.

Then some of his men began to shout and point. Morgan turned from his inspection of the fort in front of him. English colors flew stiff in the dawn breeze from the flagstaff of another fort. It had obviously just been taken by the men who had strayed from the main force in the town while the looting was in progress there, afterwards regrouped.

Morgan saw his men smile. He ordered them to collect poles for scaling ladders, and he had brought forward the large number of nuns and priests who had been captured in the town. There was no sense of mercy in him; he proposed to use the religious people as a shield when his ladders were ready. If the Spaniards fired on their own, that was their concern, not his.

He announced the intention to the Governor through an interpreter, demanded surrender. It was refused. He signed that the mute, taut group of religious be sent along to the wall.

The Better Shares

165

The Age of Piracy

They were decimated row after row by Spanish fire. Morgan took his men through the heaped wounded and dead, the scaling ladders were thrust up and climbed.

Morgan's men had fireballs and pitchers of powder in their hands. They flung them over the parapets at the Spaniards, jumped the embrasures and began the close-in cutlass, dirk and pistol fighting at which they had no equals. But the Spaniards resisted with stubborn, desperate courage. Quarter was cried and ignored, and asked only after the Governor* was dead.

He died fighting, having killed a number of his enemies, and to the end contemptuous of them.

Morgan exercised no restraint over his troops when the battle was finished. The casualty list was too great, and the savage side of his nature had been inflamed by the stubbornness of the defense. Puerto Bello, with the forts, the churches and nunneries and monasteries and churches and houses of the town, was open to rapine. Women were violated; altars were defiled; captives were tortured, their feet burned, until the demands for treasure were met.

Morgan kept himself busy at the collection of loot. He gathered in a ransom of one hundred thousand pieces of eight from the leading citizens to add to what had already been seized. Then he was informed by scouts that the President of Panamá was on his way with a large force. The redoubts in the forts were leveled with prisoner labor, the big guns spiked or tossed from their carriages, wrecked. Word had been sent for the fleet; it arrived and was loaded and provisions put aboard.

The return voyage to Jamaica was made without incident. Morgan was rowed from his ship to the Port Royal boat quay with a rather lengthy report for Modyford. He had brought back "250,000 Pieces of Eight, besides all other Merchandise." **

* The exact identity of the Governor is not known, but it is very probable that he was Don José Sanchez Ximinez, a veteran of Lowlands and West Indian campaigns.
** Exquemeling, *op. cit.*

It was Morgan's belief that Modyford, while protesting, would be pleased. He was right.

He retained the gubernatorial favor to the degree that in late 1668 he organized a larger expedition, sailed in the *Oxford,* a former Royal Navy fifth-class frigate, to gather recruits. He put the *Oxford* at anchor off Ile aux Vaches on the Hispaniola coast and on January 2, 1669, invited eight privateer captains and their senior officers aboard. They were seated with him at dinner under an awning on the quarter-deck when, through a gunner's carelessness, the main magazine let go.

Livid explosion rent the deck planks beneath the table. By some quirk of fortune, Morgan and the captains seated at his side were saved. All those opposite them were killed. The ship, torn to her keelson, sank at once, and from her crew only six men and four boys were saved. Two hundred men were either killed by the explosion, burned to death or drowned.

It was frightful disaster. Morgan could count five of his principal officers among the missing, and a quarter of his best men. But he still clung to his intention that an assault should be made upon the Spanish Main. That had been the subject of his discussion with the officers at dinner, and he persisted, although he gave up his original idea about assault upon Cartagena de Indias. A reportedly somewhat easier goal was at nearby Maracaibo.

He sailed at last with a fleet of eight vessels, some of them small, open-decked schooners. His muster amounted to five hundred men, for the most part French buccaneers. They had brought their muskets and cutlasses and knives with them in their habitual fashion, and also a large supply of *boucan*-cured meat. Morgan sampled some of it while he talked aboard his ship with a buccaneer who was to serve as guide at Maracaibo. Three years before, the man had been there with L'Ollonais and Michel le Basque; he knew the approaches to Maracaibo Lake very well.

The expedition touched at the small offshore island of

The

Better

Shares

167

Aruba to take aboard water and wood, helped by amiable Indians. Then, at night, so that they would not be sighted from the *vigilia* tower at the entrance to the lake, they sailed in attack formation. But a new fort had been built beside the narrow strait leading to the lake. They were discovered; there was an all-day fire-fight between the ships and the Spanish batteries. With the swift dusk, Morgan went in to land, leaving a skeleton crew to hold the ships offshore.

The fort was found deserted, and a keen-eyed buccaneer picked up the flicker of a slow-match fuse connected to the magazine. The fuse was stamped out; enormous quantities of powder, shot, muskets and small arms were taken, and sixteen big cannon were spiked. Morgan considered it too dangerous, though, to bring his ships in over the bar to the lake. He put the men in canoes and small boats, and with no more armament than they could carry they entered and attacked the great fort called de la Barra.

No troops were left in it. Both fort and town had been evacuated. Morgan felt flattered by the implied compliment to his skill; still he was interested in loot. He kept possession of the town for three weeks and sent parties daily to comb the jungle and bring in prisoners. The people captured were put to torture, and when Gibraltar, the town at the far end of the lake was seized, the citizens there were offered similar treatment as a means to gain confession of the location of their property.

When every conceivable amount of ready ransom and plunder had been gathered, Morgan took his little flotilla back to Maracaibo. A single sick old Spaniard occupied the place. He told Morgan, after urging, that three powerful Spanish ships lay offshore and that the fort at the strait had been repaired and remanned.

Morgan tried to treat with the commander of the Spanish warships. The man was a ranking admiral, Don Alonzo del Campo y Espinosa, and from his flagship he sent a crisply worded promise to put Morgan's entire complement to the sword. Such language made Morgan contemplative. He had the message translated into English and French and read it to his assembled force in the main plaza at Maracaibo. The men were impressed; they told Morgan that because of their lack of popularity with the admiral they were willing to fight to get to sea and keep the loot. Morgan began to plan.

There were captured ships in the lake. He armed some of them in the best possible manner, but held three out for special purposes. He sent into one of them the women prisoners and the plate, the jewels and most valuable booty. The second took aboard the male prisoners who held a ransom potential. The third was to be used as what the Tortuga buccaneers called a *brulot,* a fire ship.

He lavished his inventive talents on the fire ship. She was made to appear as a vessel carrying many guns and a big crew. Gun-ports were faked in her sides. Cylindrical drums that were the former property of Negro slaves in the town were emplaced as cannon. Figures stuffed with straw were secured at the bulwarks beside the drum cannon, and buccaneers with artistic inclinations painted faces on the canvas heads, topped them with knit wool *montera* caps worn by Spanish seamen and borrowed from a stock in the town. Then her bulkheads were cut away to allow explosion full play, and her holds were loaded with sulphur, tar, pitch and hundreds of barrels of powder.

A volunteer crew was mustered for the fire ship, and after a week's preparation Morgan sailed to make his break for freedom. Rounding into the strait from the lake, he came up on the three Spanish warships. They were abreast and at anchor right below the fort. He made a signal to his ships and they dropped anchor just beyond range and so passed the night.

Morgan gave the attack signal at dawn. The fire ship went in first, very well handled by her small crew. She closed with the *Magdalena,* the admiral's ship, and secured to her before the Spaniards recognized what she was. Her crew dived over the side up-wind and swam while the Spaniards tried to hold her off with pikes and boat hooks, cut the grapnel lines, douse the spreading fire.

The *Magdalena* was a fine frigate of thirty-six big and twelve small cannon. She was set afire and the flame licked down companionways, then along a passage to her magazine. The blast rived her; she sank a total wreck, and most of her stunned crew were drowned as they attempted to leave her flotsam. The admiral was among those saved, but he had no control over the captains of the remaining vessels.

One ran his vessel ashore below the fort, burned and scuttled her. Her crew fled into the fort while the third ship fought with spirit against Morgan. It was a sharp action and a number of men, both Spaniards and buccaneers, were killed. But Morgan's were the better gunners, and more determined. The Spanish captain was forced to surrender.

Morgan was still confronted by the strongly armed fort. He attacked it, his men going in with only muskets, cutlasses and hand grenades. They were sent back with the loss of some sixty dead. Morgan gave the recall to the boats, and the survivors were taken out aboard the fleet.

The action against the fort had been fought at dusk. With darkness, Morgan started to slip his men through the strait in canoes. His original fleet that had brought the expedition was still offshore and unharmed. It sailed in close, the men boarded from the canoes, and slowly the entire transfer was made. Morgan was able to get his loot into the ships, but he regretted that he must leave so many ransom-valuable prisoners behind. "Just as he departed Captain Morgan ordered seven great Guns with Bullets to be fired against the Castle, as it were to take leave of them. But they answered not so much as with a musket shot."*

Fierce storm was encountered on the way north to Jamaica. Many of the wounded died in the wet, cruelly pitching vessels. But every ship completed the voyage and the men

* Exquemeling, *op. cit.*

170

who survived landed in Port Royal, wealthy at least until they reached the pothouses and the doxies. Before drunkenness overtook them they admitted that Harry Morgan was the most feared, envied and respected buccaneer from Bermuda to the Main.

He returned once more to the quiet life, took up again his pursuits as a planter at his estate in the lovely Rio Minho valley. His wife was happy to have him home, and yet on his visits to Port Royal he was caught in the undertow of piracy, responded gradually to it.

Port Royal had become a fantastically evil town; it thrived on corruption, and a good deal of its arterial flow was rum. A contemporary estimate, given in 1669, stated that for each pair of men on the island there was some sort of establishment that sold strong liquor, in addition to the sugar-and-rum works which sold without license. Charles Modyford, acting as Deputy Governor during his father's absence in London, reported that there were three thousand men capable of carrying arms, exclusive of fifteen hundred privateers who manned twenty ships. Any of those ships, Morgan knew, and the pick of the men, were his for the asking.

He designed one final venture in the drowsy ease of the days at Rio Minho plantation. He determined that he would strike at the very heart of Spanish power, go after the biggest prize of all. It was the capital city of Panamá, and from it could be taken booty that would keep even his ambition-whetted appetite satisfied. He released word in Port Royal that he was in want of crews and ships.

It was the greatest and the finest buccaneer force ever mustered under a unified command in the islands. Volunteer crews came from as far away as Bermuda in their famous sloops built of cedar. Hunting parties in the remote interior savannahs of Hispaniola received the summons and at much personal sacrifice marched to join the fleet, bringing quantities of meat with them and brushing with Spanish patrols along the way as

The Better Shares

171

a warm-up for what was to come. Morgan picked, chose with more than his usual care, sailed south in 1670 with nearly two thousand men.

He first landed an attack force commanded by a veteran pirate named Captain Joseph Bradley who had been appointed "Vice-admiral." Bradley went after the formidably well-forti-fied Castle of San Lorenzo that flanked the Chagres River on the route that must be followed to reach Panamá. An almost unbelievable engagement was fought. Bradley's men, with nothing but small arms and muskets and crude grenades, climbed exposed heights beneath direct fire, entered against a greatly superior force and took the place.

Captain Bradley had both feet struck away by a cannon ball during the fighting, but he kept order among his men and sent them steadily to the attack. One man crawled so close to the Spanish ramparts that he was clipped by an ar-row, probably delivered by an Indian bowman. The arrow caused him intense pain and he yanked it out of his flesh, tied a bit of his torn shirt around the head, thrust the haft into his musket barrel and shot it back. The muzzle flash ignited shirt scrap and arrow; they fell inside a rampart where palm-thatch structures had been built to protect the troops from the sun's heat. The thatch was dry. It blazed up quickly, and afraid of the powder tubs for the guns, the Spaniards retreated.

Bradley sensed their absence when his volleys weren't an-swered. He asked his men for another attack. Up and in, they hooted from the rampart top, and the place was taken. Brad-ley, with his truncated legs, was carried to a surgeon, but that night died.

Morgan left a large detachment at San Lorenzo to secure his rear and started the march across the isthmus. He had four-teen hundred men with him and in a fleet of canoes went up the Chagres River on January 9, 1671. The Spaniards knew he was coming, and stripped the route ahead of him, laid ambushes. His men without supplies, depending on what they could take from the enemy, fought through the dense mazes of tropical jungle. For six days they found nothing and were chewing on sandal and belt leather when a crib full of maize corn was reached.

That gave its share of dysentery and added to the fever pangs. But the men kept to the trail while Morgan described with vivid oratory the quality of loot to be had at Panamá. On the ninth day a buccaneer swarmed up a cottonwood tree and shouted that he could see a church steeple, which must with certainty be in the city. Morgan took the rejoicing force ahead but, with the battle sense that had so often brought him success, changed his line of march.

Scouts gave him information about the disposition of the Spanish cannon protecting the city. He swung clear from the batteries and took up position on a ridge some little distance away. Open savannah occupied by grazing cattle was between him and the Spaniards. He held his restive men still while the Governor mustered a *caballero* force in defense. The horsemen made a brilliant sight in their silver-chased corselets and helmets and the mounts curveted when the trumpeters sounded the attack.

Morgan's men flapped their shirts at the cattle. They fired a few volleys into them and frightened them into motion towards the Spaniards. Then, while the *caballeros* slowed from the canter to the trot among the wide-horned beasts, Morgan attacked. His men passed through the cavalry, cut down the gunners that manned the culverin batteries behind, and went on into the city.

There has always been a moot point about who fired the city, Morgan or the unhappy Governor. The wooden houses, parched by the sun, burned furiously, though, and in swirls of flame, among pelting sparks and the cries of the alarmed and unready citizens, the sack began. Morgan, cleverly, restrained his men from the common buccaneer mistake by warning them that all the liquor in the city had been poisoned.

The Better Shares

He was able to send sober detachments to break into the King's storehouses.

Panamá was held by Morgan for three weeks. Scouting parties went out into the countryside and rounded up prisoners who were tortured unless they produced loot or ransom. There was rape, and murder, and very little show of mercy. Then Morgan recognized that it was time to withdraw. He left with a pack train of two hundred mules laden with gold and silver and bales and sacks of precious booty. It pleased him to give the command of the rearguard to a kinsman, Colonel Bledry Morgan. This was his greatest victory, Morgan was aware—also his last.

The Chagres was reached in March, and the men asked for their share of the spoils. Morgan was tightfisted, slow. He doled out only what amounted to £10 a man. There was resentment; he was threatened, called uncomplimentary names. He was hard enough, though, to escape personal attack, and cunning enough to sail at night, secretly, with some favored captains for Port Royal.

Deserted on an enemy coast, without ships or provisions, the buccaneers were in a desperate condition through Morgan's treachery. They built canoes, or took what they could of the local shipping, and got out before the Spaniards came upon them. What remained of the Bermudian contingent saw the voyage home as quite long.

Morgan made Port Royal in comfortable style and on May 31, 1671, he received a formal vote of thanks from the Jamaican Council, whose members temporarily forgot that the year before solemn treaty, calling for the end of depredations in the West Indies, had been signed by England and Spain. Complaint was made in Madrid and expressed at the Court of St. James. Under guard, as a prisoner, Morgan was sent out to England in April, 1672. But his ability to deal with the wily and his magnificent record as a collector of Spanish wealth had appeal to those who would condemn him; Morgan was of the stamp of Drake, if a century late. So he was knighted in November, 1674, accorded the further honor of being appointed Deputy Governor of Jamaica.

He returned home famous. The life at the Rio Minho plantation seemed like sheer monotony, although he was called upon from time to time to hang some of his old shipmates who had continued in the piratical trade. Then, more or less immobilized by gout, he spent the hours in rum and recollection and passionate talk in the Port Royal pothouses. He was over long in bad company, and he had been heard to say, "God damn the Assembly!" *

Although such remarks displeased the Governor, Morgan kept up his criticism, drank persistently to excess, dismissed his doctor's warnings, and died of a liver complaint at the age of fifty-three on August 25, 1688. His body was buried with full honors and salutes from the ships in the harbor at Port Royal. His will was in favor of his wife and her family. Word of his death, when it reached Spain, caused some relaxation at the court of His Catholic Majesty.

*Phillip Gosse, *The Pirates' Who's Who*.

The Better Shares

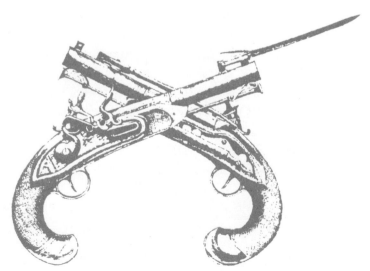

175

The Lonesome Widow

"It is no very uncommon thing for a child, that is a native of Paris, to go and seek his fortune abroad, and to entertain a fixed design of becoming a man engaged in hazardous adventure."

SIEUR RAVENEAU DE LUSSAN in the opening sentence of his book, *Journal du Voyage fait à la Mer du Sud avec les Filibustiers en 1684*

A fair amount of understatement is contained within that sentence, for de Lussan's book has the aura of an epic, and the luster and the terror of his experiences, the courage, the depravity, the astounding piety of the men with whom he served become magnificently real. De Lussan wrote in retrospect, well after the fact, yet he never forgot. Quill in hand back in Paris, he remembered each incident of the "hazardous adventure."

He was, like a number of the great English buccaneers who preceded him to the Spanish Main, of a well-to-do family. He was born, too, at a time of active martial endeavor; while still in his teens, he enlisted and fought at the siege of Condé as a soldier. At the end of the campaign he joined a marine regiment. Debt began to plague him, and it is to be gathered that he couldn't keep away from the dice box or the cards. He was very seriously troubled by this when he took part in the seige of St. Guislain under Count d'Avegean. Failing to get financial help from his family, he took the only open road away from his creditors.

He signed up as an *engagé*, indentured for three years, and sailed from Dieppe, March 5, 1679, for the then-thriving French colony of St. Domingue in Hispaniola. It was a hard life even for a tough young veteran, yet he stuck it out until the expiration of his indenture. He wanted no more of dawn-to-dusk field work, though, and disliked the lash. The King's Lieutenant, M. de Franquesnay, who ruled in the capacity of Acting Governor, took de Lussan into his own home for six months as his personal guest. Then, once more in fit shape after the vicissitudes of indenture, de Lussan learned that a buccaneer expedition was about to sail from the island.

Captain Laurence de Graff, a famous leader, was fitting out the ship, *Neptune*. She promised much in the simple fact that she was armed with fifty-four guns and would carry a muster of 210 men. De Lussan appealed to his mentor and friend, the King's Lieutenant, and was advised to join the expedition. The advice was backed up with a loan to buy gear and weapons, and de Lussan was given the rank of ensign in the buccaneer company under de Graff.

Neptune sailed from Petite Goave in Hispaniola on November 22, 1684, and at sea kept rendezvous with other French buccaneer vessels. The fleet stood to the southward and tried its luck among the small islands off the Main. Raids were made upon Curaçao, Aruba and Bonaire, then at Rio de la Hacha, but without much booty being taken. After a captains' conference, the fleet headed for Golden Island on the Gulf of Darien below Panamá. This was a small, hidden harbor known to buccaneers. Raiding parties left occasionally from there to cross the isthmus and establish themselves in the Pacific, or as the buccaneers commonly called it, "The South Sea." Disappointed by his first piratical effort, de Lussan could look forward to a wide vista of loot in the other ocean; the Pacific was supposed to have untold riches for the bold.

Three buccaneers were found at Golden Island. They said that because of sickness they had been unable to go as members of an expedition led by the French captains, Grognier and

The
Lonesome
Widow

177

The Age of Piracy

Lescuier, for the Pacific. Then some of the local Indians boarded the ships carrying letters. These men were Cimaroons of the Sambie tribe, descendants of runaway Negro slaves who had savored Spanish colonial justice for generations, taken to the bush and intermarried with the indigenous Indians. Their greatest pleasure was the destruction of Spaniards, and they welcomed anyone who would aid them in it.

The letters were from the expedition the sick men had missed. Word was given to the next body of buccaneers which arrived that Captains Grognier and Lescuier were on their way across the isthmus with two companies which had 210 men as a total muster. Ahead of them also by a few days' march was an English company of 115 men. The popularity of the Golden Island route to wealth seemed to be increasing, de Lussan remarked. While the letters were still being read and the contents debated, two other French ships came in from sea.

A long conference was held by the commanders. Some were for an expedition to the Pacific, some against it as much too perilous. De Graff appears to have withdrawn; he is not mentioned further in the de Lussan narrative. One captain decided to burn his ship as an inducement to his crew to make the march. Another, about to abandon his, gave it quite willingly to a captain who had reached the conclusion that he should retire. There was more discussion as to how much the Cimaroons should be trusted as guides; the letters from Grognier and Lescuier said that the tribe might be used if correctly treated.

De Lussan was already aware that he was a witness to the extraordinary. He went ashore and mingled with the Cimaroons on the beach. They impressed him, and he picked up all the information about them that he could, wrote later in his journal:

> They lead a wandering and vagabond life, and fix their abode in no certain place. They go naked, except it

be that they cover a part of their privities with a bit of silver or gold that is made like a candle extinguisher; and were I but satisfied that they had never seen such a thing, I should think they took their model from it.

When they feast, or hold their solemn metings, they put on a cotton robe, all of one piece, and it is usual with them, in a vaunting manner, to have a bit of gold or caracolay of an oval form hanging from their noses, which is bored through, and with this they think themselves as fine as any in the world. As for the women kind, they cover themselves from the waist downwards with an herb or cotton cloth, which they make themselves; and that they may appear finer, they color their faces with roccou, which is a small grain that dyes a brown red.

De Lussan's studies were interrupted by an order to report aboard. The captains had reached final decision. A company of 264 under Captains Picard, Rose and Desmarais would make the march across the isthmus guided by two Cimaroon chiefs with a force of forty more Cimaroons to help carry guns and ammunition. De Lussan contemplated the future a bit thoughtfully, but made no objection to being included as a member of the expedition.

March 1, 1685, the men started inland. They filed up the beach from their boats aware that there would be nothing here for them if they were able to return. Any vessel left was sure to come into Spanish hands. Before them was strange, dangerous jungle patrolled regularly from strong Spanish outposts. Capture meant instant death for the lucky, for those less so the tortures of the Inquisition or chained labor and the whip in a Spanish galley. But the men were happy as they marched. There was gold in the Pacific towns; the old-timers said the streets were paved with it.

The arduous march lasted for six days. It was the height of the rainy season; the drenched jungle stank with rot, and the men had no fire to dry themselves; food, powder and flint

The Lonesome Widow

179

were soaked; the numerous streams were in wild, muddy flow. But on the sixth day the guides put them on the Rio de la Hacha that led to the Pacific.

Shelters were made against the rain, and fires built. The Cimaroons showed the buccaneers how to construct dugout canoes, and were paid off with cloth, knives, thread, needles, scissors, hatchets and the combs and cheap glass-bead baubles the Indian women adored. The Indians gave back maize and yams and manioc, and on April first, the canoes finished, the expedition took to the river.

That was a test of seamanship. The river was very rough, with many rapids and sand bars and portages. All of the company, because of improper diet and the constant wet weather, suffered from the "bloody flux" (dysentery), and one man was so badly afflicted that he died. But with approximately twenty men to a canoe and the same number of local Cimaroon guides to aid them, they kept on towards the sea. Another man died and the rest, bleak in their discouragement, thought of the sun-filled days on the Main.

Then word was brought up-river that the English buccaneer commander, Captain Townley, had taken a pair of big Spanish provision ships bound for the supply of Quito. It was Townley who had gone ahead with his 115 men, and the French buccaneers were heartened; here was sign of what they could do in their turn. They reached the coast at Boca Chica and joined up with the rest of the companies waiting there.

Again a conference, sodden charts examined, courses laid off, distances measured. The combined force moved out in canoes for a group of islands to the east of Panamá. They met eight English ships under Captain Townley and ships commanded by Captains Grognier and Henry and Sammes and David and a number of other captains and veteran quartermasters. This amounted to a fleet that was capable of attacking the harbor at Panamá. The islands were inhabited by

Cimaroons and the buccaneers had a haven to which they might return.

A fleet of seven big Spanish vessels lay in Panamá Bay. The buccaneers went right in among them although many of their craft were no more than sail-rigged canoes. De Lussan served aboard a *barca longa,* a single-deck, lightly armed ship less than one hundred feet in length. She took into her over 120 solid shot, and was forced to fall out of the action for refit.

Captain Sammes's mate was beheaded by a cannon ball. The greater part of his ship's poop was shot away when he insisted upon close maneuver against much superior gun power. Captain David's ship was pounded until half her rudder was smashed, a man killed and six others wounded. The buccaneers in the canoes did their utmost to come within range so the sharpshooters could get to work in their famous style with the long muskets. It was impossible. The Spaniards were well-armed and determined; they repelled each attack.

The buccaneer fleet cleared the bay and sailed north. There were small coastal towns to be taken while the wounds healed. The assaults were easy, but buccaneer began to fight with buccaneer; a difference of religious belief separated Englishmen from Frenchmen. The Frenchmen, many of them Catholics by early training, resented the "impiety" of the English, who in the little chapels hacked the arms from crucifixes with their cutlasses, shot down the holy images for target practice.

Common cause against the enemy held the force together. It went on into Costa Rica and took the considerable town of Pueblo Viejo, marched for and seized after a rough, bloody fight the capital town of Granada in Nicaragua that had suffered previous buccaneer attack. De Lussan and the rest of the religious-minded Frenchmen, once Granada was secured, sang the *Te Deum* in the cathedral, set four sentries in the tower and "went to visit the houses, wherein we found nothing but

The
Lonesome
Widow

181

a few goods, and some provisions, which we carried into our court of guard."

Richer prospects could be found south of Panamá, those who had been there declared, and the expedition took to sea. On the way to Guayaquil, a prime objective, it was decided to make an assault on Queaquilla. This was a town of some consequence, but it was seized and sacked without much loot gained. The same lack of wealth was discovered aboard the Spanish ships attacked offshore. When the force entered the Guayas River to go up it to Guayaquil, the buccaneers were quite eager.

Guayaquil was built at the foot of a low mountain, guarded by three forts and numerous redoubts that were manned by a strong garrison. Scouts had made contact with the buccaneers on the river. The alarm was given to the garrison in plenty of time, yet the buccaneers attacked in broad daylight.

For some unusual reason, possibly that of pride, strict European discipline was maintained as the men moved forward. Flags were flown. Trumpets sounded and drums ruffled the cadence for the close-order ranks. But the enemy outnumbered them three to one. Intense grapeshot and musket fire stopped the attack at a ditch. The buccaneers went flat and were exhorted by their captains; a promise of one thousand pieces of eight was offered to the first ensign who sent the pirate colors aloft on the main fort.

De Lussan was still an ensign. He fought furiously when the Spanish leaped the ditch and advanced to the counterattack with the sword. The counterattack was defeated and from ditch to redoubt to redoubt the buccaneers went in. There were eleven hours of unbroken combat before the last of the Spanish troops surrendered.

De Lussan rejoiced in both his safety and the capture, although unable to claim the bonus for putting the flag on the fort. He sang *Te Deum* with his French mates in the cathedral, then took part in the search after loot. An enormous sum was uncovered, mostly in pearls and silver, and seventy thousand pieces of eight. Prisoners admitted to three million pieces of eight that had been transported up-river and secreted during the attack.

The buccaneers in anger searched the place again. They had been told of another twenty-two thousand pieces of eight and a prodigious gold-leafed eagle that weighed sixty-eight pounds and had huge rock emeralds for eyes. The Governor's family and many other principal citizens were captives, and ransom terms were established which to the buccaneers seemed only reasonable. For a million pieces of eight, plus four hundred sacks of maize to be brought from Quito, the prisoners, the town, the forts, their cannon and the various craft in the yards along the river were to be delivered.

A plea for patience was made by the Governor. He protested that he must communicate with the Viceroy at Quito, which would take time. But the buccaneers were in a bad mood; Captain Grognier had just died of his wounds, and the streets where fighting had been severe were littered with nine hundred corpses. These swelled and blackened with the heat. The town was rapidly becoming pestilential.

Part of it was burned by the buccaneers. They were drunken and disorderly, the fine sense of discipline which had shown in battle frayed by inaction. De Lussan held his poise, very much the traditional French officer. The day after the battle he was assigned to conduct a young gentlewoman to the place of safety where the rest of the prisoners were kept. She was a member of the Governor's household, served in the capacity of lady-in-waiting to the Governor's wife. Along the way, she stopped in the street, grasped de Lussan by the arm and said, "*Señor,* for the love of God, don't eat me." De Lussan assured her that while his inclinations led him to young ladies of charm, he had never yet eaten one.

The demand for ransom was refused, and this brought a

The Lonesome Widow

183

flat statement from the buccaneers: "Pay or we send you fifty heads." The expedition moved down-river, prisoners and all, and stationed itself on Puna Island at the mouth of the Guayas River, some forty miles below. An hourglass was used, and the days counted precisely off until the announced time limit was reached.

Dice were given the prisoners. They were prevailed upon to play among themselves, and four lost; their heads were cut off and sent up-river to Guayaquil. The note which accompanied this expression of purpose read in part, "Four more days and we cut off the rest."

However, the relations between prisoners and pirates did not remain strained. De Lussan wrote in his journal, "Neither did we want charms for our ears in this place, for we had all the music of the town among our prisoners, which consisted of lutes, theorvoes, harps, guitars and other instruments I never saw anywhere else, wherewith they made a fine concert."

De Lussan, stirred by the music and the lush tropical setting, found himself attracted by a young widow. Her husband had been the King's Treasurer for Guayaquil, a man of importance and not without property. While harps were plucked, guitars strummed, the widow made a proposal to her ensign captor. She said that he and she should hide in the jungle, wait for the expedition to leave. Then she would return with him to the town, where he would take over her husband's former job, his house and estate. De Lussan, although pleased by her ardor, refused, believing that the memory of the *Guayaquileños* might not favor him.

A sum of twenty thousand pieces of eight and an amount of maize were finally sent down the river. Weary of further bickering and aware of the probability of attack while they waited, the buccaneers gave up the idea of any more ransom payment and reached the conclusion that they should shove off to sea. De Lussan parted tenderly from the widow and went aboard his ship. The fleet sailed north.

It met a number of big Spanish ships along the coast and there were severe fights. De Lussan was wounded in one action and his ship took sixty-six solid shot, most of them between wind and water. But the Spaniards were beaten off from capturing her; the famous buccaneer accuracy with the musket forced the Spanish gun-ports to be shut as the gunners were riddled at the pieces. Writing later in reminiscence, De Lussan said of the Acapulco galleon which the fleet sought, "It is of a prodigious bigness, and built so strong, that she is afraid of nothing but land and fire."

Talk began in the fleet about return home. Share-out was held, but in view of the difficult overland trek across to the Caribbean, the huge sums of silver, bulky in form, appeared nearly worthless. Coined gold, because of its shape and the ease with which it could be carried, took an added worth of eighty to one hundred pieces of eight per ounce, and jewels were much more precious. The average share-out per man was four hundred pieces of eight, and the total sum the expedition had realized was estimated at a half million pieces of eight.

The fleet gave up sailing and took to gambling. Silver dropped steadily in value. The buccaneers had learned the local Spanish contempt for the stuff; the *colonios* used silver for the same purposes that steel, iron and copper were employed in Europe. When a ransom sum of silver—carried in one hundred canoes, each canoe load worth eleven thousand pieces of eight—was sent to the fleet, it was disregarded. No man wanted to leave the dice to pick it up.

De Lussan was lucky and won a lot and felt very keenly that he should start right away for home. But the temper of the expedition was different; greed was still to be satisfied; ships were sighted and fought; "descents" were made quite regularly on coastal towns. Then, north of Panamá, the final agreement was made to end the expedition.

Prisoners said that up in the northern part of Nicaragua

The Lonesome Widow

185

was a place named Segovia. They described it and the route to it, and said that after it had been reached a river of the same name could be followed across the continent to the Caribbean. The ships were abandoned to keep the Spaniards from pursuit. Four companies of seventy men each were formed for the march. There was another sharp fight to seize a town and on January 1, 1688, the men went inland to make the crossing.

De Lussan, while busy with the dice, had exchanged thirty thousand pieces of eight for coined gold, pearls and precious stones. He was advised by friends in his company that seventeen or eighteen men who had lost their share-out gambling, and were desperate, would steal from him or any winner. This could be done quite easily during an engagement against the Spanish troops who were certain to be met, and if not then, by personal ambush in the jungle. De Lussan divided his winnings secretly among his friends in their mutual sight. He promised them a percentage for their trouble in concealing his loot once they had all come to Hispaniola. The friends agreed, and hands were shaken, vows exchanged.

The last pirogue in which the buccaneers sailed was sunk on January second, yet the Spanish troops soon found the trail. They closed in on the flanks and rear of the buccaneer columns. Men turned back and fought out of necessity. Spreads of grass were set afire in savannahs to retard the enemy; ambushes were met and broken after serious losses.

There were sixteen days of this through the highlands of Nicaragua before the Rio Segovia was reached. The buccaneers worked fast. They made rafts from buoyant mapou wood, lashed with lianas, that they hoped would take them down the watershed to the Caribbean. While time lasted, some of the rafts were tested. It was learned that the best possible position for a man who mounted the structure was upright, yet when he stood so he submerged the raft two or three feet. No more could be done, though, and at the end of the river at Cape Gracias a Dios were supposed to be friendly ships. Experienced men knew of trading sloops that came in to deal with the Mosquito Indians on the coast.

A pair of men took charge of a raft. They handled long poles and immediately away from the launching shore they were in rough water. They struggled waist-deep, came to rapids, great, spume-wreathed falls and whirlpools. The rafts broke up with the shock. Men rode single logs, rebuilt below and kept on downstream. A system of "flags" was created; rags were tied to the branches of tall trees to warn the buccaneers coming behind of rapids and other stretches of treacherous water.

The only food was raw bananas. After two days on the river, the horse meat that had been taken along had become inedible. Powder was soaked, clotted in the horns. Musket locks were rusted, flint and steel too wet for use. Starvation gripped at the men. They were weak and staggered dizzily when they emerged from the rapids, climbed the bank to catch breath and rebuild the rafts. Around their necks, weighing them down, were the sacks of treasure.

Some of the unlucky gamblers had gone ahead. They waited on the banks among the fern thicknesses, the bamboos and mangroves until a more fortunate pair landed. Then they struck. The men rising exhausted from the water did not have a chance. At one point de Lussan and his raft-mate found five Englishmen with their skulls crushed, their sacks gone.

The honest protected each other as best they could. Warnings were shouted on the river, and when at night the raft crews gathered ashore, denunciations were made. Several of the number who stood in the outer darkness slipped away at the mention of names, were never seen again. But some men lucky enough to keep their lives lost their sacks of loot when rafts capsized. They hunched, staring-eyed, bent with defeat, in the shallows when the others passed.

By February twentieth the last of the rapids was behind. Here instead were shoals and snags of drifted logs, flotsam bamboo. The men went ashore and built canoes of mapou wood.

The Lonesome Widow

187

The Age
of
Piracy

They were, as much they could calculate, about sixty leagues* from the Mosquito Coast near Cape Gracias a Dios.

Shaking with fever, emaciated by the unrelieved banana diet, they came out through country where savage Indian tribes lived. But the Indians proved to be friendly and supplied food and shelter, told the buccaneers of trading vessels that touched the coast. The buccaneers waited and watched their bellies swell and their feet reduce to normal size. Then, with a topsail seen offshore, de Lussan was able to believe that his adventure was almost over.

The ship came in and anchored. She was English and small and bound for Jamaica. Her captain said he would like six hundred pounds to convert her to a transport. For the buccaneers who had suffered the loss of their booty on the river it was an impossible amount. The rest in typical fashion sat down and drew lots. Fifty of them won a place aboard, and paid forty pieces of eight a man. They insisted, though, before the captain was paid, that he take them to Hispaniola and not Jamaica.

De Lussan landed back at Petite Goave a rather sober man. He was almost overcome when he heard grammatical French spoken again; his own fluency returned, and he made a successful bid for a pardon from the authorities for any rupture he might have caused in French-Spanish relations. From Petite Goave, he went on to Paris, his loot given to him in its entirety by his faithful friends. He wrote in his journal a description that a peaceful, well-to-do existence clarified.

It told of his arrival in Petite Goave: "I had so little hopes of ever getting back, that I could not, for the space of fifteen days, take my return for anything other than an illusion, and it proceeded so far with me, that I shunned sleep for fear, when I awaked, I should find myself again in those countries out of which I was now safely delivered."

* A league is variously estimated as between three and five miles.

188

Old Friends Fall Out

Captain Jean David Nau, known to his fellow buccaneers as L'Ollonais because he was born at Les Sables d'Ollone, was the one really psychopathic pirate of whom there is record. Mixed with his frightful brutality was a peculiar cunning and audacity that often befuddled the Spaniards. He exulted in bloodshed and beside him Raveneau de Lussan's head-swapping captains were among the mildest of men. There is, in fact, nothing good whatsoever to be said about L'Ollonais. His history is cited only for the reason that it illuminates the period.

As an indentured laborer for a plantation on the island of Dominica, he came out from France to the West Indies in the middle of the seventeenth century over the same route as the Sieur de Lussan. His time up, L'Ollonais went to Tortuga and joined the Brothers of the Coast, became a *boucanier* in the true sense and made his livelihood hunting wild cattle. Then like so many of the others he went to sea.

His intelligence brought him to the attention of Monsieur de la Place, the Governor of Tortuga. Given command of a ship, he did well except that his extreme brutality with prisoners shocked the men who served under him. Somewhat in disfavor as a result, when his ship was wrecked in a Caribbean storm, his men failed to fight effectively against a Spanish force that attacked them on the beach where they had landed.

L'Ollonais was the sole survivor of the action. Wounded, he smeared blood and sand on his face, and hid among the

189

The Age of Piracy

dead until the Spaniards were gone. He got back to Tortuga and to celebrate his return stole a small vessel, sailed to plunder the Cuban coast. The Governor of Havana, hearing of his depredations, sent a large ship to catch him. A Negro executioner was aboard the Spanish ship and orders were to hang all the pirates except L'Ollonais; he was to be brought to Havana in chains for public display, then death in a rather painful manner.

But L'Ollonais met and took the Spanish ship. He put the hangman and all other hands except one to death. This man he sent to Havana with a written promise. He informed the Governor that in the future he would kill every Spaniard that came his way.

L'Ollonais pretty much kept his word. Sailing as a joint commander with a buccaneer captain named Michel de Basco, he took eight ships and a force of four hundred men to the Spanish Main in 1667. They entered Lake Maracaibo, and after assault, slaughter, torture and chase through the woods to seize captives, gathered from the towns of Maracaibo and Gibraltar the sum of 260,000 pieces of eight in loot and ransom. The share-out gave each buccaneer more than one hundred pieces of eight, plus plate, jewels and silks.

Led by blood lust and the desire for booty, L'Ollonais went to the Nicaraguan coast and acted with insensate cruelty. After many of his men had been killed in a Spanish ambush, the rest sailed off with his second in command, Moses Van Vin. Then L'Ollonais ran his big ship onto a sandbank off Honduras and lost her. He managed to build a longboat of her timbers, and went south, still indomitable, for Cartagena de Indias.

Storm caught him while at sea. He was forced to put ashore in the Gulf of Darien. The Indians there had received such a poor account of him that he was treated with special attention. He was dismembered, limb from limb, the pieces tossed into the fire, the ashes scattered so that no trace of him might remain.

The time of relatively easy sea escape at the completion of a raid, of welcome, financial help and official condonement in base ports began to run out for the buccaneers soon after L'Ollonais was offered as a Cimaroon sacrifice. Fortunes could be made by other means than piracy, and with less risk; the home governments sent forth stronger, more honest governors; guard-ship systems took effect, and treaties between nations were observed with some fidelity. Towards the end of the seventeenth century, trade closed in upon the old, free life of the Brethren of the Coast.

But the time was not entirely finished. There were still great raids to be made. Captain John Coxon, an Englishman famous among the Brethren for his cool daring, went to the Main in the spring of 1677 with a company of his countrymen. They stormed, took by surprise and swept through the important town of Santa Marta. Then they got aboard their ships with the Governor and a bishop as prisoners and sailed for Jamaica. No serious recrimination was forthcoming from any Jamaican authority, and Captain Coxon stayed on as a respected figure.

He organized in 1679 with other English captains a raid upon the Honduranian coast. It brought back a sizable quantity of coin, silver bullion, tortoise shell, cocoa, cochineal and five hundred chests of indigo. Then in December of the same year he designed even more extensively, and with a prime group of buccaneer chiefs—Captains Sharp, Essex, Row and Allison in the number—he got together a fleet at Point Morant and shoved off from Jamaica for Puerto Bello.

The place was attacked and taken on Febuary seventeenth, after an overland march of four days. The buccaneers suffered from lacerated, chigger-infested feet, and they were

Old Friends Fall Out

The Age of Piracy

weak, having been without food for three days. But they made good their attack and cleared away before the Spanish troops sent as reinforcement for the garrison could catch up to them. Each man for this effort was given one hundred pieces of eight, which seemed quite small when they heard the news from Port Royal.

Lord Carlisle, the Governor, had issued a warrant for Coxon's arrest because of the Puerto Bello sack. Then Sir Henry Morgan, acting as Governor during Carlisle's absence, issued another. The buccaneers in the Port Royal pothouses became a bit apprehensive each time the town watch passed. But nothing happened; Harry Morgan at least was still on the side of his former mates.

Coxon sailed with Captains Harris and Sawkins in April, 1680, to make an attempt on Panamá. The ships were careened in a Darien cove and camouflaged and the men began the difficult jungle march. It was not surprising that tension developed between the commanders. Coxon, known to be a man of short temper, got into a fight with Harris on the way across the Isthmus of Darien. Then he became jealous of Sawkins, younger than he and very popular with the men. He said that he would go no farther unless he led one of the companies. The town of Santa Maria was before them, though, and he calmed himself enough to take part in the pillage.

The expedition left Santa Maria in flame and went on by dugout canoe down the Santa Maria River to the Pacific coast. There they got hold of two small ships and with the canoe flotilla alongside set out for Panamá. They entered Panamá Bay and cut into the Spanish fleet lying at anchor. The action, long, often in doubt, cost the buccaneers many lives, but at last they won it.

Coxon was satisfied, not the others. He was unable to reach harmony with his brother commanders and started back across the isthmus. A company of seventy men, who also saw no reason for staying any longer in the "South Sea" went with

192

him. The remaining men, under Sawkins and Harris, were determined to raid further along the coast below Panamá.

Coxon, for the Panamá victory, gained quite a welcome home. The warrants for his arrest were not in evidence after he reached Port Royal. He was so far in the good graces of King's House that by 1682 he was commissioned to go out and catch a French pirate, Captain Jean Hamlin, who sailed in the ship *La Trompeuse* and made prizes of English vessels met at sea.

With the political fluctuations of the period, Coxon was later and more than once arrested on the charge of piracy. But he escaped the hangman and was honored with a letter of marque issued by the Governor of New Providence Island.* It did not particularly matter to Coxon that Robert Clarke, the Governor, was also accused in many quarters of being a pirate. There was a large, official seal on the document that satisfied his sense of formality.

*Present-day Nassau, B.W.I.

Old
Friends
Fall Out

193

The Gentlemanly Privateer

"Seamen love their bellies above anything else."
SAMUEL PEPYS, *Secretary to the Admiralty*
"Good liquor to sailors is preferable to clothing."
CAPTAIN WOODES ROGERS, Circumnavigator

Looking down the somber gallery of pirate portraits, the figure of Woodes Rogers stands forth in vivid color. He holds a unique position there. He associated closely with pirates, was a friend of some, and his greatest feat was the seizure of a Spanish treasure ship, yet he never considered himself as one. Late in his life while serving as an officer of the Crown, he hanged many, and believed that his action was not only logical but humanitarian.

Rogers was another West of England man. His people came from Poole, in Dorset, but he was born in Bristol to which the family had moved, and his probable year of birth was 1679. He grew up in Bristol and married, in 1705, the daughter of Admiral Sir William Whetstone, Commander-in-Chief of the West Indian Fleet, at St. Mary Magdalen Church, Old Fish Street, London.

He had already been at sea, and he began to look around for some sort of voyage that would benefit him further. There came into his hands in 1708 the journal of a French merchant ship captain, de Beauchesne Gouin, which he read with great interest. The French had taken up alliance with the Spanish, and Gouin had been sailing in the Pacific; his journal stated that in the first year on the service seventeen French ships had brought back to Europe from Spanish ports in South America treasure worth over three million pieces of eight. Rogers noted in his own journal that this was enough "to carry on the war against most of the Potentates of Europe."

Rogers recognized that the opportunity he was after was in sight. Parliament had recently passed an act to stimulate the employment of ships as privateers whose work would be legalized by letters of marque from the Admiralty. To that end, the act revoked the fifth of all prize values taken that had formerly gone to the Crown, and now all went to owner and crew.

Various conversations of a discreet nature were conducted by Rogers with the officers of the Bristol Corporation. The wealth that went from South America back to Spain beckoned to them as well as to Rogers. A company was formed, shares bought in it, and the money raised to equip an expedition. Sir John Hawkins, a former Mayor, was a subscriber; and Christopher Shuter, soon to be Mayor; and a leading seaman of the town, Captain Freake; and Thomas Clements, the Sheriff; and John Romsey, Town Clerk; and Thomas Goldney, a prominent Quaker.

The ships for the expedition were designated as "Private Men of War" and were given commissions signed by the Lord High Admiral that permitted them to wage war on both the French and Spanish. They were the *Duke,* which was the equivalent of a sixth-rate Royal Navy frigate and was of 320 tons, approximately 80 feet over all in length and 25 feet in beam, carrying a crew of 117 and mounting thirty guns; and a smaller vessel, the *Duchess.* She was of 260 tons, mustered a crew of 108 men, mounted 26 guns.

Rogers was assigned to the *Duke* as her commander. His second in command was Thomas Dover, who although a "Doctor of Physik" by profession had both invested and enlisted in the privateer enterprise and had seen to it that he was appointed captain of the marine detachment and made president of the council of officers which, while the expedition was

*The
Gentlemanly
Privateer*

195

offshore, would be charged with the decision of any important order.

Some doubt was expressed by Rogers about the doctor's capabilities away from land. Although a graduate of Caius College, Cambridge, with the degree of Bachelor of Medicine, he was admittedly quarrelsome and held a rather high view of himself as a potential seaman. But the other investors insisted, and Rogers was forced to be content with the presence in the *Duke* of William Dampier.

Here was a real seaman. Dampier had been a buccaneer on the Main and a logwood-cutter in the Spanish-infested forests of the Gulf of Campeche, and he had twice circumnavigated the world. He lacked Captain Doctor Dover's polished manners, had come home broke from every voyage that he had made. Yet he had crossed the isthmus with Coxon's expedition to Panamá, served with distinction in nearly all of the famous buccaneer raids where there was Spanish loot taken. He had also written and marvelously preserved in a bamboo tube a log book of his voyages, written another called "Discourse on the Winds." While he had held command, he no longer wished it; his last voyage, under commission of letter of marque from Prince George of Denmark, had ended in complete failure. Rogers was happy to sign him as the pilot of the expedition, and Dampier was quite willing to accept.

What appeared to be a better-integrated crew was in the *Duchess*. She had as her commander Captain Stephen Courtney whom Rogers described as a "man of birth, fortune and very amiable qualities." * His second was Captain Edward Cooke who on two occasions had had the misfortune to be captured, then imprisoned, by the French and as a result bore them a strong hatred. Serving in the *Duchess,* too, as second lieutenant was Captain Rogers's younger brother, John.

* Woodes Rogers, *A Cruising Voyage Round the World. Note:* Every quotation in this chapter is from the same source. Used by permission of Longmans, Green & Co., Inc., Publishers.

The expedition sailed from King Road near Bristol on August 2, 1708, and Rogers wrote in his journal concerning the crews, "Tinkers, Taylors, Haymakers, Pedlers, Fiddlers, etc." There was also in the *Duke* as steward, John Finch, "late wholesale oilman of London." One of Finch's duties became the care of a large bulldog, Lord Harry, mascot for the ship. Rogers entered thoughtfully in his journal: "Most of us, the chief officers, embraced this trip of privateering around the world, to retrieve the losses we had sustained by the enemy."

But while heading out to the open Atlantic an incapable Irish pilot nearly put the small fleet on a pair of rocks called "The Sovereigne's Bollacks" off Kinsale. Then, really bound away, departure was taken and the southerly course made good. The next land raised was the Cape Verde Islands, where an agreement about share-out between officers and men was accepted by all hands.

September twenty-fifth the ships crossed the Equator. Rogers wrote, "This day, according to custom, we duck'd those that had never pass'd the Tropick before." Caution was taken that the greenies were not hurt or drowned when they were slapped into the sea on a line led through a block on the main yard. "This prov'd of great use to our fresh-water Sailors, to recover the Colour of their Skins which were grown very black and nasty."

After sailing down the great western traverse, the fleet stood in towards Angre de Reys on the Brazilian coast. But the Portuguese settlement there had recently been attacked by French pirates. The boat sent ashore was fired upon and forced to withdraw. Rogers summoned his best diplomacy and within a week was on fine terms with the Governor. He and his principal officers and the fleet musicians were asked in to celebrate the ceremony of the Conception of the Virgin Mary.

The Gentlemanly Privateer

197

The Age of Piracy

Rogers described the scene:

We waited on the Governour, Signior Raphael de Silva Lagos, in a Body, being ten of us, with two Trumpets and a Hautboy, which he desir'd might play us to Church, where our Musick did the Office of an Organ, but separate from the Singing, which was by the Fathers well perform'd. Our Musick play'd "Hey, Boys, up go we!" * and all manner of noisy paltry Tunes: and after Service our Musicians, who were by that time more than half drunk, march'd at the head of the Company, next to them an old Father and two Fryars carrying Lamps of Incense with the Host, next came the Virgin *Mary* on a Bier carry'd on Four Men's shoulders, and dress'd with Flowers and Wax-Candles. . . .

Captain Rogers and Courtney marched in the procession carrying lighted candles and behind them the rest of their company. The day ended with the Protestant Englishmen being "splendidly entertain'd" first by the fathers at the convent in the little village, then by the Governor at the quarters of the local garrison. At the end of the day, "they unanimously told us, they expected nothing from us but our Company, and they had no more than our Musick."

The next day, the wind being offshore and the fleet unable to sail, Rogers returned the hospitality. He invited the Portuguese aboard and it became a merry party where toasts were exchanged, the Pope's health for the Archbishop of Canterbury's, with William Penn's thrown in. When the visitors left, they had presents of butter and cheese. "We saluted 'em with a Huzza from our Ship; because we were not overstock'd with Powder."

From Brazil the two ships proceeded towards Cape Horn. Sailmakers were kept busy aboard sewing up whatever was

* A popular Cavalier song mocking Puritan sobriety.

198

handy in the way of heavy weather clothing for the crews; in the usual heedless fashion, the men had been recruited without any sort of gear for the voyage. And Dampier took them well south of Cape Horn, to the edge of the ice fields, to make sure of the westward passage.

There was extreme suffering, a great deal of frostbite. The officers contributed what they had to spare from their sea chests, but it was not enough. Reaching up the coast of Chile, the lookouts were told to keep a sharp watch for an island where the ships might put in and the sick recuperate.

Dampier recognized the island when it was reported, located it on the chart. Buccaneers had used it occasionally in the past; it was known as Juan Fernandez, and although Spanish territory, was believed to be uninhabited. The *Duke's* pinnace was sent in to investigate and then while still about five miles off the beach, recalled. A fire had been seen burning above the beach. There was suspicion of ambush.

But the following morning, February 2, 1709, the yawl aboard the *Duke* was lowered, Captain Doctor Dover in nominal command, and shoved off with an officer and six men to investigate more closely. Officers and men were armed against possible Spanish attack. The ships beat on and off, the island under inspection through the long-glasses.

Captain Doctor Dover returned calmly enough, though, with a supply of crawfish and a man "cloth'd in Goat-Skins who look'd wilder than the first Owners of them." This was Alexander Selkirk, a Scot from Largo, in Fifeshire, who was to become later the inspiration for Daniel Defoe's character of Robinson Crusoe. He was bearded, lean and incoherent from his years of solitude on the island. It was only after Dampier recognized him that he began to talk with any real freedom.

He had lived on Juan Fernandez Island for four years and four months, to his count. Before that he had been the sailing master aboard the galley, *Cinque Ports,* a ship that was

The
Gentlemanly
Privateer

199

The Age of Piracy

part of the small fleet Captain Dampier had commanded on his previous voyage. Selkirk, a man of definite opinions, had gotten into difficulty with Captain Stradling of the *Cinque Ports;* he informed the captain that she was unseaworthy and would founder. When Stradling invited him to make his choice

between silence on the subject and marooning on Juan Fernandez, he chose the island. He was put ashore there with all his personal effects, books and navigational instruments, a musket and some shot and powder, a few other basic supplies.

Rogers was fascinated by Selkirk. He wrote about the marooned man lengthily in his journal, described how Selkirk hunted the island goats for food, then, eventually, clothing. The journal states: "He likewise tam'd some Kids, and to divert himself would now and then sing and dance with them and his Cats*: so that by the Care of Providence and Vigour of his Youth, being now but about 30 years old, he came at last to conquer all the Inconveniences of his Solitude, and to be very easy."

But while glad to see Selkirk, who, he told Rogers, had been the best man aboard the *Cinque Ports,* Dampier was depressed. He gathered from Selkirk that the ship had come to misfortune, was very probably lost. It seemed that all of his life had been the same. He had fought in the Dutch War under Sir Edward Spragge; sailed to the Newfoundland Banks and the East Indies; lived in Jamaica; lived in Virginia, made a voyage that lasted eight years and returned him to England without a ha'penny bit. He'd lost on another voyage the ship, *Roebuck,* and later the ship, *St. George,* and now most likely the *Cinque Ports* of his command was gone. Back in England, Dampier remembered, he was famous for his voyages. Fame came hard, and paid off cheap.

Rogers's gaiety restored Dampier to better spirit. It was his intention, Rogers said, to set up camp on the beach, let the sick men recoup ashore while the Governor of Juan Fernandez, as he called Selkirk, showed them the sights of the island and how to catch wild goats. A race could be arranged, too, between Selkirk; the big bulldog, Lord Harry, and the fastest men in the fleet.

The visitors marveled at the way Selkirk had built his two huts, fashioned furniture, clay pots and utensils. Rogers was further convinced of Dampier's estimate of the man when he saw Selkirk run down the goats on the mountainous ridges of the island. He determined to make Selkirk sailing master of the first Spanish prize taken along the coast.

After a stay of several weeks at Juan Fernandez the fleet sailed on a northeast by east course for the mainland, hoping to fall in with coastwise shipping that would offer booty. A small ship was seized, renamed the *Increase* and Selkirk sent

* Both cats and rats had been brought ashore by former inhabitants.

The Gentlemanly Privateer

into her as sailing master. Then a good-sized vessel, a galleon of four hundred tons, was captured off the port of Paita. But she bore little of value; the officers' council met on April thirteenth and declared the resolve to attack Guayaquil.

Rogers entered the text of the resolve in his journal. It casts a strong light not only upon the manner of his thinking but on that, too, of the officers who served with him. They were as a group, and Rogers in particular, acutely aware of their responsibility to the stockholders at home in Bristol. More, they had learned over the years of the excesses committed in Guayaquil by the expedition in which Raveneau de Lussan had served. They might be called pirates by the Spaniards whose ships they had taken, and by the inhabitants of Guayaquil, but to themselves they were honorable English gentlemen. The language of the resolve was to acquaint the crews of the fleet rather forcefully with the information. It read in part:

> And to prevent all manner of pernicious and mischievous Ill-Conduct that may accrue by Disorders on shore, we pressingly remind you that any Officer or other that shall be so brutish as to be drunk ashore in an Enemy's Country, shall not only be severely punish'd, but lose all share of whatsoever is taken in this Expedition. The same Punishment shall be inflicted on any that disobeys Command, or runs from his Post, discourages our Men, or is cowardly in any Action, or presumes to burn or destroy any thing in the Town without our Order, or for mischief sake; or that shall be so sneakingly barbarous to debauch themselves with any Prisoners on shore, where we have more generous things to do, both for our own Benefit and the future Reputation of our selves and our Country."

Then at the end was a climactic note:

> And if all the foregoing Rules be strictly follow'd, we

hope to exceed all other Attempts of this nature before us in these Parts; and not only to enrich and oblige our selves and our Friends, but even to gain Reputation from our Enemies.

Young John Rogers, the captain's brother, might well have been carried away by such grandeur of purpose. He was killed two days later during a desperate small-boat attack upon a big Spanish ship. Captain Rogers felt his loss keenly, wrote of him in his journal. John had been a bit more than twenty years old, and the captain had planned to take him as his lieutenant in the shore action.

Landing at Puna Island, the expedition put the fleet in charge of ship-keepers and started up the Guayas River for Guayaquil. There had been found at the village of Puna a copy of a warning from the Viceroy telling of the arrival of a force under "the Conduct of an *English*-man named *Dampier.*" But Rogers and the other officers were not dismayed. The seventeen-foot tide, the mosquitoes, the leeches, the heat and the chiggers were conquered and the boats brought to a position abreast the town.

Salvos were fired from the culverins and mortars aboard the boats. Fire from shore was not too heavy, and the crews went frontally to the attack. Rogers led them in and broke a formation of Spanish cavalry that defended the *plaza,* chased the cannoneers away from a culverin battery. The *plaza* and the cathedral and the main part of the town were taken, sentry posts set for the night.

The night was spent in sniping between the English and the Spanish in the jungle beyond the town. With daylight, negotiation for the ransom of prisoners was begun. But the town was conspicuously barren of treasure. Selkirk and another young officer and a picked crew of men were sent upstream to explore the jungle for loot-bearing citizens.

They came upon some miles above the town—a group of

The
Gentlemanly
Privateer

quite frightened ladies. These were dressed thinly in the tropical fashion, and the jewelry hidden on their persons was in part visible. According to Rogers's journal, the loot was taken from the ladies with the least possible embarrassment and even some delicacy. But while the find was a welcome addition to the stuff picked up in the town, Rogers had no liking for Guayaquil.

The wounded had been placed in the cathedral under Captain Doctor Dover's care. He condemned the place as a pesthole; due to a recent epidemic, scores of corpses had been buried under the floor of the building and gave off a deadly effluvium. Dover worked heroically to save the wounded, and bled each sick man, drawing off from them one hundred ounces apiece.

Rogers consulted with the senior officers. Let Guayaquil rot, they told him. The expedition should get out. Wounded and sick carried on litters to the boats, a final attempt at more ransom abandoned, the expedition left. No pursuit was given; the boats without interruption went down the river to Puna and rejoined the fleet. The assault had not been a complete failure, yet it had not brought what the men had hoped. When the fleet stood forth to sea, the talk aboard was of the wealth to be taken out of the great Spanish ships that yearly sailed from the Philippines to Acapulco in Mexico.

After weeks of tense patrol work off Puerto Seguro, Bajia California the fleet met one of the plate ships. She was huge, with plenty of armament. The English went for her in small craft or with their ships propelled by sweeps as the wind dropped. Her name was *Nuestra Señora de la Incarnacion Disenganio,* and they took her in a fight that went on at close quarters for an hour and a half.

Rogers was shot through the jaw by a pistol ball, knocked to the deck. Lying prone, he gave his orders for the rest of the action by gesture and scribbled note. Then he received the captured commander aboard the *Duke.* The man was a French noble, Sieur Jean Pichberty, and he said when questioned that his crew had amounted to 193, and that his ship had twenty big and twenty small guns. There had been nine killed, ten wounded and a number powder-burned.

This Rogers comprehended through his pain. Most of his upper jaw had been shot away, and the teeth there; he suffered from loss of blood. Yet his business instinct was un-dimmed. He dealt firmly with Pichberty, arranged for notes to be drawn on a private London bank to pay the ransom for the Spanish ship, also for Pichberty and his crew and a small vessel that Rogers indicated might be sold. There was an-other transaction that had to do with gear and cargo, and Pichberty, his credit fully established, signed all the notes, parted in an amiable style from Rogers.

The fleet went back on patrol, for a second and much larger plate ship had been reported inward-bound by some of Pichberty's men. She was found and fought, but she was far too strong for the English ships. The battle went on for over seven hours though, before she beat them off, and they learned that she was the *Begonia,* built of Manila teak in the islands, and tough and new, of nine hundred tons, with a chief gunner who knew his trade and served his pieces from behind sandbagged bulwarks.

Duchess was practically dismasted by the Spanish fire, and twenty men were killed aboard her. *Duke* was luckier; she lost only eleven wounded and three scorched by powder burns. But Captain Rogers, who had conducted his part of the ac-tion by hand signals, had been struck again. While they were close in alongside the enemy, a Spanish marine had tossed a fireball from the maintop where he was stationed. It had ig-nited a cartouche box at Rogers's feet on his quarter-deck, and his left heel was torn away by a cartouche fragment. Rogers, with a tourniquet applied and the foot propped up on a cushion brought from his cabin, continued in command to the end. His estimate later was that he had put approxi-

The Gentlemanly Privateer

mately five hundred solid shot into the Spanish ship; he had kept a record throughout of what was fired.

The fleet did its best to repair and gather provisions along the California coast after the battle. Then, in quite bad shape, it sailed for Guam in the Mariana Islands, taking departure from Cape St. Lucas on January 11, 1710. The voyage before the crews was enormous, more than six thousand miles, but the confidence in Rogers was such that the men were willing to make the attempt. Their prize, the former Acapulco ship, sailed with them, and each vessel was deep-laden.

Rogers was very ill, with a high fever, his jaw and throat swollen. He was unable to stand erect, yet he wrote his journal, kept his courage and his sense of gaiety. There was, after all, a real fortune to be taken home in the fleet. A man could think of it instead of the pain. He wrote in his journal on February 14:

> That same day, in Commemoration of the Antient custom in *England* of chusing *Valentines,* I drew up a list of the fair ladies in *Bristol,* that were anyways related to or concerned in the Ships, and sent for my officers into the Cabbin, where every one drew, and drank the Lady's Health in a Cup of Punch, and to a happy Sight of 'em all; this I did to put 'em in mind of Home.

Three days later, he was troubled by an increased swelling of his throat. He coughed up from it a piece of his jaw bone that had been lodged there since he had been first wounded. It was, he knew, most fortunate for him. He would be in much better shape, and the ships sorely needed help. They were leaking at an alarming rate, were sluggish to the helm, sailed with pitiful slowness. There were left in the fleet enough short allowances of flour, the only staple, for fourteen days to come.

Guam was sighted on March eleventh and the fleet closed in towards the land. Fast *proas* surrounded the ships. The fleet was inspected and its miserable condition reported back to the Governor in command of the Spanish forces ashore. Rogers went on into the roadstead before he dropped anchor. He was too weak to stand or walk, so he was transferred from the ship to his boat by bosun's chair. Then he was rowed in to meet the Governor.

Rogers prevailed with quiet threats. The Governor became courteous, even generous. Supplies were sent aboard the English ships. The officers of the fleet were entertained by the Governor and his staff, then, still a long way from Bristol, the ships sailed.

The course from Guam was west-southwest and Mindanao was raised, cleared; then Ternate in the Moluccas, and Morotai, and part of the vast mountainous sweep of New Guinea. Here was the strait that today bears Dampier's name. The ships worked through it with a pinnace ahead to sound the channel. They came out from the strait into the Banda Sea; across it, they touched at Buton, sailed into the Flores Sea, and along the green, lush coast of Java, where the anchors went down in the harbor of Batavia.

Rogers braced himself to deal with the Dutch. They were difficult in their transactions, and Rogers had to dig into the Spanish treasure chests to pay for haul-out, careening, repairs and supplies. He wrote about the Dutch colonial administration with some acrimony, but the ships were put in seaworthy shape, stood away cleanly enough for the run down the African coast to the Cape of Good Hope and Table Bay.

The little fleet waited there for a Dutch convoy to make up for the homeward passage. Rogers went ashore in his habitual inquiring fashion. He wrote in his journal when back aboard:

> I spoke with an *English* and an *Irish*-man, who had been several Years with the *Madagascar* pirates, but now were pardoned, and allowed to settle here: They told me, that those miserable Wretches, who had made such a

The Gentlemanly Privateer

Noise in the World, were now dwindled to between 60 or 70, most of them very poor or despicable, even to the Natives, among whom they had married. . . . Yet if care not be taken after a Peace to clear that Island of them, and hinder others from joining them, it may be a Temptation for loose stragling Fellows to resort thither, and make it once more a troublesome Nest of Free-booters.

This was undoubtedly Rogers's sincere conviction. He could look out in the bay from where he talked with the retired pirates, of course, and see the Acapulco ship that he had taken from the Spanish in violent battle. She had been renamed the *Batchelor,* in honor of a Bristol alderman, and that may have redeemed her past for Rogers. He carried, too, in his pockets Spanish pieces of eight with which he paid the price for the escort home. Yet his sincerity cannot be denied; Rogers was a devout believer in the letter of the law. Some years later, when he took over as Governor of the Bahamas, his attitude towards piracy was the same.

As part of a strong Dutch convoy guarded by men-of-war the expedition returned safely to England in October, 1711. Share-out was made without any complaint from the crews, the sum amassed from the voyage kept secret, although admitted to be around a million pounds sterling, and there was rejoicing in Bristol. Rogers sat down to write his journal in finished form. It was published the following year, and became a popular success.

Captain Doctor Dover went to London and entered medical practice, content to be done with seagoing. He saw his patients daily at the Jerusalem coffeehouse in Cecil Street on the Strand, and felt moved to write a book of his own, *The Ancient Physician's Legacy to His Country.* This ran into a number of editions, and in it he recommended the use of quicksilver for practically every form of illness. Known thereafter as "The Quicksilver Doctor", he lived until he was eighty-two, and further endowed his patients with a powder that contained opium and ipecacuanha, the root of a South American plant. It was used as a diaphoretic, and gained him more renown than his book or his experiences as a captain of privateers.

Alexander Selkirk, many years absent, returned to his home village of Largo in Fife. He was the seventh son of the local shoemaker, and in his youth had been in trouble with the authorities. A charge of indecent conduct in church had been brought against him by the Session in 1695, and again in 1701 he was criticized before the fully assembled congregation for fighting with his brothers. But the experience upon Juan Fernandez somewhat changed him.

He built a cave in the garden in back of his father's cottage. Then he sat there in long, solitudinous meditation. The people of Largo were not completely decided that he was so different, and their view was shared by a young woman, Miss Sophia Bonce.

Sophia approached Selkirk in his cave. She talked with him, and must have made known to him a few of the things he had missed in the Pacific and missed, too in his cave. He eloped with her, causing great Largo scandal, for when the couple settled in Bristol they did not marry.

Selkirk was unhappy in Bristol, though. He was charged, while living with Sophia of assault upon a shipwright named Richard Nettle. Although he drew up a will that gave his estate to Sophia, he came in contact with Mrs. Francis Candis, a widow. She was more careful than Sophia, and saw that Selkirk drew up a second will in her favor after she married him at Oarson in Devon.

Not even marriage could keep Selkirk from the sea, and in 1720 he was posted as mate to the Royal Navy ship, *Weymouth*. He died the next year. His age was forty-five and he was aboard at the time.

Woodes Rogers was almost equally restive while confined to the domestic scene, despite the fact that because of his wit and charm he was popular among the literati of the London

*The
Gentlemanly
Privateer*

The Age of Piracy

coffeehouses. Men such as Steele and Addison were his friends; he amused them with his stories of life far outside England. Then as the stories grew stale in memory, he was tempted by a government offer that would occupy every facet of his mind.

It was the governorship of the Bahama Islands, and the last few incumbents had reported it as quite unhealthy, if not highly dangerous. The Bahamas, due to their position at the head of the Caribbean, the shallow waters around them that held off pursuit from deep-draft vessels and the decline of piracy along the Main, were the final resort for those who lived on "the account."

A wild raggle-taggle of drunks, bullies, half-breed prostitutes and harbor robbers, held New Providence, the capital island. There came among them frequently men of real pirate ability who used the island as their base. They sailed from it to raid Jamaican shipping, or up the American coast, and they were a menace to organized society. Rogers believed that he could show them they lived in error.

He served two terms as Governor of the Bahamas, 1718-21, and 1729-32. His family came out there to live with him after his first indoctrination was finished. He landed calmly and with guile and rum divided one outlaw from another. A number when the royal proclamation was read to them, surrendered. They formed a double rank of a guard of honor and fired their muskets over Rogers's head. Then, promised rewards, they put to sea to catch the backsliders or those who had refused to listen.

Rogers hanged the recalcitrants in full sight of the beach. He left the corpses until the sea birds had picked them to the bone. Unprincipled violence should be checked with firmness, was his contention, and he maintained it. Hogarth, in a picture of Rogers and his family, showed him as quiet-faced, almost stolid, the eyes at rest under the powdered wig.

He died at Nassau, New Providence Island, in 1732. His name was remembered for a long time in the region. When he was done, Caribbean piracy as a common way of life was through. The major survivors of his policy had taken their ships to Madagascar, the Indian Ocean and the Red Sea, conscious that they had encountered a man much stronger than themselves.

The Gentlemanly Privateer

And We Must Die

"Some thousands they will flock when we die, when we die,
"Some thousands they will flock when we die,
　　"Some thousands they will flock
　　"To Execution Dock,
　　"Where we must stand the shock and we must die."

Captain Kid's Farewel to the Seas,
anonymous street ballad at the time of his death

His name is still commonly known in England, and is not forgotten in Europe, and at the eastern end of Long Island, his
last cruising grounds, Captain William Kidd is spoken of as a
legendary hero. The literature on his life is voluminous, and
in good part contradictory. Although he did not make many
voyages, and at present it is very dubious that he was ever a
pirate in the real sense of the term, he remains a vivid figure,
far better remembered than any other man who belongs within
the category.

Even his upbringing lends color. William Kidd was born
at Greenock, on the Clyde, about 1665, the son of the Rever-
end John Kidd. The daily round of Calvinist cant, the neat,
tight life in the gray granite town above the Tail o' the Bank,
contrast sharply with all that was to come later. He went away
to the ships when young, drawn down the glittering sea road
to the West Indies. Then he came to New York, rangy and
competent and already a respected shipmaster. His abilities
brought him the command of various privateer vessels, and he
was prosperous, settled down as the husband of an even more

prosperous widow, Sarah Bradley Cox Oort, whom he married in May, 1691, and who bore him a daughter.

He owned a large brick town house at the corner of Hanover and Pearl Streets, further property on lower Manhattan Island and at the edge of the East River in what was then called "the Harlem." Gear from a ship of his was used in the construction of Trinity Church on the Broadway, and his friends were leading city officials and several governors. But he felt himself compelled to return to the sea in 1695 on a venture that promised to pay him handsomely.

There was a great deal of talk at the time of the raids upon Red Sea and Indian Ocean shipping by pirates who operated out of Madagascar. The home government was forced to take action after the East India Company reported that all its ships must sail in convoy to be safe. Kidd's influential friends thought that he was the man to be given a ship under commission from the King to go and tend to the pirates. He sailed to London, was introduced at court and presented to King William.

The plan appealed to the King and his advisers. Kidd had sailed the Indian Ocean, knew Madagascar and had no liking for pirates. One of his early commands, the *Blessed William*, had been lost to him in the West Indies when he was ashore at Antigua, and some of his crew sailed off with the ship to go on the account. Those men were operating with Madagascar as a base, and Kidd said that he would be most happy to return them to justice.

Kidd was backed by Robert Livingston, a fellow Scot, now also a resident of New York and Secretary for Indian Affairs and member of the City Council. He had money of his own that he was willing to invest in a ship. A calculating, hardheaded Irish nobleman, the Earl of Bellomont, was impressed and went to the King to press Kidd's case. All Royal Navy vessels were actively engaged otherwise, and a privateer vessel to serve against the pirates was the logical solution to the problem.

And We Must Die

The Age of Piracy

The King listened, consulted with the Admiralty, and approved.

A courtier-directed financial pool, familiar since the time of Raleigh and Hawkins and Drake, was formed with Bellomont and practically every other prominent Whig politician as investors. The matter had duofold interest for them. They expected Kidd to catch pirates, but, further to make a nice backers' profit from the loot taken from other ships he would meet. It was rumored at Westminster that King William had personally invested in the venture.

But Kidd hesitated. His inborn Scottish sense of canniness warned him that he dealt with a cruel and subtle and self-centered group. He had witnessed enough failures, was able to contemplate what might happen to him if he did not come back with sufficient wealth. Bellomont insisted upon a decision, though, and Kidd agreed to the terms put forward.

Kidd was given two commissions. One was of the regular sort issued to any privateer vessel and allowed him the right to seize vessels of nations that were considered enemies of England. The other, which carried the Great Seal, specifically cited the police-action purpose of the voyage and named the pirates to be apprehended. A fine new ship, the *Adventure Galley,* of 284 tons and thirty-four guns, was turned over to him, and he recruited a crew of officers and men who seemed to him fully reliable. Some of his crew were taken from him by a Royal Navy press-gang, though, and he was forced to find replacements in the dockside pothouses before he sailed in April, 1696, from Plymouth.

He came into New York Harbor on July fourth, after having captured a French ship as prize. This was allowed him according to the terms of one of his commissions, and he duly paid over from her sale the amount belonging to the King and the Governor. Then he began to prepare for the arduous part of his voyage.

214

He had only a short stay with his wife and daughter before he put to sea. But he learned before he left that his London friend at court, Lord Bellomont, had been recently appointed Governor of New York and New England and was soon to arrive in the colony. His ship as ready as she would ever be, and conscious that he had powerful friends ashore to protect his interests, Kidd headed for Madagascar and the Indian Ocean.

A lot of conflicting information has been gathered about Kidd's actions after he cleared from New York. It has been established, however, that he found no pirates of any consequence or wealth in the waters around Madagascar. He proceeded north from the island and was then reported as cruising off the Malabar coast in the Indian Ocean. It was the region where the most prominent pirates worked, and they were men familiar to Kidd. Among them were Captains Avery, Thomas Tew of Rhode Island, Thomas Wake and William Mace of New York, and John Ireland, an old West Indian rover.

Kidd had no luck with them. They were too powerful for him to fight, and his ship, strained by her long voyage, was leaking badly; many of the crew were eager to join the pirates. Kidd lost his temper one sun-glazed day at sea when taunted by his gunner, William Moore. The gunner told Kidd on deck that he was not the man to command the ship.

Here was an all-but-open expression of mutiny. Moore had been sharpening a chisel, and held it in his hand. It could easily become a weapon. Kidd realized that by a single gesture the gunner might take over the ship. So he grasped a heavy, ironbound wooden bucket and threw it at Moore's head. Moore was dead within twenty-four hours of the injury, and his death, more than the charge of piracy, was to take Kidd later to the gallows.

Kidd got out of the Indian Ocean and started home in 1699. He had taken two prizes, both big ships bearing French commissions, and with the fortune in their holds and strong

And We Must Die

rooms he was satisfied that he could please his backers. He was unaware of course that in August of 1698 gossip had started in London that he operated as a pirate. Nor did he hear that a general King's pardon was issued in December, 1698. That lacked only John Avery's name and his own, a very ominous omission.

The *Adventure Galley* was no longer seaworthy, and Kidd put his crew and loot aboard the sturdier of his prizes, the fine *Quedagh Merchant,* at Madagascar. His voyage homeward bound was uneventful until he hove to off Anguilla in the West Indies and went ashore. He believed himself safe; almost his entire original crew had deserted him for the pirates at Madagascar and he had shipped workaways and passengers who paid a hundred dollars a head. But he was informed ashore that he was wanted as a pirate, and that in fact a Royal Navy squadron was out with the specific orders to bring in himself and Avery.

Kidd was in a serious dilemma. While still at Madagascar, his former crew had turned against him, broken into his cabin, rifled it and gone through his personal belongings. They had taken his journal of the voyage among other things, and he had given his oath in London to keep that at no matter what cost. He could see the first thin shadow of the hangman's noose above his head, and he moved carefully out of the anchorage at Anguilla.

The Danish Governor refused him supplies at St. Thomas and Kidd decided to call upon an old friend, Henry Bolton, a merchant who had served as Collector of Customs for the island of Antigua. He was advised by Bolton at Antigua to get rid of the *Quedagh Merchant* while he could. Kidd sailed the big ship into a backwater cove on the south coast of Hispaniola, ran her aground, transferred the best of the silks, the muslins, the money and jewel chests out of her. He put them into a sloop named the *Antonio* that he bought from Bolton, kept only the more daring of his crew and shoved off north. Whatever hap-

pened afterwards to the *Quedagh Merchant* and her remaining
cargo has not been clearly established. But it is quite probable
that Bolton, after years as a Collector of Customs, knew what
to do with her.

Kidd sailed unsighted by the King's ships that were looking for him and took the sloop as close as he believed wise to
New York. It was necessary, he recognized, to deal with Lord
Bellomont as a Governor and a principal investor in the venture, and possibly their friendship might help. He wanted from
Bellomont first off a King's pardon. Then, between them, they
might arrange for the disposition of the wealth Kidd carried in
the *Antonio*.

Kidd went to anchor at Gardiner's Island off the eastern-
most part of Long Island. He used the same strategem that was
common among home-coming Red Sea pirates at the end of
a voyage. There were men of his acquaintance, not only in
New York but in Stamford, Newport, Providence and Boston,
who were accustomed to the sort of diplomacy he needed and
were well paid for ferry service, warehouse stowage space
ashore and a lackadaisical attitude on the part of the authorities. Kidd sent a boat to the mainland with a message. While
he waited for an answer, he made a visit to John Gardiner on
Gardiner's Island.

Gardiner was accustomed to such visits. He and his wife
and family lived in seignioral ease on the beautiful, wooded
island, but they often noticed the arrival and departure of vessels sailed by pirates who favored the less visible anchorages
of Sag Harbor and Shelter Island. It caused no surprise to
Gardiner when Kidd asked him to take into his custody several ironbound chests and some bales of goods. Kidd gave
Gardiner a list of what was rowed ashore from the *Antonio*,
and he made Mrs. Gardiner a present of a superb piece of East
Indian cloth-of-gold. He told Gardiner that he would return,
and he warned him to act faithfully as a trustee. Gardiner
agreed and Kidd left the island.

And We Must Die

217

The Age of Piracy

Mrs. Kidd had arrived from New York, coming surreptitiously up the coast after having been informed of her husband's presence in Block Island Sound. They spent a few days together aboard the sloop while Kidd continued his long-range negotiations with Lord Bellomont, who was in Boston, and also released more of his cargo for safekeeping on the mainland.

The answers from Bellomont were vague, but Kidd had enough confidence in his friendship with the Governor to go to Boston. He entered a trap. Kidd was arrested on July 6, 1699, on Bellomont's order and remanded to the city jail. Bellomont let him know that he thought Kidd was a thoroughgoing pirate, then had no more to do with him except as an official. There was as yet no law that permitted trial for piracy in the colonies. Kidd protested the fact to Bellomont and realized slowly that the man was no more his friend; powerful forces, perhaps secret in London, were at work. It was Kidd's growing conviction that he had been betrayed. Bellomont held him confined until February 16, 1700, when he shipped him out to England in chains.

Kidd shared the voyage in the *Advice* with other men under the same charge, landed ill and desperate April eighth, and was sent to Newgate Prison. Scandal broke when he again made his protestations to the Admiralty, and a debate was held in the House of Commons where names were named by the Opposition and part of the financial circumstance of the case was exposed. Kidd's backers were under fire as the putative financiers of a piratical expedition, and in withdrawing from the attack, they made Kidd their scapegoat.

He was tried, not for piracy first, but on the charge of murder. He was accused of having killed William Moore, the gunner. Witnesses who had been in his original crew and who had reason to fear for their lives appeared against him. He was refused counsel. The French commissions of the two ships he had taken in the Indian Ocean, which justified entirely his seizure of them, were missing from the court records although they had been shown before during the debate in the House of Commons.

Kidd was convicted of murder, then tried on five charges of piracy. These counts he fought against as best he could, but he was ill, and there was little, now, that he could say in his defense. He was hanged at Execution Dock along with seven other men on May 23, 1701. His body rotted on the gallows within chains.

More than two hundred years after his death the two French commissions he had sought for his defense were found in the archives of the Public Records Office in London. What had happened to them in the interim is not known, but they would have cleared Kidd from the charge of piracy, quite likely would have saved his life.

And We Must Die

More Myth Than Man

"No man is a pirate unless his contemporaries agree to call him so."

SAMUEL TAYLOR COLERIDGE, in *Table Talk*

During the last years of the seventeenth century, and over into the early decades of the eighteenth, the North American colonies had great need of officials of the caliber of Woodes Rogers to stamp out piracy. It was more than a hazard to honest shipmasters all along the coast from Florida to Maine; "the account" was a recognized vocation, and many people ashore took their percentage of the booty, whether under the table or over.

Sir Thomas Lynch, the Governor of Jamaica, was instructed in 1670 by the home government to suppress piracy, but also to offer pardons to those men who would come in and surrender within a reasonable time. Very few availed themselves of the clemency. The rest, though, began to sail more frequently in northern waters when, later, Lieutenant Governor Molesworth became actively engaged against them and used Royal Navy station-ships to run them down.

This increase of popularity in the mainland ports brought a royal proclamation in 1684; the practice of entertaining pirates was to be stopped. Too many had found refuge for their ships, market for their loot and protection from various high sources. But the trade continued. Subterfuge was entered into, and excuses were made for repeated mistakes in identity. Good legal minds were hired to find loopholes by which an all-but-convicted pirate could squeak out of jail and get back to sea again.

Sir Thomas Lawrence informed London from Maryland that by his calculation about sixty pirates in from the Red Sea had landed in Pennsylvania, New York and New England. He described them as often coming ashore originally in either the Bahamas or South Carolina, where they left or disposed of their ships. Then, in new vessels, they worked up the coast. Sir Thomas complained of the large amounts of plunder carried by these men. Colonists were tempted, and merchant seamen deserted to join the rovers, and thus trade was severely hindered. It was even feared that because of their strength armed ships could be seized if the returning pirates so wished.

Little was done in response to Sir Thomas's report. Governor Fletcher of New York was in fact the acknowledged host of the more successful Red Sea rovers. They were his guests in his home. Such notorious figures as Coates and Tew and Glover and Hoare and Moston, each one an admitted pirate captain with many prizes on his record, clumped up the Governor's walk in their square-toed boots, swords at their sides and dirks in their belts, pistols in braces through frogged loops on their chest sashes.

When they dined at the Great Street taverns, they ate enormously of turkey and venison, leg of mutton steeped in wine and partridge barbecued in bear fat, Dutch cheeses and brandied plum puddings, paying with what they freely called "Arab gold" and willing to tell how they had got it. The men of the city watch knew better than to approach them when they had taken their potions of flip, rum and brandy, begun to amuse themselves with the doxies or any innocent citizen who was foolish enough to argue points of law.

While Fletcher was finally censured for his conduct after it had become scandalous, other leading citizens were known to benefit from the pirate trade. Among them was Colonel

The Age of Piracy

Frederick Philipse, for twenty years a member of the City Council; he was supposed to have sold the rovers gunpowder and spirits, flour, provisions, canvas and rope. Robert Livingstone, a colonel of militia and a manor lord, was said to be in the trade, too; and the officers of the Royal Navy station-ship, *Richmond,* were alleged to suffer abruptly from myopia when a pirate ship closed with the New York coast.

Captain Coates, for instance, in from a Red Sea voyage, anchored with some degree of political acumen off Plum Gut at the eastern end of Long Island. Then through his emissaries in the city he offered a seven hundred pounds bribe for protection while in port. This was a usual sum and in addition to it the pirates paid another one hundred pounds per man in the crew.

The foremost liaison agent was named Giles Shelley. He maintained a flotilla of neat, fast sloops off both the New Jersey and New York coasts. When a pirate ship was sighted, Shelley made contact with her, brought the captain up to date on the latest news. Messages were carried ashore, and on moonless or foggy nights, quantities of loot. Then, sanction granted, the pirates came ashore.

But Shelley was not alone in his endeavor. At the end of a voyage, some of Captain John Avery's notorious crew landed on Fisher's Island. The Deputy Governor of Rhode Island, John Greene, dealt with them in his own direct fashion. Horses were secured, and changes of clothing. The pirates went on to Boston without interruption and still carrying "great treasure."

Delaware Bay, indented by hundreds of coves and creeks where a newly arrived ship might hide, developed as a pirate retreat. Former members of Captain Avery's crew liked the region so much that they settled in retirement in Philadelphia, and one of them married Governor Markham's daughter. The rather broad-minded parental attitude aroused curiosity among the burghers and the Governor was asked why he had permitted the marriage. His answer was that the pirates he knew had always been civil with him, and they brought in money "which was an advantage to the country." * Markham had less to say when, in the fall of 1698, several pirate vessels appeared at the mouth of the Delaware and an armed group of raiders sacked Lewes, Delaware. Nothing was done by the authorities, though, and the pirates sailed free.

William Penn had his characteristic response to make when he returned to the colony at this time from England. He wrote for home consumption: "I leave to those who have been so elaborate and elegant in representing weakness of the Province of Pennsylvania since my arrival; who, if they will do me justice will have less to say to my disadvantage." (At the time of writing, Penn held two reputed pirates for trial, one of whom had served under Captain Avery, the other with Captain Kidd.) "I confess I think my interest in these cases ought not wholly to be overlooked, who as Lord of the Soil, erected into a Seigneury, must needs have a royalty, and a share in such seizures, else I am in much meaner circumstances than many Lords of Manors upon the seacoasts of England, Ireland and Scotland. . . . I do not write this to dispute any right with the King, resolving to obey his commands and submit myself to his further consideration."**

Parliament took notice at last after 1700, and an act was passed that really had an effect upon colonial piracy. The act nullified the necessity of the transportation back to England of those accused of felony, *i.e.,* piracy, and the accused were tried much more expeditiously in the colonies. Commissions were established under the Great Seal or the seal of the Admiralty with the powers of trial, conviction and sentence. These trial commissions were further allowed to extend to quorums of seven officers aboard Royal Navy ships or civilians so designated to serve as judges in the colonies. The authority granted thus enabled the establishment of a court of Vice Admiralty in any plantation, and each court had full hanging powers.

* Herbert L. Osgood, *The American Colonies in the 18th Century.*
** *Ibid.*

More Myth Than Man

223

The Age of Piracy

This was the authority used by Woodes Rogers when he later reformed pirate life in the Bahamas. But in such areas as North Carolina, with a broken coastline and venal officials, the outlaws thrived. Captain "Blackbeard" Teach, for example, enjoyed the warm friendship of Tobias Knight, Secretary and Collector of the colony, who also sat as a judge of the Vice Admiralty Court, where his decisions were given due respect by the other members because of his intimate knowledge of the subject.

Both Captains Avery and Kidd for their own particular reasons are worthy of special chapters, and will be considered later. But Captain Edward Teach, and Major Stede Bonnet also, through strange conjunction, are representative of the declining American period when pirates found a livelihood, no matter how brief, upon the North American coast. They lacked the skill or the daring to base at Madagascar and sail the Red Sea after real plunder. It was in their natures to think small and raid small, and they preferred to plunder coastal shipping alongshore, rather than go after armed deepwater ships.

Edward Teach, known too as Thatch or Thach, alias Drummond, alias Blackbeard, was more myth than man. His image has attracted public fancy; he is the storybook pirate who frightens young children. Born in Bristol, he sailed as a foremast hand in privateers, then jumped ship and settled in Jamaica. He was of huge stature, and tough-looking, would kill when he had the advantage, and he came to the attention of a pirate captain named Benjamin Hornigold.

Hornigold gave him command of a sloop and they sailed together in 1716 from New Providence to work along the American coast. Prizes were seized off Cuba, and then they careened their ships on a Virginia beach, cleaned and tallowed them and put out again. At Hornigold's insistence they went after a big French prize armed with forty guns. She fought them for some hours, but finally struck her colors, and the pirates were jubilant. They got drunk aboard her, renamed her, for no valid reason that can be discovered, *Queen Ann's Revenge.*

Teach, as captain of her, reached the peak of his career. He fought and took in a lengthy engagement the large and strongly armed *Great Allen*. Soon afterward he was pursued by *HMS Scarborough;* his gunners served him well and he escaped. Coastal waters, less strenuous opposition appealed to him, and he headed for South Carolina. While waiting for prizes, he gave thought to his appearance, which may have been a singular attempt at psychological warfare.

He let his mattress-thick black beard grow until it swept his belt buckle. He braided it and secured the braids with ribbons of various colors, twined the braids through his long, bushy hair. His clothing, floppy hat and all, was black, and he wore knee boots whose heels thwacked the deck as he walked. He festooned his chest with pistol sashes, carried an assortment of weapons in his belt, and thrust long sulphur matches under his hat brim, with the intention of lighting them to frighten the enemy. He practiced steadily at the consumption of rum and enlarged his vocabulary of dirty language.

It is not surprising that, when he met Major Stede Bonnet, the major was impressed. No two men could have had more dissimilar backgrounds. Bonnet had been raised in the narrow upper-class stratum of colonial society in Barbadoes. He had served as a King's officer, retired from the army and gone to live upon his sugar plantation, where life could have been very pleasant.

But the major was bothered by his wife. He was increasingly unhappy with her, and there was island gossip about unrelieved marital bickering in the Bonnet household. The major came to the secret determination to leave. He chose the wholly original means of buying a ship, which he proposed to sail as pirate. This historical precedent was established when he got hold of a sloop armed with ten guns; he recruited care-

More Myth Than Man

225

fully a crew of seventy men, a number of whom were pirates in temporary retirement, and he shoved off after the announcement that he was going into the interisland mercantile trade.

He did not say goodbye to Mrs. Bonnet, and he never saw her again. The veterans in his crew gave him the advice he wanted and he turned at once to piracy, taking the *Anne* of Glasgow, the *Turbet* of his home island of Barbados, the *Young* of Leith, and the *Endeavour,* each of which he burned to the water's edge after looting them. Then he put in towards the Carolina coast and took two more prizes. His crew, though, had decided that they no longer liked the idea of his captaincy, and it was suggested that he leave the ship, even if he must swim.

Bonnet refused the order with some show of force and was able to maintain himself aboard. It was still difficult for him, and lonely; he was an amateur among professionals, and resented by them. He was glad when a lookout raised Teach's ship; signals were exchanged, and Teach paid him a visit. The solution was obvious, Teach said, after the problem had been explained to him. Bonnet, being no real sailor, should get out of the sloop and she would then be sailed by Teach's lieutenant, an old-time pirate named Richards.

Bonnet acceded, and let Teach have the sloop. He was depressed, and began to think of taking the King's pardon which had been made available to all pirates on the coast. Teach set the example when he lost his own vessel in Topsail Inlet and went to Bath Town, North Carolina, and recanted to the authorities. Bonnet hesitated for a time; he reclaimed his sloop before he left her in Topsail Inlet and shared repentance with Teach at Bath Town.

He heard, while in the town, that war had broken out, with England opposed to France and Spain. This meant that he could sail as an honest man, his actions legalized by a privateer's commission, and the sea called to him. He went to Topsail Inlet to pick up his sloop and crew. But Teach was

226

ahead of him. Teach had stripped the ship and taken out of her anything of value and marooned seventeen of Bonnet's men on an isolated sand spit.

The major was furious, gathered his men and started out in pursuit of Teach. He had been informed by a bumboat man selling cider and apples to the coastal traffic that Teach was in Ocracoke Inlet with a crew of eighteen men. He missed Teach at Ocracoke and stayed at sea. It was too late now, he reasoned, to sail to the West Indies and apply for a commission as a French privateer. His pardon from the King had been issued in his own name, so he took the name of Thomas and with a free mind raided along Virginia and up into Delaware Bay.

His skill as a pirate had distinctly improved. He took a big ship and perhaps out of lingering affection for the Crown, renamed her *Royal James*. This he sailed to the mouth of the Cape Fear River to careen her for repair. News of his presence there reached the authorities in South Carolina. A formidable officer, Colonel William Rhet, fitted out two armed sloops at his own expense and sailed to catch Bonnet. One of the sloops carried eight guns and sixty men, the other eight guns and seventy men, and on September 25, 1718, the colonel found the major.

Bonnet was lying behind the Cape Fear River bar in the *Royal James,* three sloops with him. They hove anchor and made the run to cross the bar and get to sea. The *James* grounded, and in pursuit Rhet's two sloops went too close. They grounded also, but within gun range. The battle went on for five hours, then Bonnet surrendered.

Colonel Rhet took him to Charleston on October third, and the next day, after the exchange of some loot within the jail, Bonnet escaped. Rhet brought him back and Bonnet's trial and that of his crew began October twenty-eighth at Charleston. The presiding judge, Nicholas Trot, was a fervent Bible scholar and he and the prosecutor conducted the trial

More Myth Than Man

227

with long, oratorical references. A verdict of guilty was pronounced on November twelfth; Bonnet and his men were hanged at White Point, Charleston.

Bonnet died with two distinctions as a pirate. He was the first man ever in recorded history to have bought a ship with his own funds and then to have gone forth deliberately on a piratical venture. He was also, by the record, the only captain of his kind to make his victims walk the plank.

Teach did not outlive the major very long. He had taken some prizes at sea, but then chose to harass the shipping at the entrance to Charleston Harbor. Prisoners were aboard and part of his crew were sick, so he sent his lieutenant, Richards, with a letter to the Governor. He requested that a medicine chest be supplied him or he would make his next communication a set of his prisoners' heads. When the chest was furnished, he put to sea, although Bath Town where he had gone to renounce his calling held attraction for him.

He had married there during the period of regeneracy a sixteen-year-old girl. According to members of his crew who knew Teach's background in the West Indies, he had already plighted himself to twelve other women. But the Governor, Charles Eden, for reasons of friendship, performed the ceremony that united the couple.

Teach left his bride in June, 1718, and went to sea. He ran between the Carolina coast and Bermuda, taking whatever he could find. But the resentment of the Carolina people was slowly building against him. An appeal from them was sent to the Governor of Virginia; it was believed that he would take more action than was possible in local quarters.

A Royal Navy sloop-of-war under the command of Lieutenant Robert Maynard was dispatched to bring in Teach. She was the *Ranger,* and she came up the James River on November 21, 1718, and located the pirate in Ocracoke Inlet. In much the same sort of action that Bonnet had fought, Teach grounded his vessel trying to escape to sea.

The Age of Piracy

Lieutenant Maynard, a young man and deft with a sword, boarded and went for Teach. They discharged pistols at each other, then joined blades. Maynard killed Teach; he inflicted twenty-five wounds upon him before the huge, bearded figure toppled. The head made such a sight that Maynard had it severed from the body. He sailed into Bath Town with it lashed to the bowsprit as a memento of the action.

Little can be said of Teach except that he was a profligate, drunken bully who did not even respect the rights or lives of other pirates. One rum-hazed night aboard his ship a few months before the end he drew a pistol from his belt and fired it. He sat with several of his officers at the cabin table, and he fired blindly beneath it, as he explained to them, to see what would happen. The pistol ball struck his gunner, Israel Hand, in the knee and crippled him permanently. Because of his lameness Hand got out of the ship and went back to England. He became a well-known London beggar and was used by Robert Louis Stevenson as a prototype of the gunner in *Treasure Island*. Hand was not aware of the fact, but lived no doubt content that the wound Teach had inflicted meant escape from the hangman.

More Myth Than Man

229

Go Hang!

"The master, the swabber, the boatswain and I,
    The gunner and his mate
Loved Mall, Meg and Marian and Margery,
    But none of us cared for Kate;
    For she had a tongue with a tang,
    Would cry to a sailor, Go hang!"

WILLIAM SHAKESPEARE, *in The Tempest*

It was not until the trade had declined, when there was no longer any great source of booty left from Spanish wealth and the forceful leaders were either dead or gone far from the Caribbean and discipline had slackened, that women were allowed to sail with the crews of pirate ships. Anne Bonney and her sister in crime, Mary Read, are the only two of whom any record remains. But they served an ancient tradition; women had fought sword in hand beside their men in the Viking raids, and both Anne and Mary were very capable with most any kind of weapon.

Anne was born a bastard, the result of her father's attention to a housemaid. Soon after her birth her father gave up his practice of attorney in Cork, came out from Ireland to South Carolina and went to live in Charleston and became a planter. He brought Anne along, and gave her a reasonably assured place in colonial life. She was by nature, though, somewhat quick-tempered; while in her teens, she was supposed to have killed her English maid with a caseknife. This act began an alienation of her father's affection, and when she married a

230

young sailor of the port without his consent, he threw her out of the house. Bonney believed that the sailor had joined the family for financial reasons alone.

Anne made her own way in dockside Charleston after her husband deserted her. She met there Captain "Calico Jack" Rackham. He was famous on the coast for his looks if not his bravery, and his stories of piratical adventure fascinated Anne. He took her to sea with him, and during his voyages off Cuba she became pregnant.

Rackham had friends in Cuba, and Anne went to live with them until her child was born. Then, leaving the child, she returned to Rackham and the ship. She found Mary Read aboard and the two women became close friends. Mary Read was more on the burly side than Anne; she had been able to conceal her sex well enough to serve as a soldier in an infantry regiment during a campaign in Flanders. Her habitual clothing was a man's, and while this did not please her lover among the crew, she convinced Anne that it was best for their sort of work. They afterwards both wore loose cotton jumpers and bell-bottomed sailor trousers, carried a cutlass and a brace of pistols apiece.

But their ardor for combat was not enough to save the ship when Rackham was pursued by a government sloop out of Jamaica. Rackham and the rest of the men, once the sloop was alongside and the boarding party on deck, jumped below and hid. Anne Bonney and Mary Read fought without help until overpowered. This was remembered when the ship's company was taken in chains to Jamaica in October, 1720, and arraigned for trial.

Anne and Mary went before the court at St. Iago de la Vega on November twenty-eighth, and when interrogated made the disclosure that they were pregnant. Both escaped hanging, but Mary Read died of prison fever. Her death added to Anne's dislike of Calico Jack; she was permitted to see Jack the day of his hanging, and she had her speech ready. She was

Go Hang!

sorry to see him there, she said. "But if he had fought like a man, he need not have been hanged like a Dog." *

Further up the North American coast, in the Massachusetts Bay Colony, a number of men of Calico Jack's stripe troubled the authorities. Too corrupt to fish or haul cargo for a living, and lacking the courage to make the long Red Sea voyage, they frequented the inlets, the river mouths, the entrances to rivers and bays in their sloops. They were a miserable lot, and mention need not be given to many of them.

Action was taken against a pair of locally famous pirates, Thomas Hawkins and Thomas Pound, in 1689, by the people of Massachusetts. The sloop *Mary* was armed and outfitted and sent out under the command of Captain Samuel Pease. He sailed in search of them on October fourth and was given to understand that the pirate craft was in Tarpaulin Cove, opposite Martha's Vineyard, in the Elizabeth Islands.

His information was verified when he put into Wood's Hole, and he soon ran down the few miles to Tarpaulin Cove. The pirate craft was easily visible within the smooth, curved shoreline of the cove, and Captain Pease entered, came to hailing distance and called for surrender. One of the pirate captains, Pound, was on the quarter-deck and his sloop was under way and footing rapidly for Vineyard Sound. His answer to Pease was to run up a red flag on the halyards.

Pease told his gunner to lay a shot athwart the pirate's forefoot. He sailed the *Mary* close aboard and called that the red flag should be struck. Another shot was fired for emphasis. Pound had drawn his sword and he brandished it at Pease, yelling, "Come on, you dogs, and I will strike you!"** His men then let go a musket volley at the *Mary,* and a severe action started.

Pease and his men made fast to the pirate ship and went aboard her. They fought until they were in possession and her

* Charles Johnson *History of the Pyrates.*
** Exquemelin, *History,* American edition, Muzzey, Boston, 1853.

232

flag was lowered. But casualties were heavy on both sides. Captain Pease died five days later of his wounds.

John Fillmore of Ipswich in the Massachusetts Bay Colony was twenty-one when he shipped aboard the Cape Ann sloop, *Dolphin,* in the spring of 1723. He passed a profitable summer aboard her, fishing on the Grand Banks and was homeward-bound in the fall as she was seized by the pirate, Captain John Phillips. This man was more in need of crew replacements than cod, and he chose only the strongest hands out of the *Dolphin,* Fillmore being one.

Go Hang!

Then, despite all protests, Phillips put to sea for seven months. He was shown to the newcomers as a liar and a murderer, killed a member of his original crew out of spite. But he slept lightly, and his quartermaster, his sailing master and bosun were all confirmed pirates. There was nothing Fillmore could do about getting home until Phillips took a big merchant ship bound into Boston from the West Indies. She had a young captain named Harridon, and a veteran carpenter, Cheesman, and a sturdy, intelligent sailor known by his shipmates simply as "the Spanish Indian."

Harridon, Cheesman and the Indian infuriated Phillips because they refused to sign the pirate articles. Phillips threatened them violently, but they still maintained their refusal. It became John Fillmore's idea that working with the trio he might take over the ship. He spoke with them and they agreed and a plan was devised.

After a night of heavy drinking on the part of the pirates, when hangovers blurred vision, the four men took the stations they had been assigned by Fillmore. The time was noon, and Cheesman had left the more wieldy of his carpenter's tools on deck. Fillmore gave the signal and Cheesman grasped the sailing master's arms and pinned them to his sides. Then Fillmore took Cheesman's broad axe and split the bosun open from the

233

cranium to the chin. He swung and dealt in the same way with Phillips before the latter could pull his sword.

Harridon, who was supposed to have his part in the action, was rigid and useless with fright. He stood gaping. The Indian, though, was completely aware of what he should do, and when the quartermaster started up out of the main cabin in response to the sounds on deck, he was tackled. The Indian hung on while Fillmore worked with the axe and nearly severed the quartermaster's head from his body.

Fillmore had gained such a high average by now that the rest of the pirates surrendered without struggle. He brought the ship into Boston on May 3, 1724, and went on his way to Ipswich after Phillips's men were in jail. Three of them were tried, condemned and hanged in chains on Bird Island in Boston Harbor. Three more, in Phillips's former ship, Cheesman and the Indian aboard as witnesses, were sent to England.

They were tried in London, and with the testimony against them, were soon convicted, taken to what was known by pirates as "The Tree" at Execution Dock. Strung from this gallows in chains, their bodies were left to correct the errant thought of any sailor passing to seaward along the Thames. Cheesman and the Indian were "suitably rewarded," and John Fillmore lived out a full life. He was the great-grandfather of Millard Fillmore, the thirteenth President of the United States.

The Indian Ocean Breed

Captain John Avery bore the aliases of Henry Every and Captain Bridgeman, and was called among pirates "Long Ben." But ashore, in England and on the Continent, he was famous as "the archpirate." Plays, books, ballads were written about him. The books went into many editions, and the very popular play, *The Successful Pyrate* by Charles Johnson, with a character much like Avery as the hero, was produced with immediate popular response in 1695 at the Theater Royal in Drury Lane, London.

Avery was one more out of the Bristol man-power pool. He was born around 1665, brought up on the Devon coast, and went to sea as a boy. After several voyages as mate, he signed as first officer in the armed privateer, *The Duke,* under the command of Captain Gibson. She had been hired by the Spanish to combat French pirates in the West Indies and sailed from Bristol to Cadiz for orders.

Avery began making his own when the ship was at anchor in Cadiz harbor. He had talked the crew into a mutinous state of mind, and put Captain Gibson ashore before harm could come to him. Then *The Duke* cleared for the West African coast. The Portuguese settlements were raided, three English ships were taken, and a number of slaves, and two Danish ships.

But Avery was attracted to Madagascar. He had heard descriptions of the big, luxuriant island that lay off the East Coast of Africa and formed, with the mainland, the Mozambique Channel. It was a fine base for a pirate, with natives who welcomed whites as long as there was some small profit forth-

The Age of Piracy

coming to them, and to the north all the wealth of the potentates whose ships used the Indian Ocean, the Gulf of Aden and the Red Sea. What was good for the East India Company, Avery pointed out to his crew, could be better for them, and with less extended effort or investment.

Avery rounded up on the Cape of Good Hope, reached Madagascar, found conditions as he had expected, refitted his ship and set a course for the Red Sea. His objective was the Great Mogul's fleet, out of Mocha, and cruising back and forth, Avery met it. The lookouts lost sight of the fleet at night, but the next day Avery bent on full sail and drew ahead to windward. He went in after the biggest ship, the *Gunsway*, and in a savage two-hour fight took her.

She was rich even beyond his dreams. He hauled out of her holds great strong-boxes that contained 100,000 pieces of eight and another 100,000 in chequins. There was fabulous booty in precious stones, pearls, silks and damasks, and aboard her were some of the Mogul's family and his chief retainers.

Avery kept to himself the Mogul's youngest daughter when he sailed back for Madagascar. He had with him a pair of ships that had aided in the attack on the *Gunsway*, and on the return out of the Red Sea he tricked the captains of them into entrusting him with their portion of the spoils. When he dropped anchor off Madagascar and was rowed ashore with his royal captive, he believed that he had a bright future.

But the Great Mogul was both powerful and extremely angry. He protested to the East India Company: if his daughter were not freed and sent back to him, along with the plunder, he would see that every company settlement was destroyed. The man who had robbed him was English; let the English make restitution. It was, for the Mogul, as simple as that.

Word of the Mogul's attitude caused furore in London. Stories were circulated that not only was the Princess in love with Avery; she had born him a child while in residence at Madagascar. Confronted with the possible loss of their East Indian holdings which meant immense revenue to the Crown, the government moved to apprehend Avery.

Men-of-war were given orders for Madagascar, and he was forced to leave his new family. He loaded the choicest part of his loot into a sloop and shoved off towards what he hoped might be more hospitable waters. When he got into the Caribbean and touched at New Providence Island, the governor accepted his offer of twenty pieces of eight and two gold pieces for a pardon, yet Avery was still uneasy.

He left and sailed for Boston, spent bribe money and landed in 1696 with a few of his men. The colony impressed him as being small, and he was aware that too many people knew about his collection of diamonds. He went back aboard the sloop and put her under way for North Ireland. There was no pursuit, and once more he thought that he would be safe.

The sloop was sold for a fair price in North Ireland and he separated from the last of his crew, took care to enter Dublin without recognition. But it was necessary for him to sell a diamond to pay for his lodgings. He got rid of it, then too wary to stay any longer, headed for his home county of Devon.

Using an assumed name, he hid out in the village of Bideford. Men he had known in the past, Bristol merchants, came to visit him at his cottage after he had sent messages. He showed them diamonds, and some ornate gold cups he had kept. The merchants took advantage of the moment and quoted bargain rates. Avery sold the cups for a few pounds, and let the merchants take the diamonds to Bristol for negotiation there.

But the merchants sent to Bideford only small, intermittent sums as further payment. Then they stopped payment completely, and Avery's requests were ignored. He was famous, he was the arch pirate, yet he sat here and starved. Avery, weak with hunger, took to his bed in the Bideford cottage. He was still, as far as the public knew, reigning as a king on a golden throne in Madagascar. Perhaps it was better that way; he could die in peace, and the Princess would never know how.

The
Indian
Ocean
Breed

237

He Who Raised the Spanish Plate

Near this place is interred the Body of Sir William Phips, knight; who in the year 1697, by his great industry, discovered among the rocks near the Banks of Bahama on the North side of Hispaniola a Spanish plate-ship which had been under water 44 years, out of which he took in gold and silver to the value of 300,000 sterling: and with a fidelity equal to his conduct, brought it all to London, where it was divided between himself and the rest of the adventurers. For which great service he was knighted by His Majesty, King James the 2nd and at the request of the principal inhabitants of New England, he accepted the Government of Massachusetts, in which he continued up to the time of his death; and discharged his trust with that zeal for the interests of the country, and with so little regard to his own private advantage, that he justly gained the good esteem and affection of the greatest and best part of the inhabitants of that Colony.

He died the 18th of February 1694, and his lady, to perpetuate his memory, hath caused this monument to be erected.

Inscription upon the tomb of Sir William Phips
in the churchyard of St. Mary Woolnoth, London.

Phips was born in 1650 near the town of Wicasset, Maine. His father was James Phips. William was one of twenty-six children, and as soon as he was able he was apprenticed to a shipwright at Montsweag Bay. He took a ship to Boston at the end of his apprenticeship, then learned to read and write.

While sailing out of Boston as a ship's carpenter, he married.

Most of his voyages were coastwise or to the West Indies. He listened during them to a lot of the old-timers' stories about sunken Spanish treasure. Phips began to gather the stories, and disentangle the palpably false from those that might be true. He heard repeatedly in the Bahamas about a plate fleet of sixteen ships that was supposed to have foundered in hurricane some forty years before on the southern fringe of cays. It was known that the last remnants of the Lucayans, the Indian people indigenous to the islands and famous divers, kept themselves alive by salving coins and bullion.

Phips made his first investigation in 1681. He found the Indians skin-diving out of canoes and shallops and coming to the surface through shark, sting-ray and barracuda with coir baskets that held coral-crusted coins, even ingot. But he could not locate the galleon from which, obviously, they came, and he was forced to go to England with little more than his story of the probable fleet site.

He was a big, heavy-shouldered man, red-faced and red-haired; he talked with a Maine twang in not the best grammer. It took him a year to reach King Charles II, but then Charles was pleased to listen. Phips was given a small Royal Navy frigate, the *Rose,* armed with eighteen guns, and carrying a press-gang crew of ninety-five who were supposed to fight any pirates met during the voyage.

Phips sailed deeply committed to King Charles for a large part of any salvage, and put into Boston for supplies. His crew got drunk, scared a number of the inhabitants by their actions, and made Phips think questioningly of the future. But although embroiled with the judge himself, he paid the fine and herded the crew aboard. Then with another ship that sought treasure, the *Good Intent,* Phips sailed the *Rose* to the Bahama Banks. The crews searched for weeks among the shoals where the great Spanish vessels were supposed to have fetched up all-standing in the hurricane. They found nothing.

He Who Raised the Spanish Plate

239

The Age of Piracy

The crew thought they could do better as pirates, and what they needed for their purpose was the *Rose*. When mutiny broke, Phips put it down sternly, and the men admitted to a change of heart. But when Phips careened the ship at an island to clean her bottom, the men mutinied again. Phips managed to haul some cannon into place against them and keep them under control until he reached Jamaica. There he put them on the dock and hired another batch who protested no interest in either mutiny or piracy.

Phips anchored off Tortuga and started a systematic inspection of the area. He received many indications of where treasure might be along the ocean floor, yet his divers could not come upon it. When he was forced to sail for England, all he had was the hope that he could do better on the next voyage. But the *Rose* was taken from him on his arrival. Promises, he was told at court, did not represent treasure.

The Duke of Albemarle, though, and some of the other affluent courtiers still had faith in Phips. They outfitted a ship named the *James and Mary* and gave it to him in 1686 along with a tender for his diving work. He sailed again and put down anchor on the Banks and sent his divers below.

The patient, slender, small and quiet Lucayans worked for months at considerable loss of life and could raise nothing of value. Then one day a big silver ingot thick-crusted inside coral packed with sand was sent up by the divers. They were on the wreck of one of the galleons; there was no doubt. Baskets of silver ingot and pig were heaved aboard; and coins that spilled across the deck planks out of coral-clogged chunks. The galleon was in about forty feet of water, but her hold was not sealed, could be readily dived.

Phips watched the horizon and watched his crew. He was growing wealthy, but the sort of stuff that lay in the hold bred piracy. The divers had worked steadily on the wreck for more than a month, provisions were short aboard and the crew had begun the famous mutinous mumble when Phips decided

240

that he had enough. He sailed for London with thirty-two tons of gold and silver in his hold, and his share of it, after his backers were satisfied, was close to ninety thousand dollars. A popular hero, he was knighted, sent out as High Sheriff of Massachusetts, then, increasingly in King William III's favor, became Governor.

"Him who raised the Spanish plate."
Port Royal pothouse term commonly used in XVIII century
to describe Captain Henry Jennings

Another great Spanish plate fleet similar to the one whose units Phips discovered, was again lost through storm off the Bahamas. This was in 1714, and the ships were out of Vera Cruz and richly loaded and bound home. Survivors reached Havana, and the Governor immediately dispatched vessels and divers for salvage work. They located some of the wrecks, and among the treacherous reefs the men went down.

"Diving machines," * probably crude air bells of some sort, were employed, and the divers brought to the surface "millions of dollars, or pieces of eight." ** The salvaged wealth was put in a storehouse erected on a cay and was checked daily by two Royal Commissioners. They were guarded in turn by sixty soldiers from the Havana garrison.

The salvage sum had reached 350,000 pieces of eight when Captain Jennings got news of it and sailed from Jamaica. He had heard of all the hard work Captain Phips had undergone to gain his fortune, and believed his method would be simpler. For security reasons, he sailed with two ships and three sloops; they were from Barbadoes and Jamaica, and the crews were accustomed to their duties.

The visiting vessels anchored off the storehouse cay. Then the crews went ashore in small craft and chased the Royal

* Exquemelin, *History.*   ** *Ibid.*

The Age of Piracy

Commissioners and the soldiers from it. They thanked the divers for their trouble, loaded the treasure aboard their ships and sailed for Jamaica. On the way into Port Royal, they met a large Spanish ship. After they had engaged and won her, they learned that she was from Puerto Bello in a cargo of cochineal bales, casks of indigo and sixty thousand pieces of eight. They added it to the salvaged treasure and proceeded into Port Royal.

It was at a time when peace existed between Spain and England, and the defeated Spanish crew had clearly seen Captain Jennings's flotilla enter Port Royal. The Governor of Cuba made vigorous protest to the Governor of Jamaica. He was told by return message that the Governor of Jamaica was "very indignant" * at what had happened. Captain Jennings was ordered to leave Port Royal, stand to sea. But before Jennings sailed he was allowed to discharge his cargo, be paid, and take stores and munitions aboard for his next, unnamed voyage. The feelings of the Governor of Cuba were such that it was believed, in Jamaica, the peace could end at any moment.

* *Ibid.*

Jewels And All

"A short life and a merry one."

CAPTAIN BARTHOLOMEW ROBERTS, as quoted by his crew

Others took a lot more wealth and received much greater fame. But for sheer seamanly ability Bartholomew Roberts leads the list of pirate commanders. He captured over four hundred prizes at sea in a period of four years, his area of operation from the Grand Banks and Nova Scotia down through the West Indies to Brazil and across the Atlantic to the West African coast.

A tall, dark-visaged man born in Wales in 1682, he started out honestly enough in the merchant service. His skill advanced him, and he was appointed sailing master in the *Princess* under Captain Plumb. She was a London ship, bound for the Guinea Coast to load slaves. While off Guinea, she was seized by another Welshman, a pirate of reputation, Captain Howel Davis, and Roberts was forced as a prisoner to leave the *Princess*. For some time, although warmly invited, Roberts refused to turn to piracy. He listened unmoved to the stories Davis told of the big days in the West Indies, where Davis had made his name. He was one of the commanders who had accepted clemency at New Providence Island from Woodes Rogers, later at Rogers's direction sailed a sloop in trade with the French and Spanish. But the peaceful life had palled, and Davis was back at his old ways.

He went in along the Portuguese part of the Guinea Coast after Roberts was aboard his ship and attacked the settlement at the Isle of Princes. The action was conducted without too much forethought, and Davis walked into an ambush laid by the Governor. Volleys fired from out of the underbrush on the beach struck the pirates. Davis was pierced through the bowels and fell mortally wounded. Yet he was able to draw his brace of pistols and shoot two Portuguese before he died.

This made an impression on Roberts. He began to think of himself as the possible successor to Davis. There were, however, in the pirate ship quite a number of men who held the same idea. They spoke of themselves as "Lords" and meant it, and were ready to prove their right to the title. The dispute about who should assume the captaincy was marked by strong language, boasts and threats of violence. But Roberts won the vote with only a single dissension although he had been aboard just six weeks. The man who dissented left the meeting in disgust, saying that he didn't care who was made captain as long as it was not a Papist.

Roberts went immediately about his new duties; he razed the fort in revenge for Davis, bombarded the town, set two ships in the port afire after nightfall and by the light of the blazing hulks put to sea. His course was laid off for the Brazilian coast. Sailing it, he came upon forty-two Portuguese ships in the harbor of Bahia.

They were at anchor and deeply loaded and ready to sail for Lisbon. Roberts inspected the fleet through his long-glass, then gave the order to put his ship alongside the biggest. He boarded her from his much smaller ship and in a swift hand-to-hand combat captured her. While the rest of the fleet trained their pieces on him he secured from her forty thousand gold *moidores** and a cross of diamonds designed with the King of Portugal in mind. He then stood away safely out of the harbor, evaded pursuit and sailed north.

More prizes were taken in rapid succession, and he returned to the Brazilian coast to careen, clean bottom and re-

* *Moidore:* equivalent value, $6.50.

pair. His crew were highly pleased by his daring seamanship, yet they found him a strict and extraordinary commander. First off, he set himself remote from them by being an abstainer; his drink was tea. His orders were that there was to be no drinking below-decks after eight o'clock at night. It was an obvious fire-control measure, and the men respected it. They were less happy when they were informed that no women were to be allowed aboard. If a catamite was brought into the ship, or a woman in man's clothing, the penalty would be death.

Roberts, with his Welsh background, was a firm Sabbatarian; religious observances were held regularly each Sunday. The ship's musickers were an overworked group of men who in the usual pirate-ship style had previously played whenever a member of the crew requested, either day or night. Roberts said that the musickers should have Sunday as a day of leisure. Guards were set to watch all women prisoners, protect them against molestation. No fighting was permitted aboard. Any pair of pirates who could not make up their differences were to go ashore and settle the problem there. The quartermaster would take care of the details of the duel.

It was irksome for the crew, still they were aware that they had never sailed with a captain of Roberts's ability. He took prizes at an amazing rate of speed in the West Indies after leaving Brazil. There was very little left when he had finished with the unlucky vessels sailing around Barbadoes and Jamaica. When the Royal Navy station-ships came his way, he hauled for the Grand Banks.

He was a scourge in among the fishing fleet, and he raided as he wished. Cold weather sent him south again in the fall and he had his sailmaker sew up a special flag for him. This bore upon a black field a big white figure that represented himself, sword in hand. His feet rested on two skulls, one of which carried beneath it ABH, and the other AMH. When last in the West Indies, he had been given stiff fights off Barbadoes and

Jewels and All

245

Martinique, thus the initials: A Barbadian Head and A Martiniquan Head. He was determined to make the islanders remember him.

But he was already respected if not feared by them. His ships in succession had been *Fortune, Good Fortune, Royal Fortune,* all fast and well-armed, his gunners excellent men on a target, the tightly disciplined crew expert sail-handlers and helmsmen. He was in his late thirties, at the prime of his life, and sported the best clothing, jewels, rings and precious ornaments taken out of the prizes. It gave him a wild delight to run in and hammer the ports, the fortifications and shipping, issue written defiance to the various Governors, then sail off unmolested.

He became bored, though, with the lack of response. The special flag for Martinique and Barbadoes was unbent from the halyards and he set out across the Atlantic. He began to run the Guinea Coast again in April, 1721, and plundered and burned and ravaged with his habitual success. A Church of England parson was aboard one of the ships that was captured. Roberts could see the need for religious influence in the *Royal Fortune;* he offered the parson the chance to become ship's chaplain. All that the duties would be, Roberts said, were the saying of prayers and the manufacture of rum punch. The parson refused because of a previous commitment and Roberts let him go, although he kept three of the parson's prayer books and a corkscrew for use by the crew.

Roberts then sailed the *Royal Fortune* in behind the lee of Parrot Island on the Guinea Coast. He was accompanied by another pirate ship and felt himself safe. But a Royal Navy vessel, the *Swallow,* commanded by Captain Chaloner Ogle, was out after him and located the ships. Captain Ogle by a clever ruse of pretended flight drew Roberts's companion ship to sea, defeated her in a two-hour-long running fight.

Roberts still considered himself safe at his Parrot Island anchorage. He was enjoying a breakfast of salmagundi in his cabin on the morning of February 10, 1722, when men of the crew sighted the topmasts of the *Swallow* over the island to seaward. Roberts finished his breakfast before he went on deck. The *Swallow* was already in the narrow channel to sea.

Some of the *Royal Fortune* men were stumbling drunk, and slow when Roberts called his orders. The anchor cable was chopped, though, and she began to gather way as canvas was hoisted. Roberts had the intention of running squarely abreast of the *Swallow,* then, at the cost of a broadside, coming about on the other tack and standing on out the channel. It was a dangerous maneuver, but if executed promptly, could be successful.

Roberts had taken care, while still in his cabin, to dress himself in his best. His waistcoat and breeches were of red damask. He wore a red feather in his hat, and around his neck was a gold chain, pendant from it a large diamond cross. Two braces of pistols were through the loops at the end of his silk shoulder sash; he carried his fine sword in his hand.

He passed the helm orders quietly to the man at the tiller, studying the big Royal Navy ship as she approached along the passage. Yardarm would almost touch yardarm when the vessels were abreast; his men would have to step smartly when they hauled the braces and sheets for the other tack.

The bow guns aboard the *Swallow* began to fire. Then she delivered a broadside. *Royal Fortune* shivered and Roberts gave a change of course to the helmsman. He was slow to carry it out, and down on the main deck the rum-fuddled men among the crew had left their stations. Roberts started to call again to the helmsman, but a charge of grapeshot caught him in the throat.

He slumped head-down onto the deck planks, while for an instant, amazed, the helmsman stared at him. Then it was too late. *Royal Fortune* fell off the wind and *Swallow* had her. But Roberts's men still had time to bury him as he had al-

Jewels and All

ways wished. They lowered his body over the side into the sea, weapons, jewels and all, before they surrendered. Most of them were weeping, and none of them attempted to fight.

They were tried by a Vice Admiralty Court at Cape Corso Castle on the coast some weeks later. Sympathy was shown one of the musickers, whose bruises had been caused, he testified, by members of the crew who had beaten him to make him entertain them. It was also in the testimony that during his career as captain Roberts had never forced any man to turn pirate against his will.

A Mixed Muster

Captain Charles Vane, who became well known for his depredations along the Carolina coast, was one of the few pirates who ever defied Woodes Rogers when he was Governor of the Bahamas and lived any length of time to boast of it. Vane had the determination to turn down the pardon offered him by Rogers in 1718, and to make public his dislike, burned a prize he owned, and sailed out of New Providence harbor.

For a time he occupied himself filching silver bullion from a sunken Spanish galleon off Florida. Then he worked up the coast and proved so unpopular to the people of Carolina that they sent their Colonel Rhet out after him. But Colonel Rhet missed him, and instead Vane met Captain "Blackbeard" Teach at sea. The two pirate captains fired solid-shot salutes at each other, afterwards moved into a backwoods creek, tied up together and got monstrously drunk.

But Vane knew enough not to stay in Teach's company. He put to sea and, while cruising offshore, overhauled a big French ship. She was of such size that Vane was reluctant to attack her. His crew held a meeting in the traditional style and Vane was divested of his rank, just escaped marooning and was allowed to leave the ship with a few of his close followers in a small boat.

Vane, who had a real affection for piracy, was of an obdurate nature and remained with the trade. He worked himself up from the foc'sle and, as his reputation began to shine, was once more given a captaincy by his shipmates. Then, right at the height of success, a hurricane took his new command from him, his ship was sunk and he landed on the beach of a small island off the coast of Honduras.

He was alone and desperate. His condition was so bad that he had begun to beg for fish from the Mosquito Indians when an English ship went to anchor near the island. Her boat came in for fresh water and Vane learned that she was out of Jamaica and that her captain was named Holford. When the boat returned, Vane went aboard. He appealed to Holford as an old friend.

Holford answered that he would not have him aboard in any circumstances. He added that, in his opinion, Vane was of the type that would try to trick him, disaffect and take over his crew. But, he said, he proposed to be back at the island again within a month; if Vane was still alive and on it, he would take him to Jamaica to be hanged.

This persuaded Vane that Holford was no friend of his. He said a quick goodbye and left the ship. But soon after, while he was subsisting on fish borrowed from the Indians, another English ship put in at the island for water. Vane had improved his disaster story; the captain, impressed, took him aboard.

The ship had only been at sea for a day or so, though, when she was sighted by Captain Holford's ship. Holford made a signal and boarded; he was a friendly man who, island fashion, liked to gossip with his brother captains. Moving from the ladder towards the poop, Holford looked down into the opened main hold. Vane worked there in the scorching heat with great energy, the almost perfect image of the new hand.

Holford continued aft. He confided the identity of the new hand to Vane's benefactor. Then he made good his promise. He took Vane out of the ship and back to Port Royal where, duly, Vane was hanged.

Captain Henry Johnson held several minor distinctions as a pirate. Although born in the North of Ireland, he commanded a Rhode Island sloop called the *Two Brothers* and was known in the trade as "Henriques, the Englishman." Most of his crew were Spaniards, a very unusual circumstance, and he was one-armed, having lost the other in action. He was, despite his handicap, an excellent musket shot; his method was to cock the piece with his good hand, then brace it on the stump while he fired.

His area of operations was the West Indies and on March 20, 1730, he met the ship *John and Jane*. His *Two Brothers* carried eighteen guns and his crew roster was ninety. The ship against him, which was commanded by Captain Edward Burt of Jamaica, had only eight carriage guns and twelve swivel guns and a crew of twenty-five. But Burt fought the pirates for more than five hours off Swan Island before he lost her.

The pirates were furious. They boarded the *John and Jane* and stripped the few survivors naked. Their intention was to hang them in pairs from the main yardarm. Johnson and one of his English sailors, a man named Echlin, stopped this, and the prisoners were left to huddle together on deck.

Screams and oaths came from the main cabin. Pedro Poleas, the Spaniard who served Johnson as mate, had found a woman hidden in the hold. She was a Mrs. Groves, a passenger, whose husband had been killed in the action. Now Poleas had torn her clothing from her and, cursing her English frigidity, threatened her with rape.

Johnson came into the cabin with a cocked pistol in his hand. He studied Poleas over the barrel and he told Poleas to give Mrs. Groves her clothing and all her other belongings. If his order weren't carried out, Johnson said, and if there was any other attempt on Mrs. Grove's chastity, the man who made it would have his head shot off.

Poleas understood and got out of the cabin. Mrs. Groves dressed demurely while Johnson guarded her. She returned later to Jamaica, where she told the story, quite conscious that it was rare. There were not many pirate captains like "Henriques, the Englishman."

A Mixed Muster

251

The Lafittes Fight Hard

"Belles des figues! Bons petits calas! Barataria, Barataria!"
Street merchants' cry in New Orleans, Circa 1815

The Lafitte brothers, Jean and Pierre, have left behind them some of the romantic aura that attached itself to the memory of Captain Kidd. They stalk through the history of New Orleans robust and guileful, defiant of the law, yet gallant patriots. Legend has encrusted their lives; like Kidd, they are alleged to have cached huge amounts of treasure, and their actions are the source of novels and biographies. But that is understandable. They were unusual men in a turbulent, bizarre city at a time of intense crisis, and they were the last pirates of any consequence.

Their birth is supposed to have been French and by trade they were blacksmiths. They appeared in New Orleans in 1809 and soon gave up the forge, the hammer and the anvil. Smuggling tempted them; the step to open piracy was short. Jean, the more dominant of the pair, chose to make his headquarters on Grande Terre Island in Barataria Bay downriver from the city. The island had been the property of a retired pirate known as Grambo, but Jean shot him.

The Baratarian folk were somewhat lawless by disposition, and Jean and his brother were able to recruit tough, reliable pirate crews from among them. They raided around the wide bay, and down at the river mouth, then out in the Gulf of Mexico, sailing small craft for the most part and selling their booty in the city. It was not hard to find agents.

New Orleans was an almost ideal port for a pirate. The

252

frontier was right beyond, and Yankee flatboatmen in blue flannel shirts, who would be gone tomorrow, tied up their boats six-alongside at the Levée; Choctaw Indians dressed in blankets, sinuous tattoo lines on their cheeks, their hat bands decorated with pieces of tin, would for the price of a drink of rum tell about hiding places in the bayou country that no white man could ever find unaided. There was also strong dissension between the two main segments of the population, to the degree that Americans kept to the north side of St. Charles Street and the Creole native-born to the south. Thus, because of factionalism, there was not prompt administration of the law.

Jean and Pierre prospered. When in from a raid, they wore the best clothes, drank the finest wines, went to the Orleans Theater after a bit of business with their agents and an afternoon spent in the dueling masters' *ateliers* along Exchange Alley. They disregarded the warning cannon fired at eight o'clock on winter nights and nine in summer that told all sailors, soldiers and Negroes to get off the streets. Life was just about the way they liked it.

But in 1813, after many protests had been made by robbed shipmasters, the Governor declared the Lafittes to be pirates, threatened them with arrest. They denied the charge passionately, and money was spent, and months passed and they were not arrested. The Governor, though, had to satisfy the shipmasters. It was made clear to him that the Lafittes had no manifest legitimate source of income at Grande Terre Island, and did not even use the waters of Barataria Bay for fishing purposes.

The brothers were arrested and indicted. They had supplied themselves with excellent legal counsel and the jury was given to believe in their innocence. Free men, they walked proudly out of the courtroom and went back to Grande Terre. But the Governor kept an eye on them, and their further movements were hampered by a naval force sent in pursuit.

The Lafittes Fight Hard

253

Then, with the progress of the war against England that had begun in 1812, the Lafittes found themselves in a rather peculiar situation. Having been informed of their troubles with the Governor, British officers came to the island and proferred a King's commission and a large sum of money to be paid on its acceptance. Jean and Pierre put off the officers and said that they must think over the idea for a while. But they left by fast boat right after their guests were gone and went to New Orleans.

Andrew Jackson, the old Indian-fighter, was in command of the American forces, with the rank of Major General. He was a man scarred by fights, duels, backwoods altercations, and he possessed the frontier mentality. He listened to the Lafittes, took their story as truth and asked them to enlist. His forces were small, mostly local militia, and the British force aboard the fleet down-river was large and composed of seasoned professionals.

The Lafittes joined the American cause. They sent word to the Baratarians, telling every able-bodied man to muster and to report at once with what arms he could carry or transport to New Orleans. British war-sloops were active in the river, but the Baratarians got through, and they brought their weapons. Hundreds of them formed up under the command of the brothers and marched to the defense of the city.

They went out to Chalmette six miles below it with the Bataillon d'Orleans and Hind's Dragoons and Beale's Rifles and various unattached Texans and dueling masters and Mexican drovers and Ohio and Kentucky flatboatmen and trappers. There were hardly enough guns to go around, but Jackson deployed his troops behind a cotton-bale barricade at the edge of an open field and waited.

The British landed from their ships and formed to the music of fifes and drums and bagpipes. The veterans made a brave sight against the crape myrtle in their red jackets. They wore crossed breast straps that were pipe-clayed, a shiny brass buckle at the center. It was a target that would be difficult to miss.

Behind their officers and their colors, the British tried to cross the field. They were shot down rank after torn rank, and the files clambered up over the heaped dead until the call for retreat was sounded. The British losses were 1,971, and the American 13. While the retreat to the boats was made, Jackson's men rested, almost numb; none of them had ever seen such carnage, or such a waste of courage.

But before the political wind could change, Jean Lafitte took the pirates back to Grande Terre Island. It would be better, he and Pierre decided, if they abandoned the area altogether. New Orleans was no longer a port which they could use, not with a man like Andrew Jackson in command of the troops. Jean and Pierre and their followers slipped out of sight from Barataria Bay. They went westward and established themselves on an island that is now the site of Galveston, Texas.

But old habits were hard to break. Shipping in the Gulf of Mexico was again molested and in 1823 a Royal Navy sloop was dispatched to take care of the Lafittes. One account, that of Phillip Gosse, an outstanding authority on piracy, states that the sloop met the Lafitte ship at sea and in the encounter Jean Lafitte with sixty of his men were killed. There are other versions of the fashion of his death, though, and it is claimed that he died as far inland as Kansas City. Legend is not yet finished with him.

*The
Lafittes
Fight
Hard*

255

The Least and the Last

Out of the Elizabethan period emerges a figure which must be remembered by every historian of seagoing men. It is that of Richard Hakluyt, the quiet, persistent churchman who, prideful of the achievements of England's early navigators and explorers, helped her to a consciousness of her maritime power. Hakluyt knew Sir Walter Raleigh well, and others among the great English adventurers, some of whom were called pirates by the Spanish, and he left for us chronicles of them which will exist as long as any record is kept.

He had no contact with the sea except for the short, if rough, Channel crossings he made from England to France and return. But it fascinated him, and he spent many years of his life reporting voyages. He was born about 1552 in Herefordshire, and his education was at Westminster School and at Christ Church, Oxford. A man of scholarly, ruminant ways, he joined the clergy. Then as chaplain to Sir Edward Stafford, the English ambassador at the French court, he lived in Paris from 1583 to 1588. It was while he was in France that the sea began to interest him.

His scrutiny of the maritime records there brought him to the conclusion that his nation was misrepresented and that English seamen were noted for their sluggish security. This he set out to correct, and he never relinquished the purpose. He had already published, in 1582, *Divers Voyages Touching the Discovery of America* and five years later in Paris he finished a revision of Peter Martyr's work, *De Orbo Novo*.

In the same year he published "*Notable History,* containing four Voyages made by certain French Captains into Florida." His great work, which was to be later expanded, *Principall Navigations, Voiages, and Discoveries of the English Nation,* came out in 1589. When at home in England he traveled endlessly to get a sailor's story, to study a chart, or to dig into a forgotten sea chest in an attic and turn up a journal, the record of some obscure voyage.

Sir Walter Raleigh became his close friend. Raleigh's scintillant mind excited Hakluyt. He was fired by the plans of exploration that Raleigh had for the future. Raleigh aided him with the material and in the space of a summer Hakluyt wrote a book of twenty-one short chapters. It was called *The Queen's Book* and was for the personal perusal of Elizabeth. She responded to the appeal that it contained; the consequence was the Raleigh expedition to Virginia.

With the rest of his countrymen, Hakluyt shared the English hatred of Philip of Spain. He offered solutions that would bring about Philip's downfall, and wrote that if Philip were touched in the West Indies, the apple of his eye was touched. He promised that Philip would be left as bare as "Aesop's proude crowe."

But as he breathed venom against the Spanish, Hakluyt kept on at his religious duties. He became the rector at Wetheringsett in 1590 and was made archdeacon of Westminster Abbey in 1603. The enormous amount of material he had collated had not all been published at the time of his death in 1616, and another churchman, Samuel Purchas, continued his work. Hakluyt was buried in Westminster Abbey; he belonged among the really great.

Jean-Baptiste Labat was a professor of mathematics and philosophy at the University of Nancy in the latter part of the seventeenth century when a circular issued by his brother priests of the Dominican Order came into his hands. This related the many deaths, hardships and failures suffered in the

The Least and the Last

The Age of Piracy

West Indies where the order worked with difficulty to maintain itself. Père Labat talked with his superiors; he asked for release from his professorial duties and transfer to Martinique. His request was granted and at the age of thirty, tall, robust, austere in his white robes, he sailed from La Rochelle in November, 1693.

There were Capuchins and Jesuits aboard the ship and they were assigned to the same endeavor, but they soon recognized Labat's character. He was their acknowledged leader when the ship put into Martinique. The superior of the monastery, detecting the sort of man he had been given, sent him to the Macouba region in the northern section of the island. Macouba was wild and grim, and after the cloisters of Nancy it was necessary that Labat adjust himself.

Labat thrived, and soon was ordered to take over the huge sugar estate owned by the Dominicans at Saint-Jacques on the Capesterre windward coast. The estate was 700,000 pounds of sugar in debt, deserved intensive reorganization. Labat went about the task with fervor.

He became the general manager at Saint-Jacques, as well as engineer, architect and chief machinist. He invented and built new mills for sugar grinding, constructed irrigation systems that are still used, and wrote a treatise that remains a handbook for planters. But while he wrote the treatise he kept a journal and his interests were multifarious. He explored the habits of the few remaining Caribs living on the island and noted the superstitions and the music and dance patterns of the Negro slaves; he inscribed for posterity the correct way to cook a parrot. Because of the turbulence of the period, he met many pirates, and he portrayed them with the same zeal that he gave to his parrot recipe.

When he had pulled the Saint-Jacques estate out of debt, Auger, the Governor of the neighboring French island of Guadeloupe, asked for his services. He had brought the property to the profit side of the ledger in two years, and Auger had need

258

of such ability. Père Labat sailed for Guadeloupe and built fortifications for the Governor, then, as the island was attacked by
English pirates, helped man them.

The attackers killed every gunner in the emplacement
where Labat was stationed. He served the unwieldy piece
singlehanded, swabbing, loading, training and firing. After he
had thrown twelve rounds into the pirates, they retired from
his part of the fortifications and the French rested secure.

Back in Martinique, Père Labat was made the Superior
of the order, and also Vicar-Apostolic. He continued with his
construction work, built the Convent of Mouillage at St. Pierre
and a number of other structures in the lovely, hilly town. But
French buccaneers were often in the port, and for diplomatic
reasons, he was friendly with them.

They once celebrated Mass in his honor by firing off the
cannon aboard their ships at each step of the service. On another occasion, a pirate captain, to show his respect for Labat
and the sincerity of his own religious feeling, killed with his
sword one of the crew who had drunk too much rum and whose
talk interrupted the service. This, Labat reported, silenced the
man permanently, and was a costly way to maintain discipline.

Labat was tempted, though, to put to sea with some of
the French pirates. He became their chaplain, and a gunner.
Two English ships were captured, and Labat directed that his
share of the loot be turned over to charity. He was later captured by a Spanish vessel, his life threatened. He saved himself by display of a cross that had been employed by the officers of the Inquisition, and the abashed Spaniards released
him.

His shore duties were enormous, yet he took time when
the Martiniquan coast was attacked to lead a force composed
of all the Negro field hands from the Saint-Jacques estate. The
men, carrying their razor-sharp cane knives, were confident behind their commander. He led them in counterattack, and the
English pirates were driven off, sent in defeat back to the ships.

*The
Least
and the
Last*

259

The Age of Piracy

Labat was the outstanding religious if not also political figure in the French islands. It was thought wise by his superiors in Rome to recall him. He had spent twelve years in the Caribbean, and he was a *revenant,* who sought always to return after he obeyed the call from Rome. But his wish was never granted. While waiting, he wrote his nostalgic account, *Nouveau Voyage aux Iles d'Amerique.* He remained in Europe the rest of his life, and peacefully, at the age of seventy-five, he died in Paris.

The man to become lastingly and widely famous as a chronicler of the great age of piracy was a Flemish barber-surgeon who in his lifetime kept his identity secret behind a pseudonym. His real name is said to be Hendrik Smeeks, although there is a degree of doubt about that, and he is known as Alexandre Olivier Esquemelin, or Esquemeling, or Exquemelin.

Dubiety about his name aside, he came early to the West Indies after a voyage to Java. He arrived at Tortuga off Hispaniola on July 7, 1666, in the French West Indies Company ship, *St. Mary,* as an indentured man looking in the usual manner for a good-natured master. He did not find one. The Brethren of the Coast were in full operation, and the hunting of wild cattle on Hispaniola was the center of trade.

The hunters needed *valets* to assist them in their work and Exquemelin was sent out by his master, the Lieutenant-Governor. According to his account,* he suffered under the harsh treatment, became sick and was at last sold cheap to a man who served in the colony as a surgeon. His new master brought him back to health, and, moreover, taught him the profession of barber-surgeon.

Then Exquemelin started to go to sea in the buccaneer ships. He served in most of the famous raids in the Caribbean between the years 1668–74 and was one of Morgan's men at the sack of Panamá. It is difficult to tell now just how much fiction has accreted upon what he saw and put down as fact;

* Exquemelin, *History of the Buccaneers of America.*

many writers of several nationalities have worked at his copy since he finished his version.

At any rate, he went back home and wrote all he knew, perhaps a good deal more. The book was an instantaneous best seller when W. Cooke published it in London in 1684, and it had been given previous publication in Amsterdam in 1678, had a German edition in 1679 and a Spanish in 1681. Each edition was different, even at the beginning. National chauvinism colored the pages, and the hack writers and the bad translators were careless with the values of veracity.

The book was still essentially accurate, though, and held tremendous fascination for the public. Sir Henry Morgan, given prominence in the first English edition, was one of the very few to be displeased when he read it. He sued the London publisher for libel, and won his case, and amends were made; a revision of the prefatory material gave Sir Henry the highest praise. His rage subsided and the book in almost countless editions kept on selling. It is still for sale, and is regarded as a classic of its kind and time.

Basil Ringrose came to the West Indies as a young sailor in 1679. What motivated him to turn to buccaneering is described by Dampier,* who was both his fellow chronicler and comrade in arms. Ringrose was at the buccaneer rendezvous on the Gulf of Darien in 1680 and took part in the expedition that crossed the isthmus to attack Panamá. He not only kept a full diary of his experiences, but drew charts and sketches which he miraculously preserved and brought home to England.

This gave him the distinction of being the first English reporter in the buccaneer field. He served with famous captains, Coxon and Sawkins and Sharp, and raided the town of Santa Maria, fought valiantly at Panamá. Then, when dissension

* "My ingenious friend Ringrose had no mind to make this voyage, but was necessitated to engage in it or starve." William Dampier, in *New Voyage Round the World*.

*The
Least
and the
Last*

The Age
of
Piracy

separated the commanders, he chose to accompany Captain Bartholomew Sharp. The company led by Sharp sailed and sacked along the west coast of South America for eighteen months, and Ringrose steadfastly noted everything in his diary. He added to his charts and sketches while aboard ship and made the Cape Horn passage under Sharp's command in 1681, reached port at Antigua in the West Indies on January thirtieth, eager to get home to England.

He landed at Dartmouth in an English ship, all his material intact, and with some loot, on March 26, 1682. His book, *The Dangerous Voyage and Bold Assaults of Captain Bartholomew Sharp and Others* was published in London the next year. But, the book could not have paid enough, and Ringrose discovered the demand put upon all reporters: he had to return to the source of his news. He went back to sea again in 1684 with Captain Swan in the ship, *Cygnet*.

Captain Swan was an honest shipmaster. His intention was to trade peaceably with the colonial Spanish. But the Spanish refused any overtures, and once more Ringrose made the bleak Cape Horn passage. The *Cygnet* put into Plate Island on the west coast of South America (so named because of Drake's share-out there) and met a buccaneer ship. This was commanded by a well-known leader, Captain Edward Davis, and he told the newly arrived that they should go on the account with him and his men.

Ringrose agreed. The expedition moved north along the west coast, stood clear of Panamá and went ashore for a foray in Mexico. A column of one hundred buccaneers, Ringrose among them, struck at the town of Santiago. It was taken, plunder was seized, and the return march to the coast begun. But the Spaniards had gathered and laid an ambush. Fighting out of it, Ringrose was killed.

He was never during his service with the buccaneers anything more than a petty officer. His maximum duty was to lead some small landing party, or take in a boat after wood and water. But he was warmly remembered by William Dampier, who had seen him and many other men in action, and was able to recognize the brave.

Lionel Wafer, a member of the Darien expedition along with Ringrose and Dampier, enjoyed several distinctions. He wrote his own account of it, but was further portrayed by them in their books, and no company of buccaneers was ever graced by so much literary talent. Wafer was a surgeon, and when his time came to write, he followed the professional parallel of his Flemish colleague, Alexandre Exquemelin.

He was born about 1660 and passed his boyhood in the Scottish Highlands and in Ireland. His training in medicine sent him to sea as surgeon's mate under Captain Zachary Brown in the London ship, *Great Ann,* on a voyage to Java in 1677. Then he sailed for the West Indies, and attracted by the future for a man of his sort, jumped ship at Port Royal in 1679 and set up in practice as a surgeon.

A number of the pirates who frequented the port were his patients and two of them, Captains Linch and Cook, made him realize that his income would not suffer if he went back to sea. He sailed as surgeon in their ship, but afterwards left them and was on the buccaneer muster at Darien for the 1680 march. He had Dampier as an example, and could also watch the industrious Ringrose filling his diary. So he began to take close note of what went on around him.

He remarked the birds and the animals, the fish and insects of the isthmus, gave attention to the Cimaroons who had accompanied the expedition. When the leaders decided to break up the force after the Panamá attack, he chose to go back to Darien, since he lacked Ringrose's desire for marauding down the west coast. It was a ghastly return march, though, and made right at the worst part of the rainy season.

The Least and the Last

263

The Age of Piracy

The men wallowed through the quagmire that was the only trail. They were sodden day and night, and their food supplies disintegrated, and their powder, and their intelligence. Wafer wrote later in his book under the date of May 5, 1681:

> I was sitting on the ground near one of our Men, who was drying Gunpowder in a Silver Plate: But not managing it as he should, it blew up and scorch'd my knee to that degree, that the bone was left bare, the Flesh being torn away, and my Thigh burnt for a great way above it. I applied to it immediately such Remedies as I had in my knapsack: and being unwilling to be left behind by my companions, made hard shift to jog on.*

But the wound almost cost him his life. He was forced to fall behind and encountered unfriendly Indians. They were curious about him, searched his knapsack, and upon his protestation that he was a surgeon, the chief, a man named Lacentra, ordered Wafer to treat his sick wife. Wafer bled the Indian woman in the approved medical style and she recouped and became well. This so pleased Lacentra that he wanted to appoint Wafer surgeon for the tribe, keep him with it. But while appreciative of Lacentra's friendship, Wafer realized that to survive he had to rejoin his companions and make his way to the Darien coast. They parted with regret, and Wafer hurried desperately after the other buccaneers.

Luck was with them. The march had taken twenty-two days, and they were afraid of Spanish pursuit. Then, as they emerged on the beach at Darien, they found a French ship at anchor. She was commanded by Captain Tristrian, who was willing to have them aboard and sell them trade baubles to pay off their Cimaroon guides.

Wafer reached the conclusion that he had experienced a

---

* *A New Voyage and Description of the Isthmus of America, giving an account of the Author's abode there.*

sufficient amount of buccaneering. He worked his way north through the Caribbean and took advantage of King James's general pardon to pirates. Philadelphia with its prim Quaker manner appealed to him. He established himself in practice and between calls and office hours wrote his book, which was published in London in 1699.

Descriptions of piracy along towards its final decline in the last decades of the eighteenth century began to catch the public interest increasingly in America and England. Folklore tales spread. Dramatists and penny-thriller novelists and balladeers took over and the market rapidly expanded. *The Disappointment; or the Force of Credulity,* a comic opera, was published in Philadelphia in 1767. The author wrote under the pseudonym of Andrew Barton, but he was alleged to be Colonel Thomas Forrest. His theme poked bitter fun at those who indulged in the common contemporary frenzy of searching for Captain "Blackbeard" Teach's treasure. Production of the opera was stopped just before the final rehearsals and the piece withdrawn because of the satirical mention made of various Philadelphia citizens. A song set to the tune of "Yankee Doodle" was in it, and it would have been the first American production of its kind.

Some of the American novels that held American readers as late as 1840 and after were *The Deep, Deep Sea, The Pirate Boy, The Black Brig of Bermuda* and *The Child of the Wreck.* A melodrama in four acts by J. S. Jones was produced under the title of *Captain Kyd or the Wizard of the Sea.* Londoners welcomed a book of the same title, and another known as *The Death Ship; or the Pirate's Bride and the Maniac of the Sea.* This was published in thirty-two parts, and another thriller was *Jack Junk; or the Tar for All Weathers* in twenty-two parts.

But the pirates were gone. The great age was over, and fiction could not bring it back to life. Guard-ships, international

The

Least

and the

Last

265

The Age of Piracy

law, the spread of commerce and the withering away of Spanish wealth had each had their part in the decline. Richard Hughes in his *A High Wind in Jamaica* described the end very well. While he wrote in fictional terms, his pirates were real, and rather weak and indolent men. They were almost pathetic.

Afterword

There has not yet been written a fully comprehensive history of the buccaneers. Most of the information we have concerning them comes from the obvious source, Exquemelin, or the work of Funck-Brentano. More is known about their end than their beginning and their time of beatitude before the Spanish forced them into piracy.

C. H. Haring, writing in the *Encyclopedia Britannica*, says,

> Their great importance in history lies in the fact that they opened the eyes of the world, and specially of the nations from whom these buccaneers had sprung, to the whole system of Spanish-American government and commerce, the former in its rotteness and the latter in its possibilities in other hands. From this, then, along with other causes, there arose the West Indian possessions of Holland, England and France.

He gives, as does Phillip Gosse, the date of 1697 and the raid upon Cartagena de Indias as the end of the buccaneers serving together. Haring writes:

> When an expedition was projected against their traditional foes, the Spaniards, they calculated the chances of profit, and taking little account of the perils to be run, or indeed the flag under which they sailed, English, Dutch and French alike became brothers under a chief whose courage they perfectly recognized and whom they servilely obeyed. They lived at a time when they were in no danger of being overhauled by ubiquitous cruisers with rifled guns, and so long they confined themselves to His Catholic Majesty's ships and settlements, they had trusted in the immunity arising from the traditional hostility between the English and Spanish of that era.

Between 1665 and 1671 alone, the buccaneers sacked eighteen cities, four towns and more than thirty-five villages. This does not take into account the expeditions against Puerto Bello, Campeche, Cartagena de Indias and other Spanish ports raided after 1670. The

Spanish estimated in 1685 that their losses since the accession to the throne of Charles II were 60 million crowns. They had lost 250 merchant vessels and frigates. The buccaneer losses can be shown by the figures for the years between 1668 and 1671. In attacks upon Tobago, Curaçao, Puerto Bello, Granada and Panamá, they suffered approximately 2,600 men killed. This is from a force that at maximal standing could not have mustered as many as 10,000 men.

Towards the close of the seventeenth century, the buccaneers often used Portuguese letters of marque freely issued them by various governors of Tortuga. They flew a white flag while at sea. Later, Gustave Alaux reports, if they were refused surrender, they sent aloft a red flag. In the fashion of any other pirate crew, of course, they used whatever flags would help them draw alongside their prey undetected. But only when their time was almost out, and piracy in the Caribbean had spread widely and many other men practiced the trade, were they known to fly the famous black flag with the white skull and crossbones symbol, also the flag which on a black field bore a white skeleton holding in one hand a saber and the other an hourglass. It is noteworthy that this saber-and-hourglass flag is similar to that flown by the Madagascan pirates at a much later date.

It can be said unequivocally that in a ritual fashion all their voyages were begun in grogshops and ended there, from plans to share-outs. When fighting ashore, they were perhaps more formidable than at sea. They were fully conversant with the tricks and tactics of the Caribs, employed camouflage, were at ease in the jungle, could put aside their heavy if deadly muskets, and could handle very well the bow, the arrow, the lance.

Their final unified raid in 1697 was made under the command of Bernard Desjeans, the Sieur de Pointis. The war between France on one side and Spain and England on the other was still being fought. De Pointis was sent out from France with a large fleet to attack Cartagena de Indias and he anchored at Tortuga on the way to gather troops. He ordered the local governor, Ducasse, to muster the buccaneers, and 650 responded. But they refused to serve under him; he was not their kind of commander. Only when Ducasse, whom they considered to be their friend and one of them, promised to sail would they join the ships.

The fleet cleared from Cape Tiburon, Hispaniola on March eighteenth and on April thirteenth anchored two leagues East of Cartagena. The city was bombarded for fourteen days, then the

Spanish surrendered. Phillip Gosse has estimated the loot taken at £20,000,000 sterling. It appealed to de Pointis, though, to attempt to pay off the buccaneers with the same small and nominal share allowed the royal troops. The buccaneers wanted the entire sum divided man for man in their usual style.

There was a great deal of angry talk and de Pointis finally paid the buccaneers 40,000 crowns. It was all Ducasse could do to keep them from mutiny or immediate assault upon de Pointis. De Pointis sailed to get away from the buccaneers and the English fleet that was out after him. The buccaneers boarded their ships, too, and set a course for Hispaniola.

But Ducasse was sick, and the buccaneers still believed that they had been cheated. They put about and went back to Cartagena. After inexcusably cruel treatment of the citizens they rousted forth several more millions in treasure, mostly in gold and silver. Then they sailed for their old rendezvous point, Ile aux Vaches, off the Hispaniola coast. A combined Spanish-English fleet met them at sea.

Nine buccaneer ships, among them the two carrying the major part of the loot, were captured, and two more driven ashore. The rest barely made it into Ile aux Vaches, and the survivors were a broken lot. Ducasse, in his capacity as Governor, sent a mission to the King protesting the action of de Pointis and asking for restitution.

For his effort he was made a Chevalier of the Order of St. Louis. The King also promised the buccaneers the sum of 1,400,000 francs. It came out from France, but passed through many hands, and the buccaneers received very little. Those who were alive to be paid had already lost any respect for France or nationalism and served without scruples as common pirates.

Afterword

269